$ 6.95

This book may be kept
FOURTEEN DAYS

A fine will be charged for each
day the book is kept overtime.

DEC 17 '86			
JN.			

HIGHSMITH 45-226

HEREDITY
in HUMANS

All That You Inherited

was in *chromosomes*—the gene carriers—like these

1. Chromosomes of a normal human male in their doubled stage (the 23 pairs, or 46), photographed by the new fluorescent technique. (Magnification about 2,000 times.)

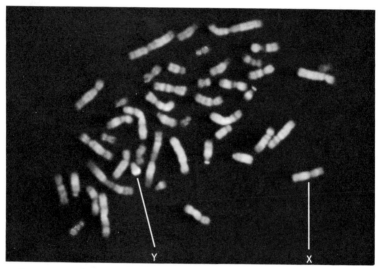

2. The chromosomes cut from above print and arranged in matching pairs *(karyotype)*, according to size and form, with their identifying numbers.

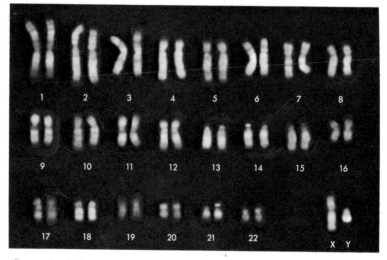

(Prepared and photographed for this book by Dr. W. Roy Breg, Dr. Orlando J. Miller, and Dr. Dorothy A. Miller. For affiliations and details, see Preface.)

HEREDITY
in HUMANS

By AMRAM SCHEINFELD
Illustrated by the Author

J. B. LIPPINCOTT COMPANY
Philadelphia and New York
1972

Based on the author's earlier work *The Human Heredity Handbook* (J. B. Lippincott Company, 1956), now completely revised and updated, largely rewritten, and with much new material added. (An earlier edition was also published in paperback, under the title *The Basic Facts of Human Heredity*. Washington Square Press, 1961.)

Library of Congress Catalog Card No.: 70–159730
Printed in the United States of America
10 9 8 7 6 5 4 3
ISBN–0–397–00820–1

To DOROTHY, RUHAMAH
and SYLVIA
and the memory of AARON

Preface

The interest in human heredity has grown steadily since the science that deals with it—human genetics—took form just a few decades ago, and is today greater than ever. For that science can now provide clear answers to more and more questions which have long been asked by people about the forces which make them, their offspring, and other human beings what they are.

Why and how do individuals develop their special characteristics? Why do children usually resemble their parents, but sometimes do not? What are the basic, *natural* differences between men and women? Which diseases, defects, and abnormalities are inherited, and in what way? How do racial and ethnic groups differ in their heredity? What part does heredity play in intelligence? talent? behavior? personality? sex life? crime?

It is the purpose of this book to throw as much light as possible—concisely and untechnically—on the foregoing and many other important questions about human inheritance.

While *Heredity in Humans* is in considerable measure derived from an earlier book of mine, *The Human Heredity Handbook*, it goes much farther on many points, reflecting the great scientific advances made in the intervening years. For instance, when the *Handbook* was published in 1956, knowledge about human chromosomes was still very hazy. Not until a new technique of culturing and photographing the chromosomes was perfected was it found that their normal quota was not twenty-four pairs, or forty-eight, as had been believed, but twenty-three pairs, or forty-six. More important, it was revealed that chromosome abnormalities

were the causes of many long-mystifying conditions, including
Mongolian idiocy, the Klinefelter and Turner sex abnormalities,
and various other physical and mental aberrations. Further findings
have greatly enlarged the knowledge regarding the roles played by
deviant genes in inherited diseases and defects; the workings of
DNA and the genetic code; and the relative influences of heredity
and environment in prenatal development, physical growth and
mental performance, sex differences, and many other aspects of
human make-up and functioning. At the same time, the new
findings have become involved in controversies regarding race
problems, women's liberation, sexual behavior, birth and population control, "genetic engineering," "genetic pollution," and
human breeding proposals. All the foregoing subjects will receive
attention in this book.

It should be emphasized that *Heredity in Humans* is definitely
not intended to compete with or approach in detail my major
work, *Your Heredity and Environment*, published in 1965 (which
succeeded my *You and Heredity* and its revised editions). While,
inevitably, the same reservoirs of scientific material have been
drawn upon in the two books, the present book is in no sense an
adaptation or abridgment. In format, style, and language, in much
of its new data, and in almost all of its illustrations, *Heredity in
Humans* is a different book. Its primary aim, as said before, is to
serve as a handy, untechnical, general guide to the subject. Should
the reader desire discussions in depth and more detailed information on many points, he is respectfully referred to *Your Heredity
and Environment* (which, among other things, has over three times
the wordage, many photographic and color plates, numerous charts
and tables, and a bibliography of 1,600 items). Contrariwise, those
who own the latter volume may find this new compact book a
useful supplement for quicker reference, and for data on some
recent findings not included in the earlier-published big book.

While conciseness has been a principal object in preparing
Heredity in Humans, there has been no diminished effort to
achieve accuracy as well. To that end, much valuable aid has been
given me in the reading and checking of many parts of the manu-
script by a number of my esteemed friends and professional
acquaintances. My thanks go especially to the following, who read
the chapters designated and offered many suggestions for their

improvement: Dr. Peter Hathaway, Division of Medical Genetics, Mt. Sinai School of Medicine, New York (Chapters 11, 12, 13, 15, 30); Drs. Virginia Apgar and Ralph W. Gause, Medical Department, The National Foundation (Chapter 2); Dr. Bruce M. Alberts, Department of Biochemical Sciences, Princeton University (Chapter 3); Dr. John Money, Departments of Medical Psychology and Pediatrics, Johns Hopkins University (Chapters 14, 24); Dr. John D. Rainer, Chief, Psychiatric Research and Medical Genetics, New York State Psychiatric Institute (Chapters 16, 17); Dr. Philip Levine, Director Emeritus, Division of Immunohematology, Ortho Research Foundation (Chapter 18); Dr. David Wechsler, Professor of Psychology, New York University College of Medicine (Chapter 20); Dr. Sophia J. Kleegman, Clinical Professor of Obstetrics and Gynecology, New York University–Bellevue Medical Center (Chapter 30).

May I add that any errors of commission or omission, interpretation or phrasing, which have survived in the book I ascribe only to myself.

For the remarkable Frontispiece, the photograph of human chromosomes made by the new fluorescent technique, and its accompanying *karyotype*, I am extremely grateful to Dr. W. Roy Breg (Department of Pediatrics, Yale University) and Drs. Orlando J. Miller and Dorothy A. Miller (Department of Human Genetics and Development, Columbia University College of Physicians and Surgeons). The photograph—made especially for this book—called for treating human chromosomes with quinacrine and photographing with an ultraviolet microscope.

Although I have drawn (with much pleasure) all the line illustrations in this book, in keeping with copyright provisions I must formally acknowledge and express thanks to the following publishers, and to myself, for permission to reproduce a number of illustrations from previous books of mine: J. B. Lippincott Company, Philadelphia, for "DNA and the Genetic Code," "How Two Homely Parents May Have a Beautiful Child," "Skin Color," "Chromosomally Caused Sex Abnormalities," "How an Rh-Disease Baby Is Produced," "Tongue Tricks," and "The Evolution of Apes and Man," all from *Your Heredity and Environment* (1965); and Harcourt Brace Jovanovich, Inc., New York, for "Sex Characteristics in Limbs," from *Women and Men* (1944).

Finally, it is my hope that the facts about human heredity as I have tried to present them in this book will do more than provide information or interesting reading. At a time when conflicts and doubts beset the world, the knowledge of how heredity and environment interoperate to make individuals and groups what they are *and can be* should help a little to promote better understanding among people and to bring greater happiness for all mankind.

Amram Scheinfeld

New York City
April 2, 1971

Contents

Illustrations

HEREDITY
in HUMANS

1

Heredity and Environment

WHY THIS BOOK? We hear people say, "I don't believe in heredity—I believe in environment." Or, "I think environment is more important than heredity." Others say, "That whole family is just no good—drunks, criminals, paupers—it's because they've got rotten heredity." Or, "Some groups are born to be superior, other groups to be inferior, and the quickest way to improve humanity is to breed out the inferior people." All such statements are based on wrong ideas as to what heredity means, how it works, and what part it does or does not play in people's lives. These misconceptions have caused much suffering, injustice, confusion, and unhappiness from the beginning of mankind's history. But at last, after decades of intensive study, the science of *genetics*, which deals with heredity, has cleared the air to a vast extent and has provided many positive, accurate answers in place of previous myths and fallacies. This book, then, will try to present the facts about human heredity as scientists now know them, and to indicate how you, the reader, can usefully apply these facts to increase your understanding of yourself, your children, and your fellow men.

WHAT IS HEREDITY? First, heredity is what makes us what we are as members of a particular species—in our case, human beings. When a woman is pregnant, we know definitely that she is not going to give birth to a little elephant, kangaroo, mouse, or bird, but to a *human* baby. We know that this child will have a *human nose*, not a snout or beak; *human* hands and feet, not hoofs or claws; a *human* brain, heart, lungs, skin, and so on. In countless details, then, it is heredity that causes human beings to produce offspring who are like themselves and like no other living things, just as it is heredity that causes all other creatures—dogs, cats, chickens, fish, apes, etc.—to produce offspring of their own kind. Further, heredity has much to do with producing the resemblances between individual parents and their offspring, and among members of the same family groups, in numerous physical and mental traits.

WHAT ABOUT ENVIRONMENT? Environment, too, is extremely important in making people what they are. By environment we mean everything *outside* the individual and his inherited factors, from conception on. Before birth the environment is the mother's womb, the nourishment she supplies to the embryo baby, and all the conditions under which he or she develops. After the baby is born, the environment includes not only what he is fed and how he is cared for, but everything he sees, hears, and is able to learn. As the child grows, his upbringing, surroundings, emotional life, hygienic conditions, medical care, experiences, playmates, schooling, attitudes of others—all of these are increasingly important parts of his environment. No matter how good a child's heredity, a very bad environment may ruin his chances of becoming a healthy, useful, well-adjusted person. Equally, no matter how good the environment, a child with very bad or defective heredity may not be able to survive, or to develop normally and successfully.

"HEREDITY VERSUS ENVIRONMENT." From what has been said, it should be clear that heredity and environment are not opposing forces, working always against each other. Rather, they are complementary forces, always working together. Every human being and every other living thing are products of both heredity and environment. Without both there could be no life, nor any particular type of creature. Everything you are, and everything anyone can be made to be, depends always on the *potentialities* of heredity, working together with the *possibilities* of environment. Very good heredity can often offset some of the disadvantages of poor environment, as has been proved in the cases of Abraham Lincoln, Martin Luther King, and many other great people who worked their way to the top against heavy odds. And very good environment can often help to make up for some of the lacks in heredity. For instance, kindly and expert training may enable a child born with inherited blindness, or some crippling condition, to become a happy and well-adjusted person. Fortunately, *most* human beings are born with pretty good heredity, and more and more persons today are growing up in good environments. **"Which Is More Important—Heredity or Environment?"** This once-popular subject for school debates or informal arguments now arouses only an indulgent smile from the scientist, who knows that the question as posed has no meaning. One can ask it only with respect to *particular* aspects or traits of inheritance. As stated before, both heredity and environment are essential to produce and sustain any living thing. So in general terms, neither force can be called "more important" than the other. However, in a garden the very same environment produces many species of flowers and vegetables, depending on which *seeds* were planted. Thus, in producing any particular kind of flower or vegetable, heredity can be called far more important than environment. Likewise, from the same prenatal environment in a mother may come two nonidentical twins—one a girl, one a boy; one blue-eyed, one black-eyed; one normal-sighted, one color-blind. In producing these differences between the children (including their sex), heredity is again vastly more important than their environment. But if a baby is born with a serious defect purely because of a prenatal accident, or some dietary deficiency, obviously in that case environment is the all-important factor. As we proceed with this book and take up particular traits of numerous kinds, we will see every degree of both hereditary and environmental influence at work.

2

The New Baby

LIFE BEGINS. The conception of a new baby takes place the instant a sperm from the father enters and fertilizes an egg waiting in the mother. Usually one egg every four weeks is produced by a woman (although sometimes two or more are produced, which may give rise to twins, triplets, and so on). The egg comes out of either of the two ovaries and moves down into one of the two fallopian tubes. Here the egg is ready to be fertilized.

Fertilization. In the act of intercourse the husband propels into the wife's vagina many millions of sperms (from 50,000,000 to 500,000,000 in an average single ejaculation). These sperms are so small millions could be packed into a pinhead. Like the tiniest imaginable tadpoles, they swim first in the stream of seminal fluid, then in the secretions of the vagina and womb. Only a small proportion get into the womb, and fewer still into the tubes. But should any sperms reach the egg, the moment a single one enters it there is an instantaneous toughening of the covering of the egg which shuts out all other sperms. Thus, of all the millions of sperms entering the race, only a single one can win out and fertilize the egg.

THE HEREDITY ELEMENTS. If we could look through a powerful microscope and follow the process of conception, we would see this: As the sperm enters the egg, leaving its tail outside, the sperm head opens and out comes a batch of twenty-three tiny little wormlike bits of living substance. At the same time a little globule inside the egg (the *nucleus*) also opens up, and out comes another batch of twenty-three of the same tiny little wormlike things. These little things in both the sperm and the egg are called *chromosomes*. They carry *everything a child inherits* from the parents.

How Heredity Works

Father's chromosomes

Each parent has
23 pairs of
chromosomes,
or 46 in all.

Mother's chromosomes

When father produces sperms,
each sperm gets only half of his
chromosomes.

When mother produces eggs,
each egg gets only half of her
chromosomes.

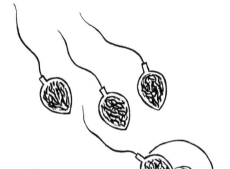

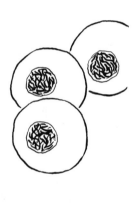

As the sperm fertilizes the egg,
the 23 chromosomes from the
father join with the 23 chromosomes from the mother.

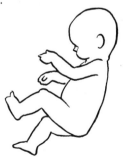

The combined
46 chromosomes
work to produce
all of the baby's
hereditary traits.

How the Chromosomes Are Paired

Chromosomes
from Mother

Chromosomes
from Father

X Y

Note that except for the father's "sex" chromosome, which may
be either an X or a Y (see Chapter 4), the chromosomes of each
pair, whether from father or mother, are the same in size and
structure (although they may differ in the nature of their genes).

The Chromosomes. As we examine them more closely, we
find that among the chromosomes in each set—whether the twenty-
three from the father or the twenty-three from the mother—one
may differ from another in shape and size. But there is a more
remarkable fact. Every chromosome from the father finds an
exactly matching type, of its same shape and size, among the
chromosomes waiting in the mother's egg. (An exception, in the
sex chromosomes, will be explained in Chapter 4.) How the
chromosomes look if those from the two parents are arranged
separately is shown in our accompanying illustration.

The Genes. Most often when chromosomes are seen under
a microscope, they are in a doubled and compressed form which
gives them their wormlike appearance. But at certain stages they
stretch out, and then we find that each chromosome actually consists of hundreds of clear, jellylike sections, strung together like
beads. These sections are called *genes* (pronounced "jeans"). And
it is these genes which act like wonderful little chemical workers
to carry out the processes of heredity. Every gene differs from the
others in some way and has some special job to do in the fashioning, developing, and functioning of a baby, from conception to
birth and beyond, for throughout life the genes continue their
work.

THE STREAM OF HEREDITY. Acquired Characteristics. One of the most important aspects of heredity is this: The genes as they pass along from generation to generation *are not changed in their workings* by any changes parents make in their own traits, or that are made in their traits by environment. Establishment of this fact has upset the old theory of the *inheritance of acquired characteristics*—that traits acquired by persons during their lifetimes, or environmental changes made in them, could indeed be transmitted to their offspring. The theory has been disproved by many experiments. Even before the science of genetics came into being, skeptical scientists had taken note of the fact that generations of binding of feet among Chinese, circumcision among Jews, mutilations among primitive peoples (enlarging lips, scarring faces, tattooing, etc.), had in no way produced any corresponding changes in their newborn offspring. Leaving no further doubts, scientists have since made countless experiments with lower animals—altering parts of their bodies, feeding them different diets and chemicals, training them in various ways for many generations—without in any way changing hereditary traits. How and why the genes retain their identity can now be best understood by looking into the processes through which eggs and sperms are formed.

Human Egg Production. When a little girl baby is born, she already has in her tiny ovaries all the eggs—in rudimentary form—which will take mature shape and emerge after she achieves puberty. And within each rudimentary egg there already are present exact replicas of all the chromosomes and genes that the girl baby received from her parents at conception, and from which will be drawn all the chromosomes her own children will receive. An immediate question, then, is this: In what possible way could the genes so tightly enclosed in the eggs (whether rudimentary or mature) suddenly be made to change in conformity with anything or everything happening to the female in whose ovaries they are? It is obviously ridiculous to think that if a dark-haired girl bleached her hair blond, that would make her dark-hair genes suddenly turn into blond genes. Or if she got her straight hair permanently waved, that would cause her straight-hair genes to change suddenly so that her baby would be born with wavy hair. But it is no less ridiculous to assume that whenever a

Human Sperms and Egg

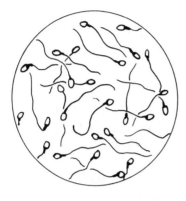

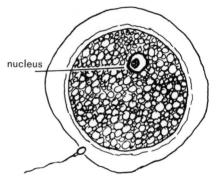

nucleus

HUMAN SPERMS
Magnified as here shown about
400 times. (Actual size of sperm
is about 1/400 of an inch long.)

HUMAN EGG
Relative size shown by sperm
entering it. The egg nucleus
contains the chromosomes.
The rest is food material.

mother, or future mother, makes a change in any other trait of her body, mind, or character (or any such change is made in her), the results will immediately cause the genes concerned with that trait to change their workings in conformity with the new requirements.

Human Sperm Production. As with a little girl baby, a boy baby, too, when he is born already has set aside within him all the "germ cells" from which will someday come his contributions to his children's heredity. A difference between the sexes is that whereas in the female the eggs themselves are already present at birth, in the male the sperms do not begin to be fashioned by the germ cells until he achieves puberty. Another difference is that although the eggs of the female are limited in number (because she will usually produce no more than one a month for a period of about thirty years), the sperm production of the male, once it begins, goes on into the billions and billions, often throughout his lifetime. But except for the difference in numbers, the sperms of a male are the same as the eggs of a female with respect to the nature of their genes. In the male, too, all the genes carried in his sperms are exact replicas of those which he received from his parents at conception, and cannot be changed in their workings by any changes that are made in his own traits. (*Note*: How some changes, or "mutations," do occur in genes in rare instances will be explained in the next chapter, and later under "The First Life-Spark," Chapter 26. These gene changes are different from those we have discussed and give no support to the acquired-characteristic theory.)

MOTHER AND CHILD. Although a child's genes can in no way be changed by the parents' acts, habits, or experiences, this hardly means that a child's *traits* will not be affected by these influences. Obviously, parents can affect their child environmentally in a great many ways, from birth onward; and in the mother's case, her influences on the child's body and mind may begin from the moment of conception. However, there has been much confusion regarding the extent to which the mother's condition is responsible for various traits appearing in babies. Often conditions that are blamed on prenatal factors are due to heredity, and at other times the reverse is true.

Prenatal Relationships. The developing baby is in no sense ever a part of the mother's body. Though growing within her, the baby is always a distinct individual (as courts have ruled). Biologically there is a porous partition—the *placenta*—between the mother and baby. The mother's blood, which carries the nourishment, stops on one side of the partition and the blood elements are broken down and strained through it. The baby manufacturers its own blood according to the formula prescribed by its blood genes. In fact, the baby's blood may be so different chemically from the mother's—for instance with respect to the "Rh" factor—that an interchange of blood substances may sometimes cause serious damage. (See Chapter 18.) Other hazards to the baby on the road to birth:

1. *Germs and viruses* in the mother of such diseases as German measles (*rubella*, especially in the early months of pregnancy), tuberculosis, syphilis or gonorrhea (capable of being transmitted during the birth process), may have serious effects on the child.

2. *Organic diseases* in the mother, including nephritis (kidney

disease), diabetes, goiter (and certain other glandular conditions), and some of the heart diseases, may affect prenatal growth and development.

3. *Drugs* (ordinary), such as sleeping pills, sedatives, and various pain killers—even aspirin,—if used in excess during pregnancy, may adversely affect the baby. The most tragic and drastic examples were the *thalidomide* babies, thousands of whom were born some years ago with absent or badly deformed limbs as the result of pregnant mothers having taken the then new, supposedly harmless sedative. The first of the babies were thought to be victims of a very rare genetic defect (acheiropodia) which similarly produces missing arms and legs, and before thalidomide was identified as the cause, the numbers born with defects it produced reached close to 15,000, of whom almost half have survived (most of the latter in Germany). There were only a few victims in the United States, where immediate suspicion of the drug curtailed its use. (Law suits to date on behalf of thalidomide victims have been settled by the drug companies involved for about $30,000,000.)

4. *Narcotic addiction* of the pregnant mother to morphine, heroin, cocaine, or opium may result in her child actually being born with all the symptoms of drug addiction. *LSD*, if used by the mother, is believed capable of producing chromosome abnormalities in the child (primarily in the egg before conception), or other abnormalities during fetal development, but evidence on this point is not yet conclusive.

5. *Smoking* of cigarettes by the mother, if excessive, may increase the risk of the child's being born prematurely or underweight. *Marijuana* smoking by pregnant women, some studies have indicated, may increase the risk of congenital defects in the offspring.

6. *Faulty diet* by the mother may result in malnutrition in the newborn child.

7. *Radiation*, through X rays that are too frequent or too heavy during pregnancy, can be hazardous to the fetus.

Any of the above-mentioned factors—which, fortunately, do not apply in most pregnancies—may disturb the normal development of a baby before birth, and can cause various congenital defects or abnormalities which may be mistakenly regarded as hereditary. However, significant hereditary defects do occur in 3 to 4 per cent of the babies who are born. (These will be discussed in later chapters.)

Mother's Age. Although the genes the mother transmits to her baby are the same whatever her age (since her eggs with their quotas of genes were formed before her own birth), her age may affect the baby she bears in several ways. First, during the final stages of egg formation, or at conception, abnormalities in the chromosomes may occur. Thus, older mothers—past thirty-five and increasingly thereafter—are considerably more likely than younger mothers to produce babies with various chromosomally caused defects, such as mongoloid idiocy, or some of the sex abnormalities. Again, aging in a woman is apt to bring more diseases, internal upsets, and organic disorders, so her prenatal environment may be less favorable for childbearing and increase the risk of congenital defects or abnormalities in her baby.

Prenatal Impressions. The basis of many popular myths has been the belief that what goes on in the mother's mind can have profound effects on the baby she is carrying: that marks or deformities could develop in a baby in resemblance to something that strongly impressed or frightened the mother during pregnancy; that by her listening to good music her child would be more musical; or that by her reading elevating books the child would be brainier; etc. Actually there is no nerve connection between the mother and the baby, and no way her thoughts could reach the child—and certainly no way that her thinking could affect the child's genes. All that might happen is that her mental and nervous state, if good, could benefit her physical state, and therefore help the child: or, contrariwise, if she is badly upset during pregnancy, the nourishment and environment for the child could be worsened.

FATHER'S INFLUENCE ON CHILD. Once a father has made his contribution to the child's heredity at conception by way of the sperm, his influence on the child's traits can be only those exerted after it is born. But often his environmental influences are confused with hereditary effects. If a father's (or a mother's) alcoholism, drug addiction, criminality, degeneracy, or other bad traits are repeated in children, this need not at all mean that heredity is responsible. Nor can the repetition of good traits of behavior and temperament be necessarily credited to heredity. In every case the home environment and the hereditary histories of *both* parents must be weighed together.

The Father's Age. Unlike the situation with the mother, the age of the father has nothing to do with the prenatal condition or prenatal development of a child. There is some possibility that chromosome abnormalities are more likely to develop in the sperms of an older man, but to a much smaller extent than they do in the aging woman; and it is also possible that more gene mutations may have occurred in a man's sperms as time goes on. But, by and large, so long as a man can go on producing fertile sperms (and some men have done so into their nineties) the genes they transmit and the traits they can produce in offspring are little different from those derived from the same man in his robust younger years. Even the fact that a man has been seriously disabled in an accident, or has acquired a serious disease, will in no wise affect the *heredity* of his children.

3

The Workings of Heredity

THE MENDELIAN LAWS. These laws refer to the basic principles of heredity discovered by an Austrian monk, Gregor Mendel, in 1857. He was the abbot of a monastery at Brno (then in Austria, now in Czechoslovakia) where he had a garden in which he experimented. One series of Mendel's experiments, cross-breeding sweet peas of different varieties, brought to light the facts about inheritance that are now called the "Mendelian laws." These laws, or principles, are:

1. Inherited traits are produced by separate factors (the genes) which pass along unchanged from one generation to another.

2. The genes come in pairs in individuals, one of every pair from each parent, and if two paired genes differ in their effects, one usually dominates the other, and may be called "dominant," whereas the weaker gene, whose effects are suppressed, may be called "recessive." A recessive will exert its effects if coupled with a matching recessive, or in the absence of the corresponding dominant.

3. When seeds are formed in plants (or sperms or eggs are formed in any animal or human), the two genes from each pair separate or segregate, and only one of each pair goes to an offspring. Which gene of a given pair goes into any seed, sperm, or egg is independent of which gene of another pair goes into the same seed, sperm, or egg. That is to say, if a plant has dominant genes producing red coloring and tallness, but also carries hidden recessive genes for white color and shortness, the red and tall genes might or might not go into the same seed. One seed could as easily get the red and short genes together, and another the white and tall genes.

Later Findings. The importance of Mendel's discoveries was not realized until after 1900, when various investigators checked and found that the Mendelian laws apparently applied to inheritance in all living things, including human beings. However, in time it was shown that these laws needed certain qualifications and modifications. The most important strides in clarifying and extending the knowledge of heredity came through the researches of Prof. Thomas Hunt Morgan and his brilliant Columbia University team, which included Prof. H. J. Muller (who, like Professor Morgan, was awarded a Nobel prize). These scientists and others, experimenting with fruit flies (Drosophila), worked out many of the detailed principles and techniques which form the foundation of the science of modern genetics. Subsequently, geneticists and other scientists in many countries greatly broadened the knowledge and produced many significant new findings directly applicable to human heredity.

THE GENES AND DNA. The special life substance in genes that endows them with their powers of transmitting hereditary traits has been identified as "DNA" (short for *deoxyribonucleic acid*). How the DNA worked and the way it sent out its genetic code messages were long a mystery until it was shown in 1953 by three scientists, Drs. J. D. Watson, F. H. C. Crick, and Maurice Wilkins (later awarded Nobel prizes), that the DNA molecule resembled an enormously long, flexible, twisted rope ladder (a "double helix"), consisting of two coiled, mated strands with rungs in between. The rungs were identified as composed of pairs of chemical bases—*adenine* ("A"), joined with *thymine* ("T"), or *guanine* ("G"), joined with *cytosine* ("C"). On any rung either of the pairs could be first or second, so there could be four types of rungs, A-T, T-A, C-G, and G-C. With successive rungs (and possibly millions of them in a single DNA molecule) there could be countless arrangements, for example, A-T, T-A, C-G, A-T, G-C, C-G, T-A, T-A, C-G, and so on for part of one gene, or C-G, T-A, G-C, A-T, A-T, G-C, C-G, T-A, etc. for part of another gene, each sequence carrying instructions somewhat like the dot-and-dash Morse code. Each gene, then, is a DNA section with a complete set of instructions for guiding the formation in cells of one particular protein (or enzyme). The different proteins made by the entire collection of genes, in turn, direct the carrying out of all the body's specific processes and functions, from the conception

DNA and the Genetic Code

own diagrammatically is a section of DNA–Deoxyribonucleic Acid–
the basis of a gene

A DNA section in its "spiral
staircase" or "twisted rope-
ladder" form

2. The DNA
"ladder" as it would
look straightened out

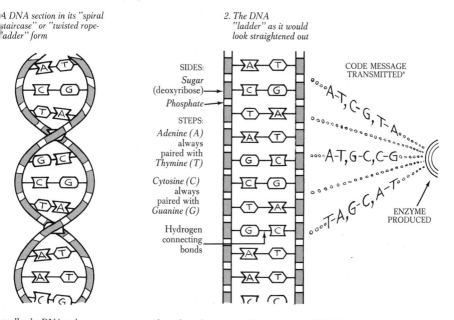

SIDES:

Sugar
(deoxyribose)—→

Phosphate—

STEPS:

Adenine (A)
always
paired with
Thymine (T)

Cytosine (C)
always
paired with
Guanine (G)

Hydrogen
connecting
bonds

CODE MESSAGE
TRANSMITTED*

A-T, C-G, T-A,

A-T, G-C, C-G

T-A, G-C, A-T

ENZYME
PRODUCED

tually, the DNA code messages are carried out through an intermediate, messenger "RNA" (ribonucleic acid). See text.

of an individual and on throughout life. Slight differences in the DNA coding of eye genes could produce one or another type of eye color; or the coding of this or that feature gene could produce any shape of nose, mouth, or ear, and so on with the coding for any other hereditary trait. Further, an error in the coding of some important gene could have serious consequences in producing a defect, disease, or abnormality.

The foregoing is a greatly simplified summary of the workings of the genetic code, with many technical details omitted. For instance, it could be noted that the DNA messages are carried out through an intermediate, messenger "RNA" (*ribonucleic acid*) and that the four-letter sequences are coded into triplets. However, the average reader may be more interested in *what* genes do than in *how* they do it.

VARIETIES OF GENES. The infinitely varied possibilities

in the DNA coding of genes can explain not only the innumerable differences in genetic traits among human beings but the great genetic differences among all the different species of living things, animal and vegetable. All animals and plants, like human beings, have DNA as the basic life substance of their chromosomes and genes, the differences between one species and another resulting from special characteristics and variations in the DNA coding of their genes. Different species also vary in the way their genes are arranged in chromosomes. For example, compared with the normal human quota of twenty-three pairs of chromosomes, a dog has thirty-nine pairs, a mouse twenty pairs, a fruit fly four pairs, a cow has thirty pairs, a gorilla or chimpanzee, twenty-four pairs. Differences in chromosome numbers among species need not be related to animals' sizes, and may mean only that the individual chromosomes of one species may carry more or less genes per average chromosome than those of another species. (The human quota of chromosomes may carry tens of thousands of genes, and the quotas of many other animals may have much the same number.) Some of the chromosomes of one species—human or lower animal—may look almost exactly like those of another species, but taken together, the chromosomes of a human being can be readily distinguished by an expert from those of any other creature through various criteria of sizes and shapes.

How Genes Work. When a baby is conceived, all the genes—collectively and individually according to their DNA codings—begin to work on the raw materials already in the fertilized egg, later on the food materials coming in from the mother. Through continuous steps the genes help to form many types of cells, produce flesh, bones, and muscles, construct organs, and get functions under way. In the first stages, when the general characteristics of the body are being shaped, all or a great many genes may work together on the same job. Later, special genes begin to work on shapes of particular features, coloring, and many other details. If we likened genes to human workers, we could find among them every type of specialist, each with his own capacities: laborers, architects, engineers, plumbers, chemists, decorators, sculptors, dietitians, doctors, etc. One need think only of the many thousands of details in the construction and functioning of the human body

Varieties of Genes

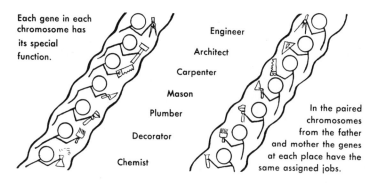

Each gene in each chromosome has its special function.

Engineer
Architect
Carpenter
Mason
Plumber
Decorator
Chemist

In the paired chromosomes from the father and mother the genes at each place have the same assigned jobs.

- But genes may do their jobs in different ways:

BULLY genes (dominant) may keep weaker ones (recessive) from working.

FREAK genes work peculiarly to produce various oddities in the body.

TEMPERAMENTAL genes (qualified) work unexpectedly and only under some circumstances.

RIP VAN WINKLE genes (late onset) may sleep for years and then awake to action.

BUSY-BODY genes (multi-action) do various jobs at once, and sometimes wreck many jobs.

VILLAIN genes produce serious defects and diseases, and sometimes cause early death.

How Chromosomes Multiply

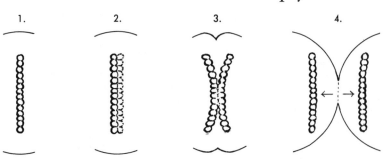

1. **1.** Section of one of the original 46 chromosomes in a fertilized egg cell.
2. **2.** Each gene in the chromosome creates a replica of itself.
3. **3.** When the genes are duplicated, the doubled chromosome splits. This has been occurring likewise in all the other 45 chromosomes in the egg cell.
4. **4.** The duplicated chromosomes move apart and the cell divides, forming two cells, each housing exact duplicates of all the original 46 chromosomes.

to realize how huge a variety of "jobs" are engaged in and directed by the genes.

GENE MULTIPLICATION. One of the most important properties of the genes is their capacity for reproducing themselves. It is mainly in this way that genes, as *living* units, differ from any mineral or nonliving molecules. The self-reproduction of the genes begins and proceeds with fantastic rapidity from the moment a new baby is conceived. As we saw in Chapter 2, the father's sperm brings into the egg twenty-three separate chromosomes—each a long string of genes. Waiting in the mother's egg are another twenty-three chromosomes. Immediately the chromosomes and their genes begin to draw material from the egg, and to fashion replicas of themselves alongside. Then each doubled chromosome splits in two lengthwise, starting from both ends, and producing, before complete separation, the sort of "X" or "plier" shape in which chromosomes are usually shown (the *mitotic* stage when they can be most easily photographed, after proper preparation, and most readily identified). Finally, as the replicated chromosomes pull apart completely, and the halves move to opposite ends of the cell housing them, the cell pinches together, so that there are now two cells, each with exact duplicates of all the original forty-six chromosomes and their genes. (See illustration.) The process is repeated again and again, the two cells becoming four, the four eight, the eight sixteen, etc., into the millions, billions, and trillions. (It is estimated that a baby at birth has about twenty-six trillion cells, with the same tens of thousands of genes in each cell.)

CELL AND CELL SPECIALIZATION. Although the chromosomes and genes that go into every cell are exactly the same, the cells as they form and develop are *not* the same. This is because with each step in the cell-multiplication process, somewhat as with material in a house being built, cells at different points are shaped and constructed in different ways. Under the direction of the "specialist" genes we mentioned previously, cell clusters take different forms. Some turn into the outer parts of the body—skin, muscles, features—some into the skeletal framework, some into the internal mechanisms—brain and nervous system, heart and arteries, digestive system, glands, etc. Precisely how this is done (or how experts believe it is done) is far too complicated to explain here. But there is no guess about *what* is done. Innumerable studies of embryos show to what point the body construction has been carried out at every successive stage. And the fact that at any given stage—four weeks, eight weeks, twelve weeks, and so on—the development of any normal baby is almost identical with that of any other is proof of how remarkably systematic and precise the human specialist genes are in their workings.

Gene Specialist Differences. Apart from completing given stages of the baby's development at prescribed times, the specialist genes are highly individual in their work, just as are human architects, carpenters, decorators, engineers, etc. One eye-color gene may make eyes dark, another may be set on making them light blue, another green, etc. For hair color there are black, brown, blond, and red genes. Innumerable other differences in genes account largely for the varieties of human features and body details, and to a greater or lesser extent for differences in physical and mental functioning, and in fitness or defectiveness (always allowing for environmental influences).

WHY CHILDREN OF A FAMILY DIFFER. The fact that

there are many differences among genes for given traits does not of itself explain why two children of the same parents are often so very different in their heredity. For if every child in a family received *all* the father's genes, and *all* the mother's genes, then one child's hereditary make-up would be exactly the same as another's. This does not happen (except with identical twins) because, as noted under the Mendelian laws, each sperm of the father carries only *half* his chromosomes, and each egg of the mother carries only *half* of hers. In other words, when a man produces sperm there is a process whereby for every two sperms, his twenty-three pairs of chromosomes sort out into two groups, with *only one chromosome of each pair* going in each group, around which a sperm then takes shape. Thus, every sperm contains twenty-three *single* chromosomes. When eggs are formed in the female there is a similar process whereby each egg gets only one of each pair of her chromosomes, so that it also carries only twenty-three single chromosomes.

Sorting Out of Chromosomes. In either parent's case, which chromosomes of any pair go into which sperms or eggs is entirely a matter of chance. The process is much like a shuffling and dealing out of cards, but with chromosomes being dealt out instead. One sperm might get a combination of chromosomes quite different or even entirely different from those in another sperm; or again, most of the chromosomes in two sperms might be the same. This is equally true for the chromosomes in the mother's eggs. But the chances that any two children in a family (other than identical twins) would get exactly the same chromosome combinations—or completely different chromosomes—is extremely remote, for reasons which follow.

Possible Chromosome Combinations. If we take at random one out of each of the twenty-three pairs of chromosomes carried by every man—this chromosome out of one pair, that chromosome out of another pair—it would be possible for a man to produce sperms with 8,388,608 different chromosome combinations. A woman's eggs, likewise, could carry any of 8,388,608 different chromosome combinations. Together, then, the sperms and eggs of any couple could produce any of over sixty-four trillion different chromosome combinations—which would be, theoretically, the possible hereditary varieties of the children they could have. Ordinarily, however, about half the chromosomes—or a few more or a few less—of any two children of a family would be the same. Nor would the *unlike* chromosomes necessarily be different in all their genes. In fact, if the grandparents on either side (and especially on both sides) were of similar stocks and alike in many traits, the different chromosomes would be carrying many matching genes. In sum, the hereditary likenesses or differences among children in a family will depend on how many genes they have in common, and what differences there are in their other genes.

Dominance and Recessiveness. How a difference in only a few genes can often produce a marked difference between two children of a family becomes clear if we recall the Mendelian principle regarding dominant and recessive genes. Suppose a parent carries a gene of each type for a given trait, and that one child receives the dominant, the other the recessive: for eye color, one child receives a black-eye gene, the other only a blue-eye gene; or for hair form, one child receives a curly gene, the other only a straight gene. In these cases, one child will show the dominant trait, and if the other child gets a recessive gene from each parent, he will show the recessive trait. The differences with respect to most traits may be unimportant. But there are some genetic situations where a single dominant gene (or its absence) in one child, and not in another, can produce striking differences in their appearance, mentality, talent, health, or strength and in the whole course of their lives. Examples of these genetic situations, and of various others, will be found in succeeding chapters.

GENE CHANGES (MUTATIONS). We have previously stated that the genes a parent passes on to a child are unaltered by any changes the parent has made (or that have been made) in given traits during his or her lifetime. But we also noted that in extremely rare instances a gene *can be changed* in its workings, though not in accordance with any change in the parent's traits. The gene change or *mutation* to which we refer may take place if a gene in one of the germ cells of a prospective father or mother is "hit" or disturbed by some outside force in such a way as to shake up, rearrange, or alter the atoms composing it, and thus change the gene's DNA coding. Under natural conditions, cosmic rays, chemicals, and perhaps other outside influences can produce mutations, as they have been doing from the beginning of life on earth. (See Chapter 26.) These natural gene changes, accumulating through the ages, have been responsible for producing the infinite varieties of genes among human beings and all other living things; and in our own time spontaneous mutations, as they have been capitalized on, have made possible the breeding of many new types of domestic animals, plants, and flowers. However, it should be stressed that in the great majority of cases mutations are very slight; that in only about 1 in 100 instances are they beneficial or useful; and that for the rest, they tend mostly to produce defects in the genes that, under natural conditions, would eventually cause such genes to be weeded out by natural selection.

Artificially Induced Mutations. How man-made mutations have been and can be produced in various ways, particularly through X rays and, on a far more serious scale, radiation from atomic and hydrogen bombs, will be told in Chapter 31. In addition to specific gene mutations, there can be radical changes affecting whole chromosomes or parts of chromosomes which can produce serious abnormalities in offspring. There is a strong possibility that LSD and certain other drugs can cause chromosome changes in the fetuses of mothers who have taken the drugs during pregnancy.

REASONS FOR OPTIMISM. On the whole, as the reader will find, the facts about human heredity uncovered by scientists are mostly on the optimistic side. Many conditions formerly regarded as due to bad or defective inheritance have been traced to bad environments or preventable mishaps; and as environments have improved, and alertness to accidental dangers has increased, the incidence of these conditions and their threats have been greatly reduced. Even where conditions are known to be hereditary, new findings have in many instances helped to lessen the fears regarding them. (Possibilities of counteracting the effects of harmful genes through chemical therapy, or even actually altering or replacing "bad" genes themselves, will be discussed in our concluding chapter.) Not least among the helpful developments has been the disproof of old theories about the inheritance of acquired characteristics (Chapters 2, 26). Parents now know that any mistakes they made, any disease, defects, or bad habits they acquired, or any shortcomings developed by unfavorable environments, did not "soak into" their genes, and cannot be transmitted to their children. At the same time, what parents have learned to advantage can be transmitted to their children through improved environment and proper training. The forces of heredity still remain and always will be vastly powerful. But more can be done now to give good heredity—with which the great majority of people are endowed—a chance to assert itself, and to keep bad heredity—which is found in only a very small proportion of people —from doing its worst.

4

The Baby's Sex

"WE WANT A BOY"; "WE WANT A GIRL." Isn't there something parents can do beforehand to make their wish as to the baby's sex come true? Not yet! Throughout the ages parents have had the same thought, and countless "sex-determining" formulas and treatments have been employed. All of those in the past were worthless because they were based on false notions and superstitions about the way in which a baby's sex is determined. But even today, although we *do* know what causes a baby to be a boy or a girl—as we shall presently see—there is still no way of ensuring the desired results. The sex of the baby continues to be a matter of chance, although it need not always remain so.

How Sex Is Determined. The sex of every baby is fixed at the moment of conception. The deciding factor comes not through the mother's but through the *father's contribution.* Whether the baby will be a boy or a girl depends simply on which *of two types of sperms from the father enters the egg first.* One kind of sperm leads to the production of a boy. The other kind of sperm results in a girl. The mother's egg is neutral: when it is fertilized it can work to produce either a boy or a girl, depending on which kind of sperm enters the egg and starts the development of the baby.

THE SEX CHROMOSOMES. Hereditary factors—chromosomes and their genes—determine the baby's sex, as they do other inherited traits. In Chapter 2 we saw that at conception every child receives forty-six chromosomes—a set of twenty-three from the father, a set of twenty-three from the mother. In each of these two sets, one special chromosome is called the "sex" chromosome because it is concerned with the determination of the baby's sex. These sex chromosomes are of two types. One type is very long,

containing many genes, and is called the "X" chromosome. The
other is very short and is called the "Y" chromosome. And the
whole difference to start with between what will be a girl and
what will be a boy is that the girl gets *two* X chromosomes, or an
"XX" combination; the boy gets only *one* X, *plus one* Y—an "XY"
combination.

How Are the Sex Chromosomes Transmitted? When a
woman produces eggs, there is a process whereby each egg receives
replicas of only *half* her chromosomes—or *one* chromosome of each
of her twenty-three pairs. Since her sex chromosomes are *both* Xs,
one X will go into every egg. Thus, the mother transmits an X
chromosome to *every* child. But the father's contribution works
differently. When he produces sperms, there also is a process
whereby each sperm receives only *one* of every pair of his chromosomes. So, since his sex chromosomes are of two kinds, X and Y,
his sperms will also be of two kinds. Of every two sperms the man
produces, an X chromosome will go into one, a Y into the other,
which means that of the tens of millions of sperms which a father
releases at a given time, exactly half are X-bearers, half Y-bearers.

The X and Y Race. As the millions of sperms enter the womb
and move up into the tube where the egg is waiting, one may
think of it as a race between the Ys and the Xs to get to the egg
first and win it for the male side or the female side. Since the egg
already carries one X, as we have seen, the baby's sex will depend
on whether the entering sperm carries another X or carries a Y.
Only a single sperm decides (Chapter 2), because the moment one
sperm enters, all the others are shut out. Thus, if an X sperm wins
out, it will join with the X already there, and an XX individual—
a girl baby—will be started on her way. But if a Y wins, the result
will be an XY individual—a boy. All of this is shown in our
accompanying diagram. Study it and fix it in your mind. The facts
will come up many times in this book, and in your life.

The Powerful Y. Formerly the little Y was believed to be only
a passive bystander—almost a blank—in the sex-determination
process. As in fruit flies, or in some species that have no Y at all,
it was thought that in human beings as well two Xs produced a
female, but only one X, with or without a Y, produced a male.
The new methods of photographing human chromosomes proved
the old theory wrong. It was shown that it was the Y which threw

How a Baby's Sex Is Determined

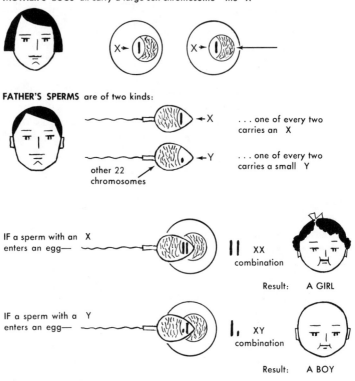

MOTHER'S EGGS all carry a large sex chromosome—the X

FATHER'S SPERMS are of two kinds:

other 22 chromosomes

. . . one of every two carries an X

. . . one of every two carries a small Y

IF a sperm with an X enters an egg—

XX combination

Result: A GIRL

IF a sperm with a Y enters an egg—

XY combination

Result: A BOY

development of a newly conceived individual toward maleness, for even in an abnormal situation when there were two or more Xs in an egg at conception, if a Y were also present the individual would still develop as a male. If there were only one X, with no Y, the individual would still develop as a female. (See "Klinefelter's Syndrome" and "Turner's Syndrome" in Chapter 14.)

Sex-Changing. Can a baby's sex be changed during the period before birth? No, once the baby has begun to develop as a boy, he cannot be turned into a girl, nor can a developing girl fetus be turned into a boy. (Even more impossible are the claims that mature men have been or could be transformed into women by "operations" or treatments. See "Sex-Changing" in Chapter 14.) However, once in a thousand times, something may happen in prenatal life to throw sexual development from its proper course, and a boy may result whose sex organs are so incompletely developed that he may be mistaken for a girl; or a girl with abnormal development of her sex organs may be mistaken for a boy. Only in extremely rare instances is there a completely "in-between" individual who is neither properly male nor properly female. (For further details about this, and also about tests for establishing sex identity, see again Chapter 14.)

WHY MORE BOYS? A remarkable fact is that year after year, among the many millions of babies born in the United States and most other countries, there is an excess of boys by almost exactly the same percentage: for every 100 girls born, there will be close to 106 boys. This is definitely not because boys are stronger and achieve birth more easily. The contrary is true, as we shall see. It is because many more boys than girls are conceived—perhaps 130 or more to 100 girls. How can this be if the male-producing sperms (the Y-bearers) and the female-producing sperms (the X-bearers) are sent out in exactly equal numbers? Apparently the Y-bearing sperms have some advantages over the X-bearing sperms in speed or chemical reactions, which enable them to win the race to the egg oftener, or to fertilize the egg more readily.

Male Fetuses Weaker. One reason why nature may cause more boys to be conceived is that they have less chance of surviving than have females. Contrary to the long-standing belief that males are hardier than females, science has now established that males actually are much likelier to be defective and less able to withstand bad conditions than are females. This applies to every stage of life, but is most significant in the prenatal stages, when the environment for males and females is the same. Among the babies miscarried in the first few months the males outnumber the females by two or three to one, and among those dying shortly before or immediately after birth there are about 130 boys to 100 girls. Moreover, the risk of being abnormal or defective is much greater for boy babies. When added to this is the fact that in almost every stage of life thereafter the male death rate is markedly higher, there is a very good reason why more males should be needed at the start.

VARIATIONS IN THE SEX RATIO. Although the *average*

sex ratio at birth, as said before, is steadily close to 106 boys to
every 100 girls, the chances of having a boy may be above or
below this average for mothers of different groups, ages, and
physical conditions. Because boy fetuses tend to be weaker, the
general rule seems to be that where prenatal conditions are best,
there is a greater chance for boy babies to achieve birth. Moreover, in each group the healthiest young mothers, aged eighteen to
twenty-two, have the greatest chance of producing boys—especially
when it is the *first* birth—whereas among mothers aged thirty-eight
to forty-two and over, the chances of having a boy may be less than
even. Thus, one explanation for the fact that the ratio of boys at
birth tends to be above average in the more favored groups and
below average in the underprivileged groups is that in the latter
groups the prenatal environments are not only inferior, but the
mothers usually have more children and continue childbearing
into the later ages which are most prejudicial to male fetuses.

Twins, Triplets. Since male fetuses suffer more under unfavorable prebirth conditions, it is not surprising that the more crowded
the womb, the less are the relative chances that males will survive.
In twin births the ratio drops to 101 or 102 boys to 100 girls; in
triplets, 98 boys to 100 girls; in quadruplets, 70 boys to 100 girls.

Wartime Births: More Boys? There is a long-standing belief
that the ratio of boys born goes up during and immediately after
wars, perhaps because nature is trying to help make up for the
men killed. The evidence for World Wars I and II supports this
theory only slightly. After World War I an increase of from 1 to
2.5 per cent in the boy ratio was reported in some countries of
Europe, and reached a high of 106.3 in the United States. During
World War II and its aftermath much smaller increases were
reported. To the extent that any increases in the boy ratio occur,
scientists ascribe it not to mysterious influences but to the fact
that in the war periods there are relatively more first births, and
more babies born to the younger, healthier mothers whose chances
of having boys are above-average.

**HEREDITARY INFLUENCES IN SEX DETERMINA-
TION.** Where parents have three or four children all of the
same sex, this may easily be as much a matter of chance as tossing
coins and having them turn up three or four heads in a row. But
where one finds families with up to twelve sons and no daughters

(or vice versa), and families heavily slanted for several generations toward children of one sex, the possibility arises that hereditary influences may be at work. The only real evidence in this direction comes from experiments with lower animals, in which strains have been bred with tendencies to produce much higher than average ratios of either males or females, as desired. Even though no such breeding has taken place among humans, it is not unlikely that in some families or individuals there also are inborn tendencies which would favor the production of offspring of one sex rather than the other. These tendencies might work directly through stronger sex genes of either type carried in the sperms or eggs, or indirectly through special factors in the environment of the mother's womb. But all of this is still theoretical as far as human beings are concerned.

Race Differences. A consistently lower ratio of boy births among Negroes than among whites seems to be genetic—at least in part—because over a period of more than fifty years since careful records have been kept in the United States, the Negro average has been no more than 102.5 or 103 boys to 100 girls (compared with the 105.5 or higher average for whites). This ratio has held despite great environmental changes and improvements in prenatal conditions. Among Mongoloid peoples—Japanese, Chinese, etc.—the reported average sex ratio has been about the same as among whites, although one study in Korea claimed the ratio at birth there reached as high as 115 boys to 100 girls.

Sex-Determining Methods. From time to time much publicity has been given to one "scientific method" or another for helping parents to have a baby of the sex they desire. As stated at the outset, none of these methods has proved to be effective. This applies, for example, to the "acid-alkali" treatment (acid for a girl, alkali for a boy). Also unproved is the theory that a boy is more likely to result if the mother conceives at some special point in her fertile period. But scientists do believe that means may eventually be found of influencing the chances of having either a boy or a girl, as desired. Possible methods may include (1) separating the father's Y-bearing from the X-bearing sperms in a laboratory and inseminating the mother with the desired type, or (2) injecting chemical preparations in the mother that will have different effects on the boy-producing and girl-producing sperms.

Forecasting the Expected Baby's Sex. If there is an urgent reason for knowing a baby's sex before birth—as in the case of threats of some inherited sex-linked disease (see "Sex-Linked Inheritance" in Chapter 11)—it is now possible to do this. The technique calls for drawing off amniotic fluid from the womb and examining the chromosomes in loose cells which have come from the fetus, to establish their sex identity. (See "Sex-identity Tests" in Chapter 14.) However, the procedure may pose certain dangers for the fetus and the mother, and is not warranted just to satisfy parental curiosity.

Your Own Chances of Having Boys or Girls. Throughout this chapter we have been speaking in terms of general averages as applied to millions of births each year. In your own case, with very few children involved, or with your mind on a single baby, the results may easily be different from the general odds. Although it remains true that young, healthy mothers tend to produce more sons than do equal numbers of older, less healthy mothers, the reader (or the reader's wife) may be a young, healthy woman and yet have three or four girls and no boy; and a much older, sickly mother next door may have nothing but boys. Nor will the fact that you have had three girls, or three boys in a row, increase the chance that the next child will be of the opposite sex. However, it is worth noting that the emphasis on having a child of one specific sex is becoming less marked in most advanced countries, particularly in the United States, where a growing number of parents see equal advantages in having girls or boys.

THE SEX FACTORS AFTER BIRTH. Do the genetic determinants of sex stop working after a child is born? No, they continue to influence the development of the body and its functioning throughout life. In the normal male the predominant "maleness" factors and the processes they set in motion will direct the production at the prescribed stages of all the many special masculine physical traits and functions—male sex organs, sex glands and sperm production, bigger and heavier bones and muscles, beard, etc. In the female the stronger balance of "femaleness" genes will direct the development of all her many special physical characteristics and functions—her sex organs and glands, egg production, menstruation, preparation for childbearing and nursing, and the various distinguishing characteristics of her body as compared with that of the male. (In later chapters we shall also see how the sex genes affect the types and incidences of diseases and defects in males and females.) Although environmental factors are also constantly at work, the sex genes largely dictate when puberty begins, when sexual development reaches its fullest point, when childbearing capacities in women cease, etc., as well as influencing many aspects of the behavior in the two sexes. (For additional discussions on these points, see Chapter 4.)

5

Twins, "Trips," "Quads," "Quints"

TWIN TYPES. The first thing to know about twins is whether they are "identicals" or "fraternals." Confusion may create many difficulties in rearing twins, in their adjustment to each other, and in medical diagnosis of their ailments.

Identical Twins. These are the "one-egg" twins, who are products of the same single egg and the same single sperm. Identical twins result when what started out to be a single baby becomes *two* babies by a splitting of the fertilized egg at a very early stage. In the process each twin gets duplicates of exactly the same chromosomes and genes, so that both have *identical heredity*. For this reason, also, identical twins *must always be of the same sex*, either two boys or two girls. But even though identical twins have exactly the same genes (and with respect to their hereditary factors are actually the same person in duplicate), their environments in the womb and after they are born may be different enough to keep them from ever being exactly the same in appearance, health, and behavior. Sometimes these differences are quite marked. Usually, however, it is hard to tell identical twins apart, and frequently their remarkable similarities continue until the end of their lives.

Fraternal Twins. These are the "two-egg" twins, products of two different eggs and two different sperms. They make up the majority of the twins—about 70 per cent. (That is, of all twins born, more than two out of three pairs are fraternals.) Even though fraternal twins are carried in the womb and are born together, they need be no more alike than any two children of a family who are born separately. In about half the cases fraternal twins are different in sex; one in four times both are boys, one in four times both are girls. Fraternal twins just happen to be con-

How Twins Are Produced

IDENTICAL TWINS
—result from the same single egg and single sperm.

After the egg begins to grow it divides into equal halves with duplicated chromosomes.

The halves go on to become two babies, with exactly the same hereditary factors.

IDENTICAL twins are always the same sex (either two boys or two girls). They usually look much alike. They have exactly the same eye color, hair color, hair form, blood types and all other hereditary traits.

FRATERNAL TWINS
—result from two different eggs, fertilized by two different sperms.

The two different fertilized eggs develop separately into two different embryos.

The two embryos grow into two babies with different hereditary factors.

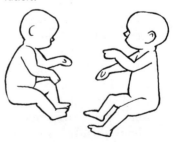

FRATERNAL twins may be either of the same sex (two boys or two girls), or different in sex (a boy and a girl). They may be different in looks, coloring, hair form, blood types, and other hereditary traits.

ceived at about the same time, when a mother produces two eggs instead of the usual one, and each egg is fertilized by a different sperm. In rare instances one of a pair of fraternal twins may be conceived several days, or even a week or more, after the other.

DIAGNOSING TWINS. Telling whether twins are identical or fraternal is not always easy, and mistakes are often made (although not nearly so much so as in the past). At birth one cannot go by the old theory that if like-sexed twins have the same placenta and fetal sac, this proves they are identical, whereas the presence of different placentas and sacs proves they are fraternal. It is now known that in up to one in four cases identical twins may develop separate placentas and sacs; conversely, in fraternal twins the sacs and placentas may sometimes be fused and appear to be one. Again, although generally true that twins who look remarkably alike are identicals, there are exceptions. Sometimes an early mishap or some unusual condition in the womb discriminating against one of an identical pair may cause him or her to look and be quite different from the other in various respects. On the other hand, just as two nontwin brothers or sisters may look remarkably alike, some fraternal twins also may look so much alike as to be mistaken for identicals.

Twin Tests. To resolve doubts, a number of tests can now be made which will prove quite clearly if twins are fraternal or identical. The first step is for the blood types—A, B, O; Rh; M-N, etc. (explained in Chapter 18). If the twins have blood-type differences, this is immediate proof that they are *not* identicals. But should their blood types be the same, this still does not mean that they might not be a fraternal pair. Further clarifying tests may be for their similarities or dissimilarities in eye color, eyesight, skin and hair color, hair form; finger-, palm-, and footprints; blood pressure, pulse, respiration, brain wave patterns; and various hereditary pecularities or abnormalities. (In cases where the problem of twin diagnosis is complex, consult one of the heredity clinics or some medical geneticist.)

Twin Transplants. An unusual and special characteristic of identical twins is that any tissue or organ from one can be successfully transplanted and take root in the body of the other. Even a whole organ, such as a kidney, has been successfully transplanted from one identical twin to another in a great many cases. But between nonidentical twins, as between any two genetically different persons, a transplant will "take" only in those instances where the tissues are not too incompatible, and where special operative measures and treatment reduce the chances that the transplanted organ will be rejected. (See also "Organ Transplants" in Chapter 12.)

Mirror-Imaging. This refers to the peculiarity, in about 30 per cent of identical twins, in which a birthmark, or some oddity in a tooth, feature, or organ of the body, appears on the right side of one twin and on the left side of the other. Such reverse patterning results from the fact that when the halves of the same embryo separate to form identical twins, certain characteristics may appear on opposite sides, somewhat as with the cut halves of an apple.

Left-Handedness. The popular belief that opposite-handedness— one twin right-handed, the other left-handed—was a common characteristic of twins has not been substantiated by careful studies which have shown that "lefties" are scarcely more prevalent among twins (perhaps 7 to 8 per cent) than in the general population. Further, the incidence of left-handedness among identical pairs is about the same as among fraternals.

Siamese Twins. These and other freak twins may result when the division of an egg or an embryo forming two identical twins is not complete. The twins may then be born joined at their breasts, hips, shoulders, or heads. (The famed circus pair born in Siam, from whom the name derives, were joined at the hip.) It is estimated that Siamese twins occur about once in 50,000 births. Few of these survive into maturity. In the past, operations to separate Siamese twins usually failed, but in recent years improved operative techniques have led to a number of successful separations. The worst freaks are those in whom the early embryonic separation is only partial, resulting in monsters with two heads and one body, or one body and four arms and four legs, etc. Most of these, fortunately, die before birth.

CHANCES OF HAVING TWINS. Most greatly affecting a mother's chances of producing twins are her age and the number of children she has had previously. In general, a mother between the ages of thirty-five and forty is about five times more likely to have twins than is a mother under twenty bearing her first baby. Since the difference involves mainly the ability to produce more

than one egg at a time, the relative twinning incidences among
the more and the less "twin-prone" mothers relates primarily to
fraternal twinning, for the incidence of identical twin births averages almost the same among mothers of all ages.

Total Twin-Birth Incidences. A marked drop in the over-all
twinning rate in the United States and other advanced countries
since the beginning of the century can be largely explained by the
decrease in childbearing by the older and more twin-prone mothers, and more childbearing by the younger, less twin-prone
mothers. Where formerly there were about 12 twin pairs per
1,000 births in the United States (among whites: see next section)
the rate is now a little over 9 pairs per 1,000, or about 1 twin pair
in 110 births. The drop, as indicated above, has been mainly in
fraternal twin births, with the ratio of fraternals to identicals
having declined from a previous 3 to 1, to a present 2 to 1 (or
more precisely, among whites, 6.5 to 3.5). In many European
countries, also, there has been a corresponding drop in twin birth
rates, although in most cases the incidences are still higher than
in the United States. In Ireland, where women marry late and
have many children into the older, more twin-prone ages, the
incidence of twinning is about the highest in Europe—over 14 per
1,000 births. Among the American Amish, whose women bear
large numbers of children into the older, more twinning-prone
ages, there also is a very high twinning frequency, reported as 15
pairs per 1,000 in one group, up to 21 per 1,000 in another group.

Race Differences. There are marked racial differences in
twinning rates, with Negroes having the highest rate, currently
about 1 twin pair in 73 births in the United States, and in some
African Negro tribes, such as the Yorubas, reportedly up to 1 pair
in 30 births. The lowest twinning rate is among Mongoloid peoples—Japanese, Chinese, etc.—with an average of only 1 twin pair
in 160 births. The racial difference relates entirely to fraternal
twins—identicals having about the same incidence in all racial
groups—so at one extreme the ratio of fraternals to identicals is
currently 7 to 3 among American Negroes, and 8 to 1 among the
Yorubas, while at the other extreme among the Japanese and
Chinese the identicals outnumber the fraternals by 2 to 1. Although
environmental factors may have something to do with the racial

differences in twinning, for the most part they appear to be genetic.

HEREDITY IN TWINNING. In addition to the racial factor, and apart from the effects of age and previous childbearing, in any group of mothers individual hereditary factors may play an important part in the chances of having twins. Repeated sets of twins occur in many families apparently much beyond random chance, as in cases of mothers who have produced six or seven sets of multiples—sometimes three or four sets consecutively, and occasionally with triplets or quadruplets among them. In general, once a mother has borne twins, her chances of a repeat twin birth may be several times the average incidence, especially if the first pair were fraternals. Adding to the belief that twins "run in families," a sister of a woman who has borne twins has twice the average chance of producing twins herself; and mothers who themselves are twins also have above-average chances of producing twins. It is estimated that perhaps one in every four or five women has a special predisposition to bear twins.

Twinning Genes. Among lower animals that ordinarily have single offspring (cattle, sheep, goats) it is well known that certain breeds are especially prone to twinning. How "twinning" genes work, whether in lower animals or humans, is not yet known. Where heredity plays a part, there would have to be different genes for the two types of twinning: For producing identical twins, the genes may be ones that cause an egg to split at an early stage. For fraternals, the genes may stimulate the mother's ovaries to produce two or more eggs at a time instead of the usual one. It may be noted that any familial twinning tendencies requiring complex genes could come through the father's as well as the mother's side. Moreover, the sperms of certain men might be more than ordinarily capable of fertilizing two eggs at a time, to produce fraternal twins, or be more prone to cause the splitting of an egg, to produce identicals. Ultimately, however, it depends on the woman to be able to carry through a twin pregnancy.

Mortality in Twins. Undoubtedly, many more twins are conceived—perhaps several times as many as achieve birth—with most being lost in early pregnancy. Further, the mortality of twins at birth and in early infancy is very much higher than of the singly born, the major reason being that over half the twins are born prematurely (with weights under 5½ pounds, much below average). Of twins born in hospitals, about 87 per cent survive.

Hormonally Induced Twinning. Recent hormone treatments to induce ovulation and conception in women who have had difficulty in childbearing have often worked all too well, resulting in the production not only of twins, but sometimes of triplets, quadruplets, and quintuplets (and in one case in New York City in 1970, of sextuplets, all of whom died). In time scientists may find a way to induce identical twinning also, when so desired, by causing fertilized eggs to divide after conception.

TRIPS, QUADS, AND QUINTS. Most of the general facts regarding two-at-a-time babies apply to the higher multiples (which have been called *supertwins*). The distinctions between identicals and fraternals also hold for triplets, quadruplets, or quintuplets, with the difference that since more than two are involved, one may find among these multiple sets combinations of both identicals and fraternals, as well as all of one type or the other.

Incidences of Trips, Quads, Etc. For large populations or the world as a whole, there seems to be a remarkable natural formula at work governing the relative incidences of twins, triplets, quadruplets, and quintuplets. Known as "Hellin's law" (after its German discoverer, D. Hellin), this formula provides that the incidences of triplets will be the square of the ratio of twins to single births; of quadruplets, the cube of the incidence of twins; of quintuplets, the fourth power of the incidence of twins. Thus, if twins occur once in 90 births, triplets should occur once in 90 times 90, or 8,100 births; quadruplets, once in 90 times 90 times 90, or 729,000 births; quintuplets, once in the latter number by 90 again, or 65,610,000 births. The ratios in the United States in recent years for triplets and quadruplets have come close to the formula, making slight corrections for the artificially induced multiples previously discussed. (Quintuplets normally are too rare for us to know how well the Hellin formula might apply to them.)

Mortality in Supertwins. Inasmuch as the prenatal and birth hazards for supertwins are higher than for twins, with most triplets and all quads and quints being premature, their mortality rates at birth are double that of twins and six times that of singly born. Of the triplets achieving birth, close to 30 per cent die in the first month, and of the quads, 50 per cent.

How Supertwins Are Formed. As with twins, the higher multiples may be all identicals from one egg, or all fraternals, from different eggs, or they may be combinations of identical and fraternal from two or more eggs. To illustrate, (1) identical *triplets* may result when a single fertilized egg first splits in half to form twin embryos, then one half remains set, to form one baby, while the other half splits again, to produce two more babies. All three carry the same genes and are as much alike one another as are identical twins. (2) Two-egg triplets start off at conception as a pair of fraternal twins, then one of these twin embryos splits to become two individuals, who are identical twins, while the triplet from the second egg is fraternal in relation to the other two. (3) Three-egg, all-fraternal triplets (probably the least common) are products of three different fertilized eggs. *Quadruplets* may be formed in five different ways, from one, two, three, or four eggs, with various combinations between all-identical and all-fraternal, while the possibilities for *quintuplet* formation are even more extensive. (Those desiring further information on these points are referred to the author's *Twins and Supertwins*, Chapter 19.)

The Dionne Quintuplets. These five girls attracted world-wide attention when they were born (near Callander, Ontario, Canada) in 1934 because they were the first recorded quintuplet set in which all survived. Further, they were proved to be an *all-identical* set, derived from a single egg which had divided and redivided. The five Dionnes remained as a unit until Emilie died in 1954 from suffocation during an epileptic attack; and Marie died in 1970 after a brief unrelated illness. These two had apparently had a special prenatal relationship, as indicated by their mirror-imaging in several details, and their having been the weakest of the five at birth. Helping the Dionnes to keep their place in supertwin history is the fact that there has been no other known surviving all-identical quintuplet set to this day. Most of the surviving quintuplet sets since the birth of the Dionnes have been either part identical and part fraternal or, in the case of those resulting from multiple-induced ovulation from hormonal treatments, all fraternal. (For additional facts about the Dionnes, see Chapter 23.)

WHY WE STUDY TWINS. If you have a set of twins (or triplets or quadruplets), particularly identicals, you will soon find that geneticists, doctors, and psychologists are much interested in them. The study of twins offers us some of our most important clues as to the degree in which human traits are hereditary or environmental. For instance, since identical twins carry exactly the same genes, any differences between them must be due to environment.* This applies to differences in stature, body build, features, or health, as well as to differences in IQ, behavior, achievement, and personality. The greater the difference in any trait between identical twins, the more strongly it points to the role of environment in helping to produce that trait. (As noted before, different environmental influences may be exerted on identical twins from the time they begin to develop in the womb.) On the other hand, where identical twins are raised in very different environments, as in cases of those separated in infancy and reared by different foster parents, remarkable similarities may yet appear in their physical make-up, diseases, and defects, and often in mental qualities and capacities. These similarities offer evidence of the role of heredity. Finally, when identical twins are compared with fraternal twins, the relative degrees of similarity or difference between paired twins of the two types may offer important clues as to the comparative influences of heredity and environment. (Twin studies will be dealt with again at later points in this book. See Index for specific references.)

---

* In very rare instances an accident during the initial egg division may result in a chromosomal difference between identical twins, such as one developing with a loss of a chromosome or part of a chromosome. For example, in identical twins from an XY egg, one twin may develop with the X and Y sex chromosomes, producing a male, whereas the other twin, losing the Y, may develop into an abnormal "XO," Turner's syndrome, female. (Chapter 14.)

6

Predicting Children's Looks

WHY PARENTS ARE INTERESTED. People wonder what their children will look like for more reasons than mere curiosity.

Pride. Individuals are flattered when their children resemble them (at least in the desirable aspects), and relatives may be partial to the child who is most like them or their side of the family.

Jealousy. Suspicious husbands are reassured if their children have some of their distinctive traits.

Good Looks. Of most concern is that the child—particularly a girl—be good-looking. On the latter point, fortunately, the chances that a daughter will be pretty or a son handsome are much greater today than ever before in most countries. The genes for looks have not changed, but environments have. Great improvements in diet, health, living conditions, and medical and dental care are steadily helping to produce better-looking better-built, and taller young people, and very few grow up to be really homely.

FORECASTING A CHILD'S LOOKS. If human beings were bred as are cats, dogs, or blooded livestock, predictions regarding the looks of an expected child would be easy. Through many successive generations of controlled breeding of domesticated animals, the genes of particular breeds have been so selected and fixed that there is little doubt about the size, shape, coloring, and feature details of offspring of a given mating. But human beings have at no time been bred so deliberately. Every person today is a descendant of a great many ancestors of varied types, and carries a haphazard collection of hundreds of genes governing body structure and outward appearance. Many of these genes—the dominant ones—reveal themselves by the surface traits they produce. But many other genes—the recessives—may have their effects suppressed in the parents, though they can assert themselves in a child. It is in the latter way that various unexpected and sometimes baffling traits may appear in children.

Specific Feature Forecasts. Any forecast of what the expected children of a given couple will look like is largely a matter of knowing or guessing what genes for the traits in question the parents carry, and then estimating the chances that their children will inherit the gene combinations required to produce these traits. If the parents are fairly similar in coloring and important features, and are of the same ethnic and/or racial stocks, they are likely to be carrying many matching genes for the traits they themselves show. Their children, then, are apt to inherit gene combinations that will make them resemble not only their parents but their brothers and sisters in many details. But when the parents are very different in coloring and features, and are of different stocks, their children can inherit any of numerous gene combinations. In such cases it is possible for a child to look not only unlike the parents but unlike other children in the family. However, conclusions about this cannot be drawn until maturity, because family resemblances often come out and increase with age.

ODDS IN FEATURE INHERITANCE. With respect to many traits that given couples show, geneticists can say there is an almost 100 per cent chance that these will reappear in their children. But there are many other traits where the expectancy of appearance in children can be stated only in terms of odds, such as a "one-in-two chance," or a "one-in-four chance," or even more-reduced chances. All such fractional forecasts are based on the knowledge of how the genes for a given trait work according to the principles of *dominance* and *recessiveness*, explained in "The Mendelian Laws," in Chapter 3. Here are some of the possibilities of transmission:

1. If *either* parent has a dominant trait (such as dark eyes) and the other parent has the corresponding recessive trait (such as blue eyes), there is at best a fifty-fifty chance any child will show the recessive trait. This will depend on whether the parent with the dominant trait is also carrying a hidden recessive gene

for the trait. But if this parent is not carrying the recessive gene, every child will show the dominant trait.

2. If both parents have a given dominant trait (such as dark eyes or dark hair), there is at best only a one-in-four chance a child will show the corresponding recessive trait (such as light-colored eyes, or blond hair). This can happen only if each parent is carrying a hidden recessive gene for the trait, paired with the dominant gene, and the two recessive genes come together in a child. Obviously, if both parents carry only dominant genes for a trait, there is no chance a child will show the recessive trait.

3. If both parents show a recessive trait (blue eyes, or blond hair, etc.), which means neither is carrying the corresponding dominant gene, every child will show the recessive trait. (Rare exceptions will be dealt with in later chapters.)

Uncertain Odds. There are some genes which may produce particular effects only if they are coupled with unidentified other genes, or only if there are certain special factors in the environment. In such cases the odds for the appearance of the trait in question may be uncertain, and one may speak of inheritance in terms such as "probable," "possible," "not too likely," etc.

Unexpected Results: Beauty and Homeliness. It sometimes happens that two very handsome parents will have a child who is definitely not good-looking. If this is not because of some prenatal condition, or some disease, accident, or other environmental factor, heredity may be involved in this way: Each of the good-looking parents could be carrying recessive genes which, coming together in a child, would produce homely features. Fortunately, a much more common situation these days is for two homely parents to have a very good-looking child. This, again, may be for two reasons: (1) Bad environmental conditions in the parents' childhood may have kept them from becoming as good-looking as their genes would have permitted. With more favorable environments today the same genes would make their children better looking. Or (2) each parent could be carrying genes that in new combinations with the genes from the other parent would produce better looks. (See accompanying chart.)

Laws of Chance. Whenever fractional odds are given that a child or children will or may inherit some trait, the reader should bear in mind that these odds are only in terms of averages. The

How Two Homely Parents May Have a Beautiful Child

FATHER

Bald

Murky-green eyes; lashes lost through disease

Misshapen mouth due to bad teeth

Bad nose due to accident

MOTHER

Dull, dark straight hair

Dull-brown eyes; drooping eyelids

Bad skin (local disorder)

Protruding under-lip

BUT they may carry and pass on to their child hidden genes for

—Blond, curly hair
Blue eyes
Long lashes
Pretty nose
Cupid's-bow mouth
Lovely complexion

RESULT: A BEAUTY CONTEST WINNER

How Two Handsome Parents May Have a Homely Child

FATHER

Curly, black hair

Large, dark eyes, long lashes

Well-shaped mouth and chin

MOTHER

Wavy, blond hair

Blue eyes, long lashes

Regular teeth, pretty mouth

BUT they may carry and pass on to their child hidden genes for

—Dull-brown, straight hair

Murky-green, small eyes with short lashes

Protruding jaw and teeth

Other irregularities, added to by environmental factors

RESULT: AN UGLY DUCKLING

results in the case of a single child or a single family need be no more certain than the results in any game or venture where chance is involved. For instance, if a parent carries a dominant gene for a trait, paired with a recessive gene, the chance that a child will get one or the other is like tossing up a coin. On the average the chances for heads or tails are exactly even. But sometimes one may get three or four heads in a row, and sometimes a run of tails. Likewise, when we say there is a fifty-fifty chance that a child will show a given inherited trait, it is possible in the case of a particular family that this trait may turn up in two or three, or even four, children in a row, or in none at all. (This is similar to the situation with regard to the chances of having boys or girls, discussed in Chapter 4.) Again, if we say there is a one-in-four chance that a recessive trait may appear, it is possible that in one four-child family, two or three children may have the trait, whereas in another four-child, or even six- or seven-child family, no one will have it.

How Odds Remain the Same. One important point that many persons find hard to accept is that the stated odds for the appearance of any trait *remain the same for each successive child* in a family, regardless of what has happened with the others. Again it is like tossing coins: If the chances are fifty-fifty for a head or a tail, one may toss three heads in a row, and there will still be the same fifty-fifty chance that the next toss will bring a head or a tail. So if first-time parents are told there is an even chance they will have a blond baby, and their baby is dark-haired, the chance for their second baby being blond is again no greater or no less than fifty-fifty. Only when one checks the results with large numbers of children does one find that the predicted genetic odds work out very closely.

7

Coloring:
Eyes and Hair

HUMAN COLORING. Human beings are much less gaudily or variably colored than are a great many, if not most, species of other animals; and the human coloring processes are generally simpler. In fact, all the colors of eyes, hair, and skin found among human beings of every type and race are produced in much the same way and with the same few basic pigments. The main pigment, or coloring ingredient, is *melanin*, a brownish substance. The amount and strength of this coloring matter, and the way it is distributed, is the chief factor in making eyes, hair, or skin darker or lighter. In addition to melanin there are several other pigments that produce special color effects. How the coloring process works in given individuals is determined largely by the activity of the "color" genes they inherit, although various environmental factors can modify the results.

EYE COLOR. This depends mainly on how the basic pigment, melanin, is distributed in the *iris*, the disclike part of the eye with the pupil at its center. The less pigment there is in the iris, the lighter the eye; the more pigment, the darker. As to particular eye colors, they are not produced by different colored pigments (like painted objects), but are mostly the *effects* of the way the same melanin pigment is concentrated in the eye, and how it reflects the light. In *blue* eyes, for instance, there is no blue pigment in the iris, but the blue effect results only from the way the light is reflected back to the viewer by the pigment particles in the rear of the iris—just as the sky is made to appear blue through an optical effect. In *gray* or *gray-blue* eyes, some extra pigment is distributed in the front of the iris in such a way as to give the grayish effect. In *green* eyes a special scattering of yellow pigment (possibly diluted melanin) in the front of the iris converts the bluish effect into green (somewhat in the way that yellow dots stippled on blue produce a greenish effect). Different amounts of light-brown or yellow pigment in the iris, and different patterns of pigment distribution, produce the various other light eye colors. The darker eyes, ranging from *brown* to *black*, result from the heaviest concentrations of pigment. (See illustration.)

THE EYE-COLOR GENES. Although the inheritance of eye color is sometimes complex, the main results are usually determined by a few key genes. A "strong" eye-pigment gene produces dark eyes. "Weak" eye-pigment genes produce the lighter-colored eyes. Should a child receive a strong gene from one parent, a weak gene from the other, the stronger gene will dominate and the child will have dark eyes (with only occasional exceptions). To have blue eyes, or any other lighter-colored eyes (light gray, light brown, green) a child must therefore get weaker color genes from both parents. When the parents have light eyes of different colors, the tendency is for the blue gene to be dominated by the light-brown, gray, or green genes, although it is quite possible that the nonblue-eyed parent may also be carrying hidden genes for blue eyes, and that the child will have blue eyes. Some shades and gradations of eye color may be influenced by structural details of the eye, iris patterns, blood vessels in the eye, chemical influences in the body, and the state of the person's health.

Albino Eyes. True albino eyes have no pigment in them whatsoever. The "pinkness" of these eyes results from the tiny blood vessels in the otherwise colorless iris, and the reflection from other blood vessels inside the eye. The absence of eye pigment is due to a pair of abnormal genes which also interfere with the coloring processes of the hair and skin. (Further details on albinism and its inheritance in later chapters. See Index.)

Unmatched Eyes. In occasional instances a person may have one eye dark and the other light, or each eye of a different shade or color. This condition (*heterochromia iridis*) may result in several ways, and sometimes heredity may be involved. For example: (1) A person may inherit one brown-eye gene and one

Eye Colors

*All eye colors are effects of how genes work
to produce pigment deposits in the iris*

BLUE EYES

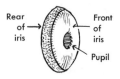

Light deposit of pigment in rear of iris, but not in front. "Blue" is only an optical effect. (See text.)

GRAY EYES

Light pigmentation in rear, as in blue eyes, but also some scattered dark pigment in front, which "grays down" the blue effect.

GREEN EYES

Rear of iris pigmented as in blue eyes, but scattered yellow pigment in front: Yellow over blue effect gives the green hue.

BROWN EYES

Heavy deposit of pigment in rear of iris, and also some pigment in front.

BLACK EYES

Very heavy deposit of pigment in both rear and front of the iris.

ALBINO EYES

No pigment at all in iris —"pink" effect due to reflection of blood vessels inside.

blue-eye gene. Normally this would produce brown eyes; but if in an early embryonic stage the brown-eye gene is knocked out of action on one side of the face, the blue-eye gene may take over on that side, producing a blue eye, whereas the other eye with its brown gene working as usual becomes brown. (2) In an embryo with light-eye genes something may happen to increase pigment production abnormally in one of the eyes, causing it to become much darker, or different in color, from the other. (3) Although either of the foregoing situations may be purely environmental, it is also possible for an inherited abnormality to produce unmatched eyes. The condition, either dominant or recessive, runs in some human families, but is much more common among cats, dogs, rabbits, and other animals.

Rare Eye Colors. "Tortoise-shell" eyes (mottled yellow and black) and "ruby" eyes are among rare types found in individuals. They may possibly occur through mutations in the eye-color genes.

Changes in Eye Color. Whereas most persons' eyes remain the same in basic color throughout life, it should not be overlooked that eye colors are capable of being modified by inherent chemical changes, aging effects, and various environmental factors. At birth most white babies (and many Negro babies) have slate-blue eyes, which in some may presently become heavily pigmented, turning brown, and in others may turn clear blue, depending on the types of genes they received. Sometimes a child's true eye color does not become set until it is several years old, and often there is a change at puberty. Diseases or nutritional deficiencies may affect eye-pigment production, leading to either darkening or lightening. Cataracts may make dark eyes bluish, as may aging effects.

PREDICTING CHILDREN'S EYE COLORS. The facts given in preceding sections, and in those which follow, should enable most prospective parents to make fairly accurate guesses as to what the eye colors of their children will be—or, at least, what the odds are that given types of eye color will appear in them.

Both Parents Dark-Eyed. All children will have dark eyes— *unless each parent* has some light-eyed close blood relative (particularly one of his or her parents, or a brother or sister), in which case there is a chance (but no more than one in four) of having a light-eyed child (blue-, gray-, or green-eyed). Only rarely do two dark-eyed parents with no known light-eyed blood relatives produce a light-eyed child, but it can happen. Once two dark-eyed parents have had a light-eyed child, there is a one-in-four chance of having another or others.

One Parent Dark-Eyed, the Other Light-Eyed. If the dark-eyed parent has no light-eyed close blood relative, there is little more chance of the couple's having a light-eyed child than if both mates are dark-eyed. (See preceding section.) But if the dark-eyed mate does have one or more light-eyed relatives (par-

ticularly a parent), there is up to a one-in-two chance of producing a light-eyed child or children in conjunction with the
light-eyed mate.

Both Parents Light-Eyed. It is about 98 per cent certain each
is carrying only light-eye genes and that all their children will
be light-eyed. Should both mates be blue-eyed, their children will
have approximately the same eye color. But if the eyes of one or
both parents are green, gray, or very light brown, a child's eyes
may be any one of these colors, or blue. But no child's eyes in a
mating between two light-eyed parents are apt to be much
darker than the eyes of either parent. However, in about 2 per
cent of the cases this may happen if one of the parents is carrying
a hidden dark-eye gene which for some complex reason failed to
assert itself. (The fact that a wife and husband are blue-eyed and
that a dark-eyed child is born to them is therefore by no means
proof that the child is not legitimate. See "Disputed Parentage
Cases" in Chapter 29.)

HAIR-COLOR INHERITANCE. This follows the same
principles as in eye-color inheritance. The degrees of darkness in
hair depend on how strong or active the hair-pigment genes are,
mainly with respect to how much of the basic brown pigment,
melanin, they produce. In black hair the hair cells are heavily
filled with melanin; in brown hair there is less; in light, blond
hair there is very little; and in white hair virtually none. Special
hair-color effects may result from the addition of other pigments
(as in red hair). Shades of the same hair color may be influenced
by the way the hair cells are constructed, their oiliness or dry-
ness, changes in the body chemistry, and other factors, in all of
which hereditary tendencies, as well as environmental influences,
play a part. In children light hair tends to darken somewhat
with puberty, blond hair often becoming brown, while in later
ages, of course, hair may become lighter through the weakened
action of the pigment genes and changes in the hair cells. (Natural gray hair and premature gray hair are due to special factors
to be discussed later.) All the various influences on hair color
must be taken into account in tracing hair-color inheritance in
any family.

The Hair-Color Genes. As is also true in eye color, the
strongest and most active hair-color genes almost always domi-

The Hair-Color Genes

*All human hair-color differences are due mainly to how genes work
to deposit the basic brownish pigment, melanin, among the hair cells.*

BLOND HAIR

Dilute melanin pigment gives yellowish effect. The less the pigment, the lighter the shade of blond.

RED HAIR

A special gene works to produce red pigment, diffused with scattered melanin pigment.

BROWN HAIR

Heavy deposit of pigment. The more pigment, the darker the shade of brown.

BLACK HAIR

Extremely heavy deposit of melanin-pigment granules.

NOTE: Various internal and external influences can modify the effects of the hair-color genes. See text.

nate the weaker ones, so that if a person inherits a dark-hair gene from one parent, a light-hair gene from the other, the hair will be dark. For the same reason, a dark-haired person may often be carrying a hidden gene for any of the lighter hair shades, but a fair-haired person cannot be carrying a dark-hair gene (except in rare instances).

Red Hair. This results from special genes, which produce a reddish pigment. The degree to which the red shows through depends on the activity of the other hair-color genes the person carries. When coupled with a gene for black hair, the effects of the red gene will be obscured. But when the red-hair gene is coupled with genes for lighter hair shades, the results may be reddish-gold, chestnut, or vividly red hair. The red-hair genes are found in all racial groups, including pure Negroes, among whom red hair sometimes appears when their dark-hair genes are not strongly active. (See also last paragraph of this chapter.)

White Hair. This can be due to several causes: (1) Defective genes (as in albinos), which prevent the production of any pigment in the hair cells; (2) very weak blond-hair genes which produce almost no pigment; (3) disease, hereditary or environmental, which interferes with the hair-pigmenting process; or (4) aging effects. In the latter case, the approximate stage in a person's life when his hair begins to gray and then turns white is often governed by heredity, with the graying taking place in some families much earlier than others. Even though nerve disorders, diseases, or shocks may affect hair cells and the hair-pigmentation process, causing new hair to grow out white, it is a myth that a person's whole head of hair can turn white "overnight."

Eye and Hair Color. In most cases very dark eyes and very dark hair go together, almost invariably so among pure Negroes and Mongolians. But among whites it is not uncommon to see a person with very dark hair and blue or light-gray eyes, or, conversely, blond hair and dark eyes. Among mulattoes and other racially mixed persons, also, dark-light combinations in eyes and hair (or vice versa) are seen. This is proof that the eye-color and hair-color genes may be inherited separately and work independently.

FORECASTING CHILDREN'S HAIR COLOR. In trying to guess what an expected child's hair color will be, parents must first seek to determine what hair-color genes they carry. They can be guided in this by being clear as to the *natural* color of their hair, ruling out any changes produced artificially or by acquired diseases (which can have no effect on their genes), by what their own hair color was in childhood and at puberty, and by types and shades of hair color in their parents, brothers and sisters, and other close relatives. With these facts in mind, the following general forecasts may be made:

Both Parents Dark-Haired. All children will have dark hair— *unless each parent* has some light-haired close blood relative or relatives (or is otherwise carrying a hidden light-hair gene), in which case there is a chance—but no more than one in four—of having a light-haired child. In any case, once a dark-haired couple has had a fair-haired child, there is a one-in-four chance of having another or others.

One Parent Dark-Haired, Other Light-Haired. If the dark-haired parent has no light-haired close blood relative, which strongly indicates he or she is carrying only dark-hair genes, there is little more chance of the couple's having a light-haired child than if both parents were dark-haired. (See preceding section.) But if the dark-haired mate does have one or more fair-haired close relatives (particularly a parent), there is up to a one-in-two chance of producing a fair-haired child in conjunction with the light-haired mate.

Both Parents Brown-Haired. Most children's hair will be brown, possibly a little darker or lighter than the parents', and with a chance that some child may be blond.

Both Parents Blond. Their children are almost certain to be blond (especially if the parents are light blond or flaxen-haired). But occasionally blond parents may produce a brown-haired child.

Red Hair. Two true redheaded parents are likely to have all redheaded children, but light-brown or blond hair may also appear among their offspring. If one mate is redheaded, the other blond, there may be an even chance of having a redheaded child, with a reduced chance if the other parent is dark-haired. Redheads also appear sometimes when both mates are dark-haired, but only very rarely if both parents are blond.

8

Skin Color

HUMAN DIFFERENCES. Even though there are marked differences in skin color among individuals—especially of different races—we noted in the last chapter that all human beings have the same basic skin-coloring elements, although in varying proportions as governed by particular genes. *Melanin* is the chief skin-coloring pigment, as it is in eye and hair coloring. There are several additional skin pigments, among them *melanoid* and *carotene* (yellowish or yellowish-red), and several blood pigments in the skin which contribute to its coloring. Also influencing the skin color of individuals is the structure of the skin and its thickness and oiliness, to which heredity may contribute. Environment can modify skin color through such factors as exposure to the sun (to be discussed later), changes in the person's health, and age. But since the effects of environment cannot be inherited, the big differences in human coloring everywhere are those produced by the genes people inherit.

THE SKIN-COLOR GENES. What chiefly determines a person's skin color is the way that certain genes work to lay down deposits of the two brownish pigments, melanin and melanoid, in the skin cells. The relative amounts and strengths of these pigments, and how they are combined in persons, account for many grades of skin color, from almost black through dark brown, light brown, and light. In other words, the most active melanin-melanoid genes are in the darkest Negroes, the least active in the "whitest" whites. In addition, an especially active carotene gene contributes to the yellowish skin of Mongolians and the bronze skin of their relatives, the American Indians. However, the terms "black," "yellow," "red," and "white" to describe races are highly inexact, because few Negroes are really black, no Mongolians are really yellow, no Indians are red, and no whites are white. But more than this, some whites, such as those found in India and the Arab countries, have blacker skins than many Negroes, even of certain native African tribes.

Skin-Color Mixtures. In offspring of persons with markedly different skin colors there may appear to be a "blending" of the colors, but actually, the effects are only those of new combinations of the skin-color genes. There is an important difference here from the way the eye-color or hair-color genes work. In producing eye color, if a dark-eye gene is coupled with a light-eye gene, the dark-eye gene dominates the process (as we saw in the preceding chapter), and the child has dark eyes. The results with one dark-eye gene are the same as with two dark-eye genes. (This is also true of combined dark and light hair-color genes.) But in skin color, if one dark-skin gene is coupled with one light-skin gene, there is no dominance of the first over the second. Instead there is an in-between result.

Negro-White Matings. How the skin-color genes work is best shown in the results of (1) a Negro-white mating, producing mulatto offspring, and (2) a mating between two mulattoes. As indicated in the accompanying illustration, a pure Negro carries several pairs of dark-skin genes and a pure white several pairs of white-skin genes. (There are probably more than the two pairs shown for each.) In the first mating, each of the offspring receives one set of the Negro-skin genes, and one set of the white-skin genes, which produces in each much the same in-between skin color. But when two mulattoes mate, their different skin-color genes sort out independently to form any of various combinations: One child may get *all* Negro-skin genes, and be as dark as the darkest Negro grandparent; another child may get *all* white-skin genes, and be as light as the lightest white grandparent; or a child may get any mixed combination of the genes and have any skin color in between these extremes. However, since the feature genes (which we will deal with in the next chapter) are also inherited separately, a child of two mulattoes who has the lightest skin might have features that are much more Negroid than those of his darkest brother.

"Throwback" Children. One of the most persistent popular myths is that two white parents sometimes produce a "coal-black"

Skin Color

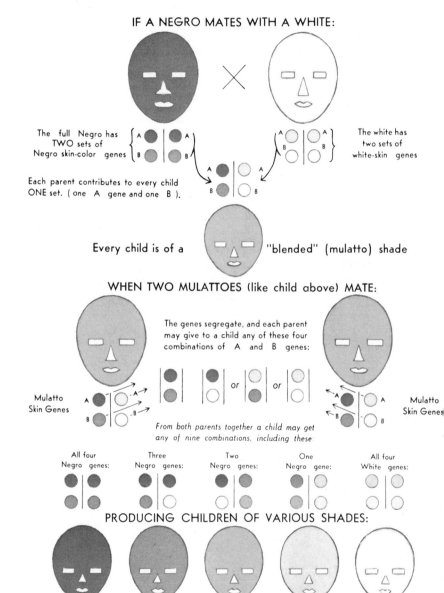

IF A NEGRO MATES WITH A WHITE:

The full Negro has TWO sets of Negro skin-color genes

The white has two sets of white-skin genes

Each parent contributes to every child ONE set. (one A gene and one B).

Every child is of a "blended" (mulatto) shade

WHEN TWO MULATTOES (like child above) MATE:

The genes segregate, and each parent may give to a child any of these four combinations of A and B genes:

Mulatto Skin Genes

or   or

Mulatto Skin Genes

From both parents together a child may get any of nine combinations, including these:

| All four Negro genes: | Three Negro genes: | Two Negro genes: | One Negro gene: | All four White genes: |

PRODUCING CHILDREN OF VARIOUS SHADES:

Black   Dark   Medium   Light   White

NOTE: Only two types of skin color genes are shown, but there probably are more.

(Adapted from The New YOU AND HEREDITY. Copyright, 1939, 1950, by Amram Scheinfeld.)

baby if one of the parents has some long-hidden "Negro blood." This cannot really happen, first, because a very dark-skinned baby can be produced only if it receives Negro skin-color genes from *both* parents; and, second, if one parent alone carried skin-color genes strong enough to make the baby "black," that parent would not look white. Wherever these "black-baby" cases have been tracked down, either they are found to be untrue or else the parents involved were both racially mixed and may or may not have been passing as whites.

American Negro-White Mixing. Contrary to popular notions, there is probably less Negro-white mixing in the United States today than in former times, and the Negro population as a whole is not becoming lighter in skin color. (See Chapter 27.)

ENVIRONMENT AND SKIN COLOR. All that environment can do with respect to skin color is to increase or decrease the *effects* of skin-color genes to a certain extent. Under a hot sun the pigmentation process is speeded up to lay down more pigment particles in the skin and thus give it added protection. This is what happens when a person tans during the summer. If a white man lives a long time in the tropics his skin may become very tanned, but no matter how dark it gets it will never look like true Negro skin. Nor will his children be born any less white than if he lived in Norway. Once the same white man leaves the tropics and remains away his skin will become progressively lighter. Pure Negroes, however, have much the same basic skin color whether they live in Africa or in the United States, although those exposed continually to hot sun will be somewhat darker, everything else equal, than those who are not. But even in Africa, as elsewhere, under the same conditions some strains of Negroes are always much darker than others. Nor need it be added that the dark skin of Negroes is due solely to the fact that they have inherited dark-skin genes, and not to centuries of exposure to the sun (as Shakespeare's Othello thought). Just as white children continue to be born to heavily tanned white parents in the tropics, dark Negro children continue to be born to Negroes who for generations have lived in northern American cities.

Negroes "Turning White." Such rare reported instances may be the result of an inherited disease, *vitiligo*, which gives affected Negroes an albino appearance. However, while sometimes the whole face may whiten, the skin whitening is usually confined to white patches over the body.

Sunburn. Heredity plays a considerable part in the way different skins react to the sun. In some white persons the pigment genes will be quickly stirred to added activity under a hot sun, and they will tan easily and with no discomfort. Other persons—particularly fair-skinned redheads and those with "milky-white" skins—will simply *broil*. But even some Negroes sunburn painfully.

PREDICTING CHILDREN'S SKIN COLORS. Because of the complexity of skin-color inheritance, only a few general observations can be made other than those with respect to Negro-white or mulatto matings. Among whites, where one parent has darkish, swarthy skin (as in Italians, Arabians, and other Mediterranean peoples) and the other parent is fair-skinned, the children are likely to be of in-between shades. Again, if both parents are of mixed stock, each with some swarthy and some fair-skinned relatives, their children may also be any of these varied skin-color types. Familial resemblances in skin color are apt to become stronger with aging.

Freckles. The tendency to freckling often runs in families, with inheritance by way of a *dominant* gene. Transmission of freckling is especially likely when red hair is also present.

9

The Features

ONE'S PHYSICAL LOOKS. Many things can make people look the way they do. Heredity, obviously, is almost the sole factor in making humans distinctive in every detail of their looks from all other animals. But it is the relatively minor differences in appearance among humans themselves which we have in mind when we speak of inheritance of features. As a rule, then, the genes set the pattern for the way individual characteristics in features develop in the growing child, the shapes they take at maturity, and the changes they undergo in later years. One of the clearest proofs of this is that identical twins, who have the same genes, usually preserve a remarkable resemblance to each other throughout life, even when living apart under different conditions. However, environment can often do a great deal to modify the features, although much more, usually, with respect to their outer forms than to their inner construction. The changes in underlying fat, tissue, and muscles of the face and its parts are what we chiefly notice when we remark upon the differences in a person's looks that result from disease, state of health, or age.

The Feature Genes. There are a great many feature genes which work together to shape both the face as a whole and its separate details. For instance, the shaping and appearance of the eyes will depend not only on the specific eye genes but on the way other genes help to construct the brows, forehead, nose bridge, and cheekbones, and to lay down fatty tissue in the region. Other features are similarly influenced in their appearance by surrounding details.

Sex Differences. Although men and women inherit the same feature genes, the effects of these may be considerably modified in one direction or another by basic sex differences in body chemistry.

Thus, just as the XY and XX sex-chromosome mechanisms cause the sex organs of males to develop differently from those of females, in a more limited way they also affect the features, causing males as a group to have relatively heavier brows, squarer chins, heavier facial muscles, and more facial and body hair, and women to have softer facial contours and relatively smaller noses, ears, and mouths. (For sex differences in stature and body form, see next chapter.)

THE EYES. Shapes and appearances of persons' eyes result mainly from the way the key eye genes construct the eye sockets, eyeballs, and eyelids, as well as the surrounding bony structures of the face and their fleshy parts. Moreover, the width of the nose bridge has an important influence on the spacing between the eyes.

Mongolian and Slant Eyes. The distinctive inherited eye shapes of the Mongolians (Chinese, Japanese, Eskimos, etc.) result from fatty underpadding of the lids, and thick folds (*epicanthi*) overlapping the inner corners, giving the eyes almond-shape or oblique effects. Mongolian eyes should not be confused with the true "slant" eyes found among whites and other peoples, in which the inner skin folds are absent and the eyes really slant upward toward the outer corners. Moreover, the genes for the two types of eyes work differently, the genes for Mongolian eyes being dominant, those for true slant eyes recessive. Thus, in matings between a Mongolian and a white, the children will almost always have Mongolian eyes. But if in two white parents one has slant eyes, the other straight eyes, the children are likely to have straight eyes.

Other Eye-Gene Workings. *Wide or Large Eyes.* The genes tend to be dominant. If one parent's eyes are wide and/or large, the other parent's narrow and/or small, their children will tend to have the wide or large eyes. (Abnormally small eyes: See "Eye Defects" in Chapter 15.)

Deep-Set Eyes. The genes are usually recessive. If only one parent has such eyes, the child is not too likely to have them.

Long Lashes. The genes are dominant. If one parent has them, they are likely to reappear in a child.

Drooping Eyelids. This abnormality is dominant. (See Chapter 15.)

Dominance and Recessiveness in Features

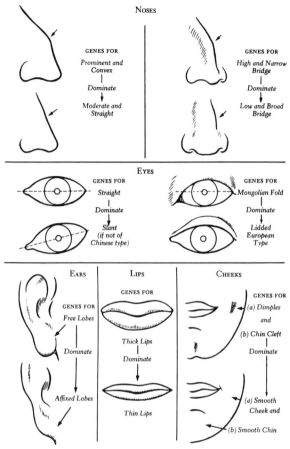

NOSES

GENES FOR
Prominent and
Convex
|
Dominate
↓
Moderate and
Straight

GENES FOR
High and Narrow
Bridge
|
Dominate
↓
Low and Broad
Bridge

EYES

GENES FOR
Straight
|
Dominate
↓
Slant
(if not of
Chinese type)

GENES FOR
Mongolian Fold
|
Dominate
↓
Lidded
European
Type

EARS

GENES FOR
Free Lobes
|
Dominate
↓
Affixed Lobes

LIPS

GENES FOR
Thick Lips
|
Dominate
↓
Thin Lips

CHEEKS

GENES FOR
(a) Dimples
and
(b) Chin Cleft
|
Dominate
↓
(a) Smooth
Cheek and
(b) Smooth Chin

* It should be kept in mind that it is not one feature itself which dominates another but the genes for a given feature which dominate other genes.

THE NOSE. Although one hears it said, "He has his father's nose," this organ is not inherited as a unit. Its shape and size result from the action of a number of separate genes, governing the sizes and forms of its different parts—the bridge, nostrils, "bulb" or tip, and the junction with the upper lip. If a person does have a nose which seems almost a replica of that of one parent, it is likely he received a combination of the nose genes from the one parent which dominated those from the other parent. More often a child's nose will resemble that of one parent in only one or two main details, while also showing some characteristics of the other parent's nose. But in all cases due allowance should be made for aging effects and environmental influences on nose shapes. In addition to radical changes in nose shapes at puberty, less perceptible and gradual changes may occur through the years as part of the normal maturing and aging processes. Often family resemblances in noses become most evident in the older years. On the other hand, hereditary nose characteristics may be masked or canceled out in individuals by accidents, disease, plastic operations, effects of abnormal diet or heavy drinking, and other environmental factors. All the foregoing facts must be taken into account when tracing inheritance of nose shapes in any family.

Nose Inheritance Predictions. If two parents have very different nose shapes—one straight and moderate-sized, the other prominent, hooked, high-bridged, humped or pug-nosed—the genes for the more prominent or extreme details usually dominate, and these tend to reappear in a child. If both parents have rather small, straight, regular noses, the children all are apt to have noses of the same type. However, since the various nose genes may sort out and work independently, one child in a family may have a small nose with large nostrils, another a long nose with small nostrils. Varieties of noses may be found especially in offspring of two mulatto parents who carry both white and Negro nose genes. In matings between whites and Negroes, the children's noses tend to have the high and narrow bridges of the White parents and the broad nostrils of the Negro parents.

MOUTH AND TEETH. Inheritance of mouth shapes may be even more complex than that of nose shapes. Not only is the mouth much influenced by the structure of the jaws, teeth, palate, and surrounding muscles, but being so movable and in such constant use, its form and appearance are continually and throughout life affected by the person's talking, eating, and sleeping habits, facial expressions, and moods. In addition, there are the marked changes in mouth shape that illness and aging can produce. Hereditary factors in mouth shapes can therefore be identified only after environmental influences are ruled out, and this is not easy. To date, conclusions have been arrived at only with respect to the more marked racial differences and a few odd or abnormal conditions.

Negro and White Lips. In mixed matings, the genes for the thick Negro lips tend to dominate. If the Negro parent has no white genes, the offspring are all likely to have thick lips. In matings between mulattoes, the offspring may have various types of lips and mouths, showing that a considerable number of different genes are involved.

Hapsburg Lip. The peculiarity of a protruding lower lip, usually with a narrow, undershot jaw, is named after the royal Spanish and Austrian families in which it has been prevalent for generations. It is dominant in inheritance.

Dimples. Dimples are usually dominant. If they are found in one parent, a child is likely to have dimples too.

Chins. Receding chins tend usually to be recessive to straight chins; narrow or pointed chins recessive to wide chins. In matings between parents with these different chin shapes, the children are more likely to have straight rather than receding chins, and wide rather than narrow or pointed chins. *Clefts* in the chin (vertical) or grooves (horizontal) are likely to be dominant in inheritance.

Teeth. There are marked family tendencies toward various types of teeth and the manner in which upper and lower teeth are set together. But eating habits, diet, tooth care, and other conditions may also contribute to these family resemblances. Where direct evidence of inheritance in teeth can best be seen is in the abnormal conditions described in Chapter 13.

HAIR FORM. Natural differences in hair form, from curly to poker-straight, are determined chiefly by the way genes cause the hair to be shaped and to grow out of the hair follicles in the scalp. The genes for the frizziest or curliest types of hair usually dominate those for straighter hair. Most potent is the woolly gene, found largely among Negroes, but sometimes also, though rarely, in whites who have no Negro blood. Next in order of potency, the kinky gene dominates the ordinary curly; the curly dominates the wavy; the wavy dominates the ordinary straight. However, the very thick, straight Mongolian hair is of a special type, and the gene for this may dominate all the others. Thus, in matings between pure Mongolians and whites, and usually between Mon-

The Hair-Form Genes

*One's inherited hair form depends on how genes work to shape
the hairs and the follicles out of which they grow*

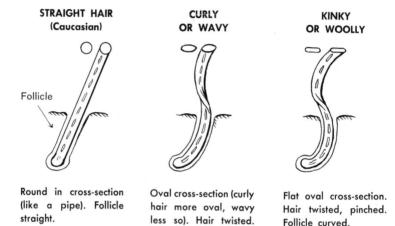

STRAIGHT HAIR (Caucasian)	CURLY OR WAVY	KINKY OR WOOLLY
Round in cross-section (like a pipe). Follicle straight.	Oval cross-section (curly hair more oval, wavy less so). Hair twisted. Follicle curved.	Flat oval cross-section. Hair twisted, pinched. Follicle curved.

(For inheritance workings, see text.)

golians and Negroes, the offspring will all have the thick, straight
hair. Likewise, in matings between white persons and Negroes
with woolly hair, the Negro type of hair will tend to appear in
offspring.

Hair Inheritance in Whites. If we rule out any artificial
changes made in parents' hair, and keep in mind that hair form
may change with age—wavy or curly hair often becoming straighter
—here are some predictions of what a child's hair form will be:

Curly Hair. A child has little likelihood of being curly-haired
unless at least one parent has natural curly hair. If both parents
are curly-haired, the chances of the child's being so increase and
become almost certain if all the parents' close relatives are curly-
haired. Should there be relatives with wavy hair and/or straight
hair, these hair types may also appear in children of curly-haired
parents, though with less frequency than curly hair.

Wavy Hair. A child with such hair results most often if both
parents are wavy-haired, or if one parent and all his or her close

relatives are the same. If one parent has wavy hair, the other straight, the chances are even for either type to appear in a child.

Straight Hair. If in both parents, their children are almost certain all to have straight hair.

Kinky Hair. If just one parent is kinky-haired, and comes from a family with that hair type, the children are all likely to be kinky-haired. But if the one parent has some nonkinky-haired relatives and the other parent has curly, wavy, or straight hair, there is an even chance any of their children's hair will not be kinky.

Hairiness. The tendency to have much or little hair on the head or body, or both, is strongly influenced by heredity. Race differences offer the best examples. Mongolians (especially full-blooded American Indians) have the least facial and body hair, Negroes have more, and whites have the most. The hairiest of all peoples are the primitive Ainus of Japan, who are of white origins.

Heavy eyebrows growing together are most common in Greeks, Turks, Armenians, and other Mediterranean peoples, but also are sometimes found in other groups, including the Irish and Welsh. Apart from the gene workings, hormonal factors may have much to do with the extent of hair growth on the face or body. The most marked differences in this respect are between women and men, with the male sex hormones tending to stimulate such hair growth.

Baldness. See special discussion in Chapter 13.

10

Shape and Stature

HUMAN SIZES. The general sizes of all human beings, as of animals of other species, are determined by their heredity. The human genes dictate that no person can grow to be as big as an elephant, nor as small as a mouse. Moreover, human stature genes work within a much narrower range than do those of many other species. For example, there are no such size differences among human beings as among dogs—a giant Saint Bernard or a pint-sized Mexican Chihuahua. It is because the differences in human stature are so limited that we often attach such importance to a few inches more or less in height. At the same time, the limited differences have made it difficult to study stature inheritance, with added complications resulting from the fact that the influences of environment on stature must always be taken into account.

Biggest and Littlest. In terms of groups, the very tallest human beings today are African Negroes of the Lake Chad tribes, near the lower Nile, whose males average 6 feet 1 inch in height, with many 7 feet and over. (These towering Negroes are often shown in movies.) The smallest humans are the pygmy Negrillos, also of Africa, whose adult males average 4 feet 6 inches. (Midgets and giants are in the abnormal category. See Chapter 13.) Apart from these extremes the differences between people of stocks we call "tall," such as the Swedes, and those we call "short," such as the Japanese or Italians, may be a matter of only 2 or 3 inches on the average. The principal reasons why the stature differences of the various human ethnic stocks are not greater is that there has been constant interbreeding among them, and that no attempt was ever made to breed human groups deliberately for tallness or shortness.

Sex Differences. In any group and under any conditions, a major factor in determining height is an individual's sex. Given exactly the same stature genes, a male will grow about 6 per cent taller than a female, or somewhat over three quarters of an inch more to each foot of her size. Thus, younger American men at this writing (under age thirty), average over 5 feet 9 inches in height (with the college group reaching an inch more), while young women (aged eighteen to twenty-four) average about 5 feet 4½ inches. This sex difference can be little more attributed to environmental factors, such as work activities, diet, living habits, etc., than can the differences in size between bulls and cows, or roosters and hens. Obviously, the internal chemical differences between the sexes, set in motion by their respective XX and XY chromosome mechanisms, cause their skeletal and bodily developments to diverge not only in size but in proportions. (Further discussion under "Sex Differences in Body Form," p. 72.) But this indicates that in individuals of either sex, special internal chemical factors may also modify the activity of their stature genes and the development of their bodily details. Some of these factors may be hereditary, some environmental, and some a combination of the two. (For extreme examples, see "Stature Abnormalities," in Chapter 13.)

Environment and Stature. Just as plants and flowers grow taller if they are in good soil and are properly watered and tended, or can be stunted if conditions are poor, so the statures of human beings can also be considerably influenced by their environments. Although human genes have changed little in thousands of years, people of modern times are considerably taller than were those of ancient and medieval periods. Most noticeable have been the changes in the past half century, with the new generations of Americans being taller than their grandparents by an average of 2 to 3 inches. Especially marked increases are found among off-spring of various immigrant stocks, with frequent cases of sons 4 to 6 inches taller than their fathers. In most European countries, and in many other advanced countries, including Japan, increase in stature has also been noted. For the most part this increase has been attributed to great improvements in diet, living conditions, and medical care. However, some scientists believe that changes in the earth's climate, and in meteorological and cosmic conditions, have added to the stature increase.

How Much Taller Can People Grow?   Many experts think that in about two hundred more years the average height of American males will be at least 6 feet, with a great many up to 7 feet or somewhat over, while the average American woman will be about as tall as the average man now is. Any much greater height may bring difficulties. As will be noted in Chapter 13, giants of 8 feet or over have tended to be weak glandular cases, usually short-lived.

FAMILY STATURE INHERITANCE.   Whatever the environmental conditions may be anywhere, it is evident that tendencies toward greater height run in some families, and in some racial or ethnic groups, and toward lesser height in others. Among American Negroes, for instance, probable descent from the tall African strains is indicated by heights in men of up to 7 feet, and by many towering women. Also, Americans descended from northwestern Europeans tend to be taller than those from south-European stock.

Stature Genes.   How the stature genes work is not precisely known, but as a rule it appears that the shortness genes dominate the tallness genes. This means that a tall person probably is not carrying any shortness genes, and that if two tall persons mate, all their children will be tall, except in individual cases where disease, dietary deficiencies, hormonal upsets, etc., may stunt normal growth. Short persons may or may not be carrying hidden tallness genes; they probably are not if they are of short stocks on both sides and if this shortness was not due to environmental factors. But if they had or have some close relatives who are tall, they may very well be carrying hidden genes for tallness, and may produce children much taller than themselves. This is especially likely to be so with persons who had grown up under unfavorable conditions, as with those of various immigrant groups. (See preceding sections.) Where one parent is genetically short, and the other tall, the odds are somewhat greater that the children will be short rather than tall.

Age Changes in Stature.   In judging inheritance of stature, or drawing conclusions with respect to individuals, full allowance should be made for age changes that have taken place or may take place, and for the fact that different individuals have different growth rates, even with the same stature genes. Males sometimes do not reach their full height until age twenty-three or twenty-four, females not until twenty-one or twenty-two. Some shrinkage in height in men and women may begin to occur as early as age thirty, becoming more pronounced with added years, so that by age seventy a man may be about 1 inch or more shorter than he was at twenty-five.

BODY FORM. Although skeletal structure is largely determined by heredity, as is stature, a person's "upholstery"—the muscles, fat, and outer tissues—can be strongly influenced by environment. Thus, where an individual's height remains almost the same from maturity on (except for the slight decline with aging, just noted), the outer body form may change frequently, and sometimes radically within a short time. Moreover, occupations and living habits can do much to influence the structure and outer form of the body or its parts, as is shown in certain bodily characteristics common to farmers, sailors, dancers, etc. Such environmental characteristics may be mistaken for inherited traits when they appear in successive members of families who have worked at the same tasks for generations. Nevertheless, with full allowance for the environmental influences, definite tendencies toward given proportions and details of the body are strongly conditioned by a person's genetic make-up.

Changes in Dimensions. Going with the increases in stature have obviously been increases in weight. But there also have been changes in bodily proportions. The younger adults in proportion to heights tend to have relatively broader shoulders, narrower hips, and longer limbs than their parents, and on the whole they are what would be considered "better built" men and shapelier women.

Growth and Puberty. Contributing to and accompanying the increase in stature has been much more rapid growth in childhood and much earlier puberty. In many places today children at age five are 2 to 3 inches taller than their grandparents were at the same age; and where at the turn of the century most men did not attain their full height until about age twenty-six, they are now usually doing so in the United States and Europe by age twenty. The onset of menstruation by girls in advanced countries—at an average age now under thirteen—is about two or three years earlier than it was in their grandmothers or great-grandmothers. Even though heredity sets the potentials for childhood growth and puberty onset among human beings, and influences the growth rates in individual families and groups, the big general changes in recent decades in these respects have been due largely to such environmental factors as better nutrition and hygiene, reduction of childhood diseases, and more healthful exercises.

Obesity. This bodily characteristic has received much attention in the current period when so many people are weight conscious. Although many complex factors, both physical and psychological, are generally involved in obesity, there is evidence that tendencies toward fatness or slenderness may have a hereditary basis. In lower animals some strains of a species have been bred which are excessively fat, others lean. Also, in human beings, studies of twins show that obesity is far more often a common trait of both members of an identical pair than of a fraternal pair, or of non-twin siblings.

Obesity Genes. These genes, it is believed, work mainly through the glands, causing certain individuals to put on much more fat per pound of food consumed than do others, or increasing the proportion of weight gain that is fatty tissue. This does not mean that even glandular obesity is always, or most often, due to heredity, since many of these cases are traceable to acquired diseases. (See "Extreme Fatness," Chapter 13.) Further, when all members of a family are fat it may often be because of their similar diets and ways of living. But when environmental causes are minimal, genetic studies indicate that a predisposition toward obesity may be produced by *dominant* genes, with tendencies toward leanness produced by *recessive* genes. Thus, on this basis, slender parents, carrying no obesity genes, will usually have only slender children. But fat parents, while tending to have fat children, may be carrying hidden slimness genes, and so may also have some slender children.

SEX DIFFERENCES IN BODY FORM. Whatever the special effects of body-form genes may be, a most important fact is that their general workings are very different in males and females. Just as the same stature genes produce greater height in the male than in the female, the same body-form genes, as in a brother and sister, have divergent effects on almost every detail of

Sex Characteristics in Limbs

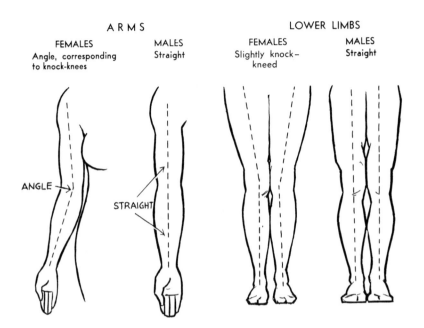

ARMS

LOWER LIMBS

FEMALES
Angle, corresponding
to knock-knees

MALES
Straight

FEMALES
Slightly knock-
kneed

MALES
Straight

ANGLE

STRAIGHT

their skeletal structure and fleshy parts. In the male the bones are relatively thicker and heavier, as are the muscles; the chest is larger and broader; the hands and feet are longer, blunter, and heavier. In the female the shoulders are relatively narrower and more sloping; and the hips are wider and bigger, because the hip structure is both broader than in the males and covered with more fat. The extra fatty layers found in females, as a rule, in addition to their softer muscles, contribute toward making their contours more rounded than those of the male. A seldom-noted sex difference is in the alignment of the arm and leg bones: In the male the upper and lower arms are usually in line when the arm is held straightened out against the side, whereas in the female the lower arm tends to jut out from the elbow. (See the accompanying illustration.) Also, females tend to be more knock-kneed, in part because their hips are wider and their thighs heavier.

Breast Shapes. Different sizes and shapes of breasts in women may result from different types of breast genes, although diet, health factors, physical activities, and childbearing and nursing are modifying influences. Some of the most striking hereditary breast types are found in women of certain African tribes. The genes for any type of female breasts, it should be noted, can be transmitted as easily through the father as through the mother. This explains why, in many cases, a mother may note that a grown daughter has distinctive breasts, not like hers, but like those of the husband's mother or one of his sisters. (A son, similarly, can inherit through his mother male bodily traits that are like those of her male relatives rather than his father's.)

Glandular Factors. Much of the work of the sex genes in shaping bodily details in either male or female directions is carried out through the way they construct and influence the sex glands—the testes in the male, the ovaries in the female. This is shown by what happens if these glands are removed, or if the production of their normal quotas of male and female hormones is radically changed. If a male is castrated before he achieves puberty, his body will develop many of the feminine characteristics (wider hips, soft muscles, lack of facial hair, etc.). If the sex glands in a young woman do not function properly before or during puberty (or if they are removed through operation as is sometimes necessary), her breasts, hips, and contours may not develop in the normal female way. Often in these cases a girl may also grow unusually tall. (Proper medical treatment given in time, with the supplement of the required sex hormones, may help to prevent or correct these deviations from normal body development.) However, if the glandular changes or upsets occur *after* puberty, when the skeletal structure is set, the effects on the outward sex characteristics are much less. Castration of an adult male will in time make him flabbier and fatter in his tissues; but in a woman, removal of the ovaries after maturity usually has very little outward effect.

HEAD SHAPES. Whether a person is roundheaded (*brachycephalic*), or longheaded (*dolichocephalic*) in maturity depends largely on heredity, but diet and living conditions are modifying influences. Even though all shapes of heads are found among all peoples, round heads (broad oval) predominate among the Mongolians, long heads (long oval) among Negroes. Among whites one head shape may be more prevalent in some groups, another head shape in other groups. As a rule, if parents have different head shapes, the roundhead genes tend to dominate those for long heads. But any predictions of head-shape inheritance should take into consideration environmental influences. For instance, stature has a relationship to head shape, since a lengthening of the body bones may also bring a lengthening of the skull. Thus, the increase in stature in the United States has brought some lengthening of heads, and particularly in immigrant stocks offspring may have head shapes somewhat different from their parents. The tendency away from the round head and more toward the egg shape has also been reported among peoples of Western Europe.

Other Bodily Details. Inherited factors in shapes of hands, feet, chests, muscles, etc., have been studied mainly with respect to abnormal traits, to be discussed in Chapter 13.

11

The "Wayward" Genes

INHERITED FLAWS. Although improvements in environment and medical science have made human beings healthier and sounder in body than ever before in the world's history, there unfortunately are a great many inborn defects that continue to assert themselves. Some of these affect outward appearance; others affect some inner organ or process. Of greatest concern are the inherited defects or abnormalities that severely handicap the person, or doom him to suffering, or cause premature death. Fortunately, most of the serious ills and defects produced directly and chiefly by heredity are not too prevalent; many of those in which heredity plays an indirect part may often be prevented by early safeguards; and even hereditary ailments that have already asserted themselves may in many cases be eased or cured by prompt and effective treatment. (It is a common mistake to assume that because a condition is hereditary nothing can be done about it.) Another fact on the optimistic side is that many human afflictions which in the past were blamed on bad heredity have now been proved to be mainly or entirely due to bad environment. In every case, then, when individuals or members of a family are concerned about a given disease or defect which they know, believe, or suspect is hereditary, it is important that they have the essential facts. These facts, with respect to all except very rare conditions of limited interest, we shall try to present in this and succeeding chapters. However, it should be understood that any vital judgments or decisions involving inheritance of specific defects and diseases should not be made without consulting competent medical and genetic authorities. (See concluding section of this chapter, under "Cautions." Also see Chapter 30, Parenthood Problems.)

WHEN IS A DEFECT HEREDITARY? There is much confusion on this point. For instance, even doctors sometimes wrongly use the terms *congenital, familial,* and *hereditary* as if they meant the same thing. But this may or may not always be so. Here are the differences:

Congenital Conditions. *Congenital* refers to a condition present at birth. This need not mean that it is hereditary. While heredity is responsible for or involved in many congenital abnormalities, perhaps the majority are purely environmental. That is, they are *acquired* by the developing baby at some stage before birth, through various unfortunate conditions that may arise in the mother's womb, such as improper nourishment, lack of certain needed substances, hormonal upsets, or prenatal accidents. (Discussed in Chapter 2.) Also, if there are menacing germs or infections in the mother, these may affect the baby and cause it to be born with a congenital disease. *Congenital syphilis* is one example of a disease that can be present at birth and not be hereditary. Although it was long thought that syphilis could be inherited (the theme of Ibsen's famous drama, *Ghosts*), we know now that neither this nor any other germ disease can be passed along through a parent's genes or chromosomes. The only way any germ disease can appear in a newborn baby is through infection from the mother. (Sometimes a mother can unknowingly carry the syphilis germs received from the father.) In all, it has been estimated that about 20 per cent of congenital defects are directly inherited, 20 per cent are purely environmental, and the remaining 60 per cent are the result of complex interactions between hereditary and environmental factors.

Familial Conditions. The mere fact that a disease or defect is repeated in parents and children, or has run in a family for several generations, is again no proof that it is hereditary. Very often the condition is due solely to such environmental factors as dietary deficiencies, bad living or working habits, lack of hygiene or proper medical care, infections, diseases, or other harmful influences. It may be only these same influences running in a family which produce the same given diseases or defects. If the environments are changed, such familial conditions will disappear. On the other hand, whereas a great many familial conditions which assert themselves are wholly or in some degree hereditary, it quite often

happens that a disease or defect which apparently is not familial—
that is, not known before in the family—is in fact hereditary.
(See next section.)

Hereditary Conditions.   A defect or disease is called hereditary
if it is produced by a gene or genes carried in the chromosomes
received from the father and/or mother. Aberrant genes may work
in a wide variety of ways, and at different stages of life. Some
hereditary conditions are also *congenital,* but a great many others
are not, since they may not appear until late in childhood, or
maturity, or old age. Similarly, as previously indicated, some
hereditary conditions may not be familial if the genes producing
them are not sufficiently simple and direct in their workings to
cause a given condition to reappear in members of a family for
successive generations. Likewise, nonfamilial hereditary conditions
may occur when the required two rare recessive genes are brought
together by a husband and wife in neither of whose families the
resulting disease or defect had previously appeared. In other conditions complex gene workings, and perhaps special environmental
factors as well, may keep a hereditary disease or defect from crop-
ping out except in occasional instances. And sometimes a harmful
gene may have suddenly arisen through a change (mutation or
accident) in the mother's egg or father's sperm, so that there
would have been no family history of the condition. (Mutations:
see Chapters 3, 26.)

Chromosome-Defect Transmission.   In certain cases (perhaps
1 in 200 children) congenital defects are due to abnormalities in
chromosomes transmitted to offspring. There may be a whole
chromosome or part of a chromosome missing, which can interfere
with some vital processes; or there may be one or more extra
chromosomes present which may disrupt normal development.
(Conditions resulting from these chromosome abnormalities—
among them *Mongolian Idiocy* [Down's syndrome] and Klinefelter's and Turner's syndromes—will be discussed in later chapters.)
In most instances the chromosome abnormalities result from some
first-time accidental upset during the processes of sperm or egg
formation, or during conception, and are not likely to be repeated
in other offspring of the same parents. In only a small percentage
of the cases are the chromosomally caused defects hereditary and
transmissible, whether the persons carrying the abnormal chromo-

somes do or do not show their effects.

Nonhereditary and Hereditary Distinctions. The greatest importance lies in this fact: If a condition is proved *nonhereditary*, it offers no threat of repetition in the affected person's children— or, if it is in a child, in other offspring of that person—unless it is a contagious or other environmentally caused disease or condition for which no remedy has been found. However, once such a disease or condition is identified and cured or eliminated in the individual, all threats of transmission posed by him or her to others are eliminated. But if a condition is *hereditary*, the threat of transmission is always there no matter whether the person carrying the genes for it is himself afflicted or was afflicted and had been cured. In short, any nonhereditary disease or defect could be wiped out completely if one could change the conditions causing it. But hereditary conditions will continue as long as the genes producing them are passed along.

HOW WAYWARD GENES WORK. Wayward, or aberrant, genes, are in many ways like individuals who misbehave, or don't do their jobs properly, or create serious difficulties for others. Some wayward genes may be recklessly overactive, producing too many fingers or toes, or too much of some chemical in the body. Other genes may be shiftless and underactive, not completing the job to which they are assigned and leaving serious flaws in some vital part of the body or its functioning. Still other genes work properly only up to a certain stage of life, and then become irresponsible or worse. Again, many wayward genes produce only a single, distinctive defect, without impairing anything else in the body's workings. But other wayward genes, if they are in a key position—particularly at the beginning of life—may start off a chain of defective processes, creating many defects. Such multiple defects that arise from the workings of a single gene are called *syndromes*. Finally, as with human workers, some wayward genes go wrong only if in the company of certain other genes, or only in certain environments. Examples of all these types of genes will be found among the specific conditions to be discussed in the following chapters. (See also illustration, p. 19.)

Predispositions and Tendencies. Some persons, because of wayward genes, have a special weakness in one part of the body or another—in the brain, heart, lungs, digestive system, nervous system, or elsewhere. Under average or favorable conditions, these persons may function normally. But if there is some unusual stress, or some adverse factor in the environment (infections, dietary deficiencies, etc.), they may have breakdowns or develop diseases, whereas individuals with properly working genes would escape these ills. In all such cases affected persons are spoken of as having inherited "predispositions," "tendencies," or "susceptibilities" to given diseases. As will be noted in later chapters, many mental disorders, heart afflictions, and other serious ailments may depend for their development on degrees of such inherited predispositions.

Phenocopies. These are environmentally caused traits that have all outward evidences (*phenotypes*) of being copies of genetically produced conditions. The thalidomide babies (Chapter 2) were striking examples. Many other defects, diseases, and abnormalities which can be either genetic in causation or phenocopies will be discussed in the following chapters.

Penetrance. Geneticists use this term to describe the relative force with which a gene works among people who have that same gene. If it shows its full effects under all circumstances, it is said to have "100 per cent penetrance"; if only in half the cases, "50 per cent penetrance," etc. Thus, a condition caused by a single dominant gene with 100 per cent penetrance may appear without a break in generation after generation of a family. But should a gene be incompletely dominant, with partial penetrance (75 per cent, 50 per cent, 40 per cent, or whatever), its effects may be discontinuous, failing to show through in many individuals who inherit it.

Expressivity. The same gene may express itself in different degrees or forms in different persons. Sometimes in a given family the effects of a gene may be much more marked and severe in one member than in another. These varying effects of the same gene should not be confused with the actions of two quite different genes.

Incomplete Recessives. Just as many dominant genes are not always completely dominant (see above), many if not most genes for recessive diseases may produce some mild effects even in the single state when coupled with a normal dominant gene. The importance of this fact will be discussed in a later section, "Tests for Detecting Carriers."

Newly Mutated Genes. In extremely rare instances two normal parents may unexpectedly produce a child with a defect that is known to be always caused by a single gene (either a simple dominant or, in sons only, a sex-linked recessive). When it is clear that neither parent could have inherited the gene from his or her family, it may be assumed that the child's defective gene had arisen through a new mutation in a germ cell of one of the parents. Geneticists estimate roughly that on the average a gene mutates about once in 100,000 times or even less often; also, some genes are more unstable than others, and mutate considerably more often than the average, whereas some very stable genes mutate much less frequently.

Errors of Metabolism. Many of the serious mistakes made by bad genes in their behavior involve specific metabolic processes— the chemical functions of given organs or systems in the body. These genetic errors may result in inadequate or improper production of given important enzymes or hormones, with the effects ranging from a single disease, disorder, or deficiency, to a syndrome, or combination of a variety of defects. *Diabetes, gout,* and *phenylketonuria* are among the most common of the genetic errors of metabolism, but scores of others have been identified. Many of these will be dealt with in later chapters.

Biochemical Individuality. Whatever the threats of a hereditary disease or defect may be, the biochemical make-up of the individual has an important influence on whether it develops or, if it does, how serious the effects will be. Just as no two individuals look alike, no two are exactly alike in their inherited chemical make-up and functioning. This kind of chemical individuality can cause the same gene to have different degrees of effect in different individuals. Similarly, it can result in different reactions to germs, drugs, stresses, or other environmental influences. Of special importance is the role played by biochemical individuality in organ transplants, determining whether an individual will accept or reject a grafted organ from another person. (See next chapter.)

MALES AND FEMALES. Apart from the individual biochemical differences, there are many important ways in which males and females differ with respect to hereditary or other afflictions—*usually to the disadvantage of the male.* In some conditions the hereditary action is direct, as when it involves genes in the sex chromosomes. (See "Sex-Linked Inheritance," following.) In other conditions there are general inborn sex differences, in body construction, chemistry, organs, and functions, which produce differences in the susceptibility or resistance of males and females to given diseases. In still other conditions the environmental differences between males and females (in their jobs, parental roles, activities, or habits) may be mainly responsible for the different ways or degrees in which they are afflicted; but even here, inborn sex factors, as well as social or psychological factors associated with them, may have much to do with directing the lives of males and females into different channels. Altogether, it is now recognized that in almost every important disease—mental, organic, functional, infectious—the sex of the individual plays a role in its development and severity. And most amazing, it is becoming increasingly clear as environments are now constituted that *males, not females, are the weaker sex* biologically. For, as a group, males are more often born defective, are more likely to suffer hereditary ailments, are inherently more susceptible to most major diseases, and when afflicted are more likely to succumb. Females are inherently at a disadvantage in only a minority of the categories, the most important being afflictions linked with childbearing and their sex organs, cancers restricted to their sex, gallstones, and diabetes, goiter, and certain other glandular diseases.

Prenatal and Childhood Sex Differences. The fact that inborn, and not environmental, factors are mainly responsible for the greater biological weaknesses of males is clearly shown by the situation before birth. Among unborn babies the males who die off are markedly more numerous than the females, ranging from perhaps twice as many in the first months after conception, to about 30 per cent more in the later months. Among defective and abnormal babies, miscarried or born, the proportion of males is again very much higher. And in infancy and early childhood— before environments or conditioning become different—males continue to die off, become diseased, or develop defects at a higher rate than females. The same is true among many lower animals, from insects to the higher mammals. There seems little doubt, then, that females are endowed with many genetic advantages over males.

Environmental Changes. The reason the inborn advantages of human females were not so apparent in the past was that they were so often canceled out by the strains and mortality tolls of unlimited childbearing. Another reason was (and still is in many less advanced countries) that very poor environments give the female's minor inherent advantages less chance to assert themselves. But today, as environments have steadily improved, and the special hazards of women have been greatly reduced—much more so than the special hazards of men—all women's biological advantages are being manifested to an increasing extent. (See also "Sex Differences in Longevity" in Chapter 19.)

SEX-LINKED INHERITANCE. Hereditary conditions are called *sex-linked* when the genes responsible are in the X chromosome. Since females carry two Xs, but no Y, and males carry only one X, coupled with a Y (Chapter 4), wayward sex-linked genes work differently in the two sexes, with the males much more often affected. The reason is mainly that if a female receives an X chromosome with a wayward gene of the *recessive* type, her other X chromosome usually has a normal matching gene to block the effect of the wayward one. Only in infrequent cases do both X chromosomes of a female carry the same bad gene. However, if a male's single X chromosome has one such gene, it alone usually produces a defect in him, for in no known case does the small Y chromosome carry a matching normal gene. Thus, a great many inherited conditions strike at males far more often than at females, the best known of these being *color blindness* and *hemophilia*, with others including certain eye defects, errors of metabolism, and muscular defects. Males also are affected with *speech disorders* and *reading disabilities* in much higher proportion than females, but to what extent genetic factors have anything to do with these conditions, or how far they are due to psychological or other environmental factors, has not been established. Also uncertain is whether the small male Y chromosome—while clearly exerting a powerful effect on sex determination—carries any genes directly involved in producing specific diseases or defects.

Sex-Linked Inheritance

If a defective gene is in the X chromosome (as in color blindness)—

FEMALE (Carrier) X   X

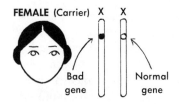

Bad   Normal
gene   gene

With two X's, a female carrier usually has a normal X gene to block
the bad one, and is herself normal.

X   **MALE** (Afflicted)

Bad →
gene

Y

With only one X, male has no
normal gene to block the bad
one and develops the defect.

WOMAN CARRIER'S SONS

One in two gets
mother's bad X
gene and has the
defect.

One in two gets
mother's normal
X and is not de-
fective.

AFFLICTED MAN'S SONS

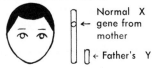

Normal   X
← gene from
mother

← Father's Y

No son gets father's X, so every
son is free of the defect and
cannot pass on the bad gene.

WOMAN CARRIER'S DAUGHTERS

One in two gets
mother's bad X,
and is a carrier like
mother.

One in two gets
the normal X, and
cannot pass on de-
fect.

AFFLICTED MAN'S DAUGHTERS

Every daughter gets the
father's bad X, and is a carrier (like woman at top left of
page).

AFFLICTED FEMALE

Only when a female
gets an X with a bad
gene from both par-
ents will she develop
the defect.

Every one of her sons
will have this same
defect. Every daugh-
ter will be a carrier of
the gene.

Transmission of Sex-Linked Defects. In all conditions where the defective gene is in the X chromosome, transmission to a male can obviously be only through his mother, from whom he receives his single X. Thus, if one of the mother's two Xs is defective and one normal, the son has an even chance of either inheriting the given defect or escaping it. Should both the mother's Xs carry the same defective recessive (which means that she herself would show the affliction), no son could escape inheriting the defect. An afflicted male, in turn, cannot transmit a recessive X gene condition to his son, who receives only his father's Y chromosome. As for a daughter, even though she is certain to get any defective gene carried in the single X chromosome she receives from her father, it will usually cause no damage unless she receives a matching X-chromosome gene from her mother. (See preceding paragraph.) In the great majority of cases, therefore, sex-linked recessive defects skip a generation, passing from affected fathers through unaffected daughters to affected grandsons.

Dominant X-Chromosome Genes. A small number of detrimental genes in the X chromosome are of the dominant type. In these cases, if a mother is afflicted, there is the same fifty-fifty risk for her sons and daughters alike. But an afflicted father will transmit any such genes and the resulting condition to *each of his daughters*, but to none of his sons. This accounts for the much higher incidence in women of a few rare inherited conditions, such as one type of defective teeth with brownish enamel.

The Lyon Hypothesis: Mosaic Sex-Linked Inheritance. According to findings by Dr. Mary Lyon, only one of a female's two Xs functions in a given cell, the other being inactivated, with the choice of the functioning X being a matter of chance. Thus, if one of the Xs carried a gene for some defect, it could assert its effects wherever the X with the normal gene was inactivated. The result would be a *mosaic*, or patchwork, of cells defective and normal for the given trait. For example, if the female had one X with a color-blindness gene, the other X with a normal gene, her eyes would have part color-blind cells and part color-seeing cells, causing a partial deficiency in color vision. Similar partial deficiencies could occur in a female in other sex-linked conditions wherever her cells were a mixture (*mosaic*) of functioning and inactivated normal X genes, and deficient X genes.

FORECASTING DISEASE INHERITANCE. Doctors recognize that knowledge of hereditary diseases or defects in a patient, or in members of his or her family, may prove important in various ways. This is why they ask details about family histories. Often the information is highly useful in diagnosing early symptoms and taking preventive measures. Where a hereditary condition has already made serious progress in a patient, examination of close blood relatives, particularly younger ones, may often reveal similar hereditary threats, which can be staved off through prompt treatment. Apart from this, the facts about disease inheritance may have great importance to parents or prospective parents who know, or suspect, they carry genes for one undesirable condition or another, and can weigh the dangers to their children.

Tests for Detecting Carriers. What has proved to be among the most important findings of medical genetics is that persons who are themselves not afflicted (or not yet afflicted) by various hereditary diseases, but are carrying genes for them, may be identified by certain special characteristics in their blood, or body chemistry, or eyes, etc. This applies particularly to individuals carrying a single gene for conditions whose serious effects are produced by a pair of the genes. The most striking examples to date are the carriers of single *incomplete dominant* genes for either *sickle-cell anemia* or *Mediterranean anemia*, who show easily detectable signs in their blood. (See Chapter 18.) Also, as previously noted under "Incomplete Recessives," many recessive genes in the single state, even when coupled with normal dominant genes, may nevertheless show some effects. Thus, tests may also often (but not always) identify in both sexes unafflicted carriers of single genes for such conditions as galactosemia, Wilson's disease, glycogen storage disease, cystic fibrosis of the pancreas, phenylketonuria, and Tay-Sachs disease, and in females, X-borne genes for color blindness, the Duchenne type of muscular dystrophy, and primaquine sensitivity (favism), among other conditions. In time it is hoped that tests will also be able to identify younger adults who carry genes for, and are threatened with development of, such menacing diseases as Huntington's chorea, hereditary ataxia, and several others with late onset.

(Problems of prospective parents who are carriers of harmful genes will be discussed in Chapters 30 and 31.)

METHODS OF INHERITANCE. In the case of any given hereditary condition, an absolute essential is that the doctor and the afflicted person (or one who fears transmitting the genes for it) should know the precise mechanism of its inheritance wherever established. Thus, throughout our disease and defect chapters, the known or suspected gene-working for every condition will be given. In order to save space, abbreviations will often be used. A guide to the meaning of these abbreviations, and the nature of each type of gene, follows immediately. Those desiring a general knowledge of all disease and defect inheritance should study this guide and try to retain the basic facts. Those interested mainly in a few conditions may refer back to this guide as the need for specific information arises. But with regard to taking any specific action, one should observe the cautions expressed at the beginning of this chapter, and again in the concluding section of the guide.

GUIDE TO GENE TYPES
(Meaning of abbreviations used in later chapters)

Dominant Genes (Dom.)

Dom.: Simple-Dominant Defect. A single gene will produce the condition. If only one parent is afflicted, there is a fifty-fifty chance any child will also be afflicted. If both parents have the dominant condition, there is a three-in-four threat to any child. (Examples: Huntington's chorea, inner-ear deafness, drooping eyelids.) In the case of some conditions, if a child gets the *double dominant*—one from each affected parent, as could happen in one in four children of such parents—the effects may be prenatally fatal or especially severe. (Examples: brachyphalangy, telangiectasis.)

Inc. Dom.: Incomplete Dominant. One gene produces a mild effect, but two of the same produce a marked effect. (As in sickle-cell and Mediterranean anemias.)

Dom.-Q.: Qualified or Irregularly Dominant Gene. The effects may depend on other genes and environmental factors.

Recessive Genes

Rec.: Simple-Recessive. Two of the same genes, one from each parent, are needed to produce the condition. If both parents are afflicted, every child will be. If neither parent is afflicted, but each is carrying a hidden gene for the condition, there is a one-in-four chance the child will develop it. If only one parent is afflicted, and the other does not carry the gene for the condition, no child will develop the affliction. (Examples: amaurotic idiocy or Tay-Sachs disease, albinism, Friedreich's ataxia.)

Rec.-Q.: Recessive-Qualified. The pair of recessives that cause this condition do not always show their effects, or the effects may vary, because environmental factors, or some other genes, may be involved. (Examples: anencephaly, cleft lip with or without cleft palate.)

Rec.+: Recessive-Plus. Two of the same recessive genes *plus* some other genes or environmental factors are required to produce this condition. Inheritance is less certain than in the case of simple recessives. (Examples: schizophrenia, middle-ear deafness [some cases].)

Sex-L. Rec., or *Sex-L.: Sex-Linked Recessive.* The conditions are caused by a gene in the X chromosome, whose effects are linked with the sex of the individual. (See "Males and Females" in this chapter.) Only one such gene will produce its effect in a male, but two genes are needed to produce an equal effect in a female. If a father has the condition (examples: color blindness, hemophilia), no son will inherit it, and no daughter will have the condition unless the mother also carries a hidden gene for it; but otherwise every daughter of an afflicted man will be a carrier of the gene and can transmit the condition to one in two sons, on the average. If a mother is herself afflicted with the condition, each of her sons will be afflicted, and each daughter will be a carrier of the gene. (For sex-linked dominants; see p. 85.)

Sex.-Lim.: Sex-limited. In these conditions, the genes are on chromosomes other than the X (autosomes), but even though inherited equally by both sexes they may express themselves principally in one sex. (Example: baldness, afflicting males.)

Cautions

1. The nonmedical reader should not try to draw precise conclusions about the hereditary threats of any condition without

having had competent medical opinion beforehand, so that he will be sure the condition is the one referred to in the text and is inherited in the way stated.

2. In many cases the same or similar conditions can be produced either by heredity or by environmental factors (as with various types of deafness, blindness, muscular defects, etc.). The doctor should study the family history and, if necessary, check medical literature and/or consult with a medical geneticist to make sure the condition in question is or is not of the hereditary type. (Further, many similar conditions can be inherited in different ways.)

3. The *time of onset* is important in many conditions that appear at different stages of life: at birth, in childhood, or not until middle age or old age. (Example: chronic simple glaucoma.) Where the same condition appears in some families only at one stage of life, in other families at another stage, different genes working in different ways may be involved. Thus, in checking on some variable-onset conditions, not only the precise nature of the disease or defect but the approximate age of members of a family when afflicted must be known.

12

Inheritance in Major Organic Diseases

HEART AND BLOOD-VESSEL DISORDERS. These now account for more than half the deaths in the United States annually. Chief killers among them are high blood pressure (*hypertension*), hardening and thickening of the arteries (*arteriosclerosis*), and *rheumatic heart disease* (or *rheumatic fever*). Medical authorities believe that hereditary factors are involved in all these conditions by way of some degree of predisposition. This means that where any one of these conditions runs in a family, an individual member may have an above-average risk of developing it. The threat is considerably greater as a rule for males, whose death rate from heart and arterial ailments is about 50 per cent higher than that of females. The difference cannot be ascribed entirely to the greater strain under which men live and work, or to other environmental factors, for there is evidence that inborn male weaknesses are also involved. (See "Males and Females" in preceding chapter.)

Hypertension (High Blood Pressure). This condition may result from other diseases, or may also lead to other diseases, such as enlarged heart and heart failure, coronary artery diseases, with blood clots, apoplectic stroke (or brain hemorrhage), or kidney disease. It is very probable that a predisposition to hypertension is hereditary, although environmental factors are also important in bringing it on. Although no specific genes for this disease have been identified, it is advisable that in families with a history of hypertension the adult members have medical checkups to reveal possible threats.

Arteriosclerosis. This disease—the cause of 25 to 40 per cent of heart deaths—involves thickening and hardening of the arteries, with impairment of blood circulation, leading to heart pains (*angina pectoris*) or damage to heart muscles (*coronary thrombosis*), and strokes or brain damage. Suspicion of heredity is greatest in cases of *atherosclerosis*, where there are fatty deposits in the arteries caused by improper conversion or production of cholesterol. Certain errors in fat metabolism, inherited through *dominant* or *semidominant* or *recessive* genes, may predispose individuals to the more severe form of this condition, and if not treated properly, coronary thrombosis may also result at an early age. The danger is greatest for men. In susceptible women, atherosclerosis is usually later and milder.

Congenital Heart Defects. These comprise a variety of conditions, most of them due to prenatal mishaps or other purely environmental factors (such as German measles in the mother, or other causes listed in Chapter 2). But some types are due to genetic defects, or to chromosome abnormalities. The gene-caused congenital heart defects may often appear in successive generations of a family. If not fatal in early life, they may cause serious heart conditions in later years.

Rheumatic Fever (or Childhood Rheumatism). This severe and puzzling condition (one of the symptoms often being St. Vitus' dance) afflicts mostly children (about 1 in 100 of school age), and in many cases adults with previous heart damage. Although the *susceptibility* to the disease may run in families, rheumatic fever is triggered by a streptococcal infection of the nose and throat. Prompt treatment of such an infection greatly reduces threats of the disease.

Varicose Veins. The principal causes and factors are probably in most cases environmental, the condition being most common among persons whose work requires continued standing and among women after childbirth. In some families, however, a tendency to varicose veins may be inherited through an irregular dominant gene.

CANCER. There is no proof as yet that heredity is directly responsible for any of the *common* cancers, although some rare forms of cancer are definitely inherited; and there is much to suggest that different individuals are born with varied degrees of susceptibility to given types of common cancer. The term "cancer," it should be understood, relates not to one specific disease but to a great many different types of malignancies, which may arise in different ways at different places. Cancers are known to develop when a group of cells and their chromosome mechanisms, in any part of the body, "go haywire," or begin to behave abnormally, producing malignant growths. As these cancerous cells multiply they invade, starve out, and destroy surrounding tissues and vital organs, and then may metastasize— break loose and range like outlaws through the blood stream or lymphatic vessels, coming to rest and growing in other organs or areas of the body, thus creating havoc and finally bringing death to the individual.

Causes of Cancer. Both hereditary and environmental factors may be involved in producing cancers. Heredity may predispose given individuals to the development of malignancies (1) by making their tissues or certain organs unusually susceptible to any cancer-inducing agencies and/or cancerous changes; (2) through the production in their systems of unusual quotas of chemical substances or hormones (particularly in the older ages when body tissues weaken) which might irritate cells into becoming cancerous; (3) through the improper construction of some cells so that cancer could easily develop under various irritating influences; or (4) through abnormalities in chromosomes which could unbalance the cell mechanisms. As for environmental agencies, *viruses* able to disrupt the proper workings of the genetic codes in cells are now regarded as a major factor in inducing many types of cancer.* There also are hundreds of known cancer-inducing irritants (called *carcinogens*), among them a great many kinds of chemicals and abrasive dusts, radiation particles, and ingredients of *cigarette smoke.*

Cancer-Inheritance Theories. Establishing heredity in cancer is complicated by the fact that the many different types of the disease—often several forms appearing in the same family—may arise from different causes that have not been identified. What is known to date is only that (1) the incidence of cancer of the breast, prostate, lung, stomach, or intestines is considerably above average in some families, and where a particular type of cancer has appeared previously in a person's close relative, he or she has

---

* Viruses themselves contain sections of DNA or RNA, and can impose their own alien code on the normal DNA coding of cells, causing cancerous changes to occur.

a greater than average risk of developing the same condition; (2) among identical twins, if one has cancer, the other is more likely to develop cancer of the same type, and sooner, than is the case with fraternal twins; and (3) "cancer-susceptible" strains have been found in lower animals, and one can breed strains of mice and other experimental animals which will develop given types of cancer according to regular rules of inheritance. Nonetheless, the reader is cautioned not to draw conclusions about hereditary cancer threats in his own case until a medical expert has confirmed the facts. As previously noted, different types of cancer need not be related. Moreover, the same type of cancer may run in a family only because the members for successive generations have been exposed to the same cancer-inducing influences. (Some clearly inherited predispositions to cancer will be discussed presently.)

Sex Differences. The many important differences in the incidence and nature of cancers in the two sexes arise mainly from differences in the sex organs and breasts. But differences in their body chemistry, hormones, body functioning, work, and external environments also are involved. Females naturally run the risk of developing cancers of the womb, cervix, ovaries, and breasts, whereas males have a considerably smaller cancer risk, associated with their prostate glands and testes. On the other hand, in the nonsexual cancers of the skin, lips, mouth, tongue, throat, lungs, and stomach, the male death rate is very much higher. Whether this is entirely due to the greater exposure of males to cancer-inducing conditions and irritants is doubtful (except possibly with respect to *lung cancer*, in which the much greater amount of cigarette smoking by men is a factor, and cancers of the lips and mouth, in which pipe and cigar smoking may have an influence).

Breast Cancer. Despite conflicting reports and theories, there is enough suspicion of hereditary influence in breast cancer so that if several women in a family have been or are afflicted by it, the daughters or sisters should have frequent periodic examinations in their mature years, and prompt treatment if there are any questionable symptoms. Also to be kept in mind is that any genes predisposing to cancer could be just as easily transmitted through a father to a daughter as through a mother, so one should also be alerted if breast cancer has run among women on the father's side. However, the appearance of breast cancer in several successive generations—grandmother, mother, daughter—need not of itself prove inheritance, first because the condition is so common that it could be merely coincidence; second, because the breast cancers in different members might be of different and unrelated types, which had started out at different locations.

Leukemia.   Although formerly classified as a blood disease, leukemia is now regarded as a type of cancer of the blood-forming organs, revealing itself through abnormal white cells in the blood stream. There is some suspicion of heredity, but no evidence of any direct gene action. However, a rare type of leukemia—the *chronic myelocytic* form—has been found associated with a chromosome abnormality (called the "Philadelphia" chromosome) which may in some cases be hereditary. Leukemia in another form may be a by-product of several rare congenital syndromes with chromosome abnormalities, such as *Bloom's syndrome* and *Fanconi's anemia* (both inherited as recessives).

Skin Cancers.   There is little evidence that any of the *common* types are hereditary, the principal causes being clearly environmental. However, a person's inherited skin pigmentation may affect his chances of developing skin or lip cancer under exposure to the sun. Thus, fair-skinned persons in hot climates run a much higher chance of developing skin cancer than do the dark-skinned inhabitants. Where there are special threats are in certain kinds of *hereditary* skin conditions which include, among the cancerous ones, *malignant freckles* (*xeroderma pigmentosum*) induced by exposure to the sun if the inherited tendency (recessive) is present, and which may appear in childhood and soon prove fatal. Also, *epiloia* (*tuberous sclerosis*)—tumors of the skin and brain—causing mental derangement and usually early death, and *neurofibromatosis*, associated with numerous lumpy growths on the skin and in the brain and nerves, are dominant-qualified in inheritance.

Other Rare Inherited Cancers.   Among these are *familial polyposis of the colon*, growths in the large intestine which can become cancerous (dominant). A similar cancerous colon condition, *Gardner's syndrome*, due to a different dominant gene, includes among its peculiar symptoms bony lumps on the fore-head, as well as lumpy tumors of the jaw, and coffee-colored spots. Also inherited is a cancer of the eye, *retinoblastoma*, appearing in early life and fatal unless the eye is removed. (See Chapter 15, p. 120.)

(*Note:* Although cancer is commonly thought of as a degen-erative disease of the middle and older ages, there is a menacing incidence of cancer among children, with malignancies of the blood, eyes, kidneys, bone and skin causing, collectively, more deaths at ages one to fifteen in the United States than any other disease.)

DIABETES. In most cases this common disease (*diabetes mellitus*, or the "sugar sickness") may be the result of a predis-position inherited through recessive genes. This means that the inheritance must come through both parents, one gene from each. (The theory that in some instances the disease can be produced by a dominant gene is in doubt.) The cause of diabetes is inadequate utilization of blood sugar, which involves impair-ment of the insulin-producing and/or insulin-releasing function of the pancreas, leading to excess sugar in the system which may have serious results unless preventive measures are taken. Unfa-vorable fatty diets, obesity, overeating, nervous strains, infections, and the effects of certain other diseases may serve to bring on diabetes or worsen it; but there is no definite evidence that the disease will develop without some inherited tendency. Especially significant is the fact that many hundreds of children each year in the United States develop diabetes, in most cases despite good diets and wholesome conditions, leading to the conclusion that they are victims of marked diabetic heredity. Additional evi-dence: (1) One in four diabetics has diabetic relatives, a far higher than average incidence. (2) Twin studies show that in identical twins, if one has diabetes, so has the other in almost every case, whereas in fraternal twins diabetes affects both together no more frequently than it does two nontwin siblings. (3) Diabetes has been shown to be inherited in some strains of mice, independently of any environmental influences.

Sex Differences. Diabetes is one of the few major diseases which afflict women more than men. The reasons are women's generally greater susceptibility to glandular diseases; childbearing effects; and the longer life span of women, bringing more of them into the diabetic ages.

Diabetes Insipidus.   Often hereditary but sometimes not, this condition has no actual relationship to true diabetes. The only similarities in symptoms are an abnormal thirst and frequent urination, but without abnormal production of sugar, or any danger of the condition's developing into common diabetes. It can be caused by a lack of the pituitary hormone which directs water reabsorption in the kidney, or by a failure of the kidney to respond to the hormone. Where hereditary, it may be dominant or sex-linked.

Sugar Urine (*Renal Glycosuria*). Although it involves excess sugar in the urine, this condition has none of the harmful effects of diabetes. It is usually dominant in inheritance.

TUBERCULOSIS.   The only possible role that heredity can play in this germ-caused disease is to make some persons more susceptible to the *tubercle bacillus* and others more resistant. Studies among twins in families where tuberculosis has appeared, and with experimental animals, indicate that the chances of developing or resisting tuberculosis, and the degree of its threats, may be considerably influenced by inheritance. However, any inherited susceptibility or resistance factors are definitely very complex and are greatly overshadowed by the environmental influences. This is clearly shown by the enormous drop in the general tuberculosis death rate which has come with marked improvements in living conditions and medical care in the United States and other countries. At the same time, the tuberculosis rate remains high wherever environments continue to be unfavorable, as in slum areas and in disadvantaged foreign countries.

GOITER.   The possible part played by heredity in this disease remains doubtful because development of the common, simple form of goiter depends largely on lack of sufficient iodine in the food or drinking water, causing a strain on and swelling of the thyroid gland. However, even under the same conditions there is evidence that members of some families are much more likely than others to develop goiter, leading to the belief that weakness in the thyroid gland may be inherited, possibly through a dominant-qualified gene or recessive genes, but this is uncertain.

Should there be any susceptibility, the females in a family run about four times as great a risk of developing goiter as do the males, since the female system apparently needs more iodine. A special danger is that when a mother has a thyroid deficiency, there is an increased chance of her giving birth to a *cretin* (a type of mental defective: see Chapter 17). In any family where goiter has appeared, a first precaution is to see that there is always enough iodine in the diet.

Exophthalmic Goiter (Graves's Disease). While similar to common goiter in a number of ways (though more likely to be fatal) the cause of this condition is predominantly related to an excess in a pituitary hormone which overstimulates the thyroid. It most frequently afflicts young women who are highly nervous and slender, which may either go with the condition or result from it. Possible inheritance, as in common goiter, may be dominant-qualified or recessive, though not established.

ULCERS OF THE STOMACH AND INTESTINES. These afflictions are considered to be principally brought on by nervous strain, but some authorities believe there is a possibility also of inherited predispositions. For one thing, stomach ulcers are now being found in many young children; also, there is a much higher than average incidence in some families, and duodenal ulcer shows a higher proportion in persons with blood group O. Further, the very much higher incidence and seriousness of stomach ulcers in men (with four times the female death rate from this disease), may be related in some degree to inherent biochemical differences.

PYLORIC STENOSIS. This condition, a stricture of the passageway from stomach to intestines, is usually congenital. It occurs in about 1 in 300 babies—four fifths of them boys—pointing to sex-influenced inheritance, probably multiple Dom.-q.

CYSTIC FIBROSIS (FIBROCYSTIC DISEASE OF THE PANCREAS). This serious metabolic disorder, which strikes at and is fatal to many children, is inherited as a recessive, manifesting itself in about 1 in every 1,000 to 2,000 children at birth. The cause is an inherent failure of the secretory glands in the pancreas and lungs to function properly. Until recently the disease in its serious forms was almost always fatal in childhood, but new treatments are enabling many of those afflicted to live into maturity. (Cystic fibrosis primarily affects whites, occurs infrequently in Negroes—very rarely in African Negroes—and is also very uncommon in Mongoloid peoples.)

KIDNEY DISEASES. It is uncertain whether the common type of kidney disease, *nephritis*—one of the leading causes of death—is directly influenced by heredity, although a genetic predisposition may possibly exist with respect to the reaction to the strep infection usually involved. However, a rare type, *polycystic disease of the kidneys* (especially serious to pregnant women) appears to be inherited as a qualified dominant. Another type of kidney disease, with deafness, which strikes particularly at young males (*Alport syndrome*) is also dominant-qualified in inheritance. *Cystinuria*, a condition which may produce kidney stones, occurs in three types, two recessive, one incomplete dominant in inheritance. *Vitamin-D-resistant rickets*, due to defective kidney functioning which resists treatment with vitamin D (as in ordinary rickets), is a sex-linked incomplete dominant (meaning that the gene for it is on the X chromosome, and being dominant—though incomplete—poses an increased threat for females. (See "Dominant X-Chromosome Genes" in Chapter 11.) It should be added that a score or more of other inherited structural and functional defects linked with the kidney have been identified.

ORGAN TRANSPLANTS. Hope—realized or in prospect—for saving many individuals with hitherto fatal afflictions of the kidneys, heart, and other organs, is being held out by operations in which defective organs are replaced by healthy ones from other individuals. Successes, in a large number of cases, have been mainly in *kidney transplants,* and also in *bone-marrow transplants.* Much less successful have been *heart transplants,* with only one person of scores involved having survived to date beyond two years after receiving another heart.

The Rejection Element. A major problem in all organ transplants has been the fact that the recipient's tissues may be immunologically incompatible with those of the grafted organ and prevent it from taking root. Thus, the most effective and lasting organ transplants—of kidneys—have involved identical twins as donor and recipient, their tissues being genetically the same biochemically. Transplants of kidneys from other near relatives (parent-child, brothers, sisters) are also often, though not always, successful. (A person can usually get along safely with one healthy kidney.) But whether the donated organ is from a relative or an unrelated person, success of a transplant depends primarily on how closely the tissues of the donor and recipient match immunologically. If the conflicts are not too great (as determined in prior tests), they may be overcome or subdued by radiation and/or chemical treatments. A great difficulty is that the same treatment that induces the recipient not to reject the foreign tissues may also reduce his resistance to germs and viruses which he would normally fight off. With advances in combatting rejection threats it will be possible to widen greatly the use of many kinds of organs from deceased persons (perhaps stored in "organ banks") to save the lives of living ones.

13

Outer Defects
and Abnormalities

STRUCTURAL DEFECTS. Most recognizable of the human defects and abnormalities are of course those which strike our eyes instantly—unusual sizes and shapes of bodies, peculiarities in bodily details, odd skin conditions, etc. Many of these are inherited, in some cases appearing at birth, but often not until much later. But there also are many similar abnormalities that are purely or mostly due to environmental mishaps or deficiencies in prenatal life. Lack of sufficient oxygen or of needed chemical elements for the developing baby may be among the causes. Very often an environmental abnormality is mistakenly thought to be hereditary, and sometimes the reverse is true; or it may be hereditary in one family but environmental in another. A knowledge of the facts is especially important to persons who have had close relatives or children with any one of the conditions to be described.

STATURE ABNORMALITIES. Human stature tends to be so fairly uniform that a difference of a foot or so above or below the average height range is apt to be considered abnormal. As noted in Chapter 10, human beings as groups have never been deliberately bred to produce extremes in size. Even if this were attempted, it is doubtful if we could produce breeds of healthy humans averaging more than 7 feet 6 inches tall, or smaller than 3 feet 8 inches to 4 feet. At least, that conclusion is suggested by such degrees of human stature as have so far appeared.

Dwarfs. These are of several types, with heredity working differently to produce each.

Midgets (*"Lilliputians,"* or *Ateliotics*). Classed as such are the doll-like persons with normal proportions who do not reach beyond about 3 feet 7 inches in height. (The smallest adult

Human Stature Variations

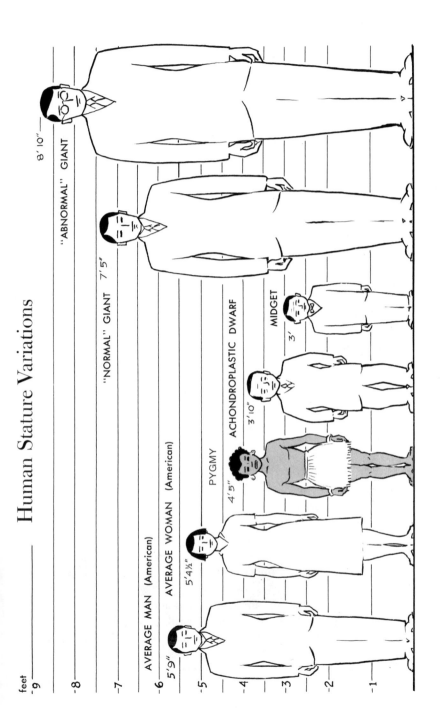

midget on record was 21 inches.) Failure to grow results from an
inherited deficiency in the pituitary, probably due in most cases
to two separate recessive genes. Most midgets are born of normal-
sized parents (sometimes two or more appearing in a family)
because midgets themselves are usually sterile. When midgets
reproduce in rare instances they are likely to be those whose
pituitary dysfunction is limited to a failure of the growth
hormone.

Achondroplastic dwarfs. These are persons in whom only the
arms and legs are stunted, while the trunk is normal. They also
usually have oversized heads and pug noses. Even though many
do not survive to birth or beyond infancy, those who do, unlike
midgets, may be fertile, and often produce children like themselves. In most cases the achondroplastic condition is directly
inherited through a single dominant gene: If one parent is a
dwarf of this type, there is almost an even chance a child of the
same type will result; and if both parents are achondroplastic,
the chances are that two in four children will be dwarfed, one in
four (with the double-dominant) will die early or be severely
affected, and only one in four will be normal. (In many communities there are whole families of such dwarfs. Among lower
animals, dachshunds and bulldogs are achondroplastic, and there
are or have been breeds of cows and sheep with the condition.)
Occasionally an achondroplastic child is born to normal human
parents, possibly as the result of a mutation, or sudden change,
in one of the parent's genes; or because the gene-workings had
previously been held back for some reason.

Pygmies. These undersized people average about 4 feet 6
inches in height. Whole tribes of them are found in Africa, New
Guinea, Malaya, and the Philippines. Differing from both
midgets and achondroplastics, Pygmies are not abnormal in any
way, but are merely undersized because of genes that produce
small stature.

Giants. Tallness up to a certain point—7 feet or so—is inherited through tall-stature genes, probably working as recessives
(as was explained in Chapter 10), which are given full opportunity for expression. But extreme heights much beyond that—up to
8 feet or over—are usually due to a glandular abnormality, most
often a "runaway" pituitary, which gives little evidence of being

hereditary. Most of these pituitary giants grow weaker as they grow taller, and usually do not survive beyond early maturity. (In the record case, an American youth, Robert Wadlow, reached 8 feet 10 inches and was still growing when he died at age twenty-two, in 1940.)

EXTREME FATNESS. Circus "fat ladies" (and men of the same type) are almost always the result of a glandular disorder. (The condition differs in origin from that of ordinary obesity, discussed in Chapter 10.) The record for a fat woman is 772 pounds; for a fat man, 1,000 pounds. Whether heredity plays any part in these extreme conditions is uncertain. Although extremely fat women sometimes have similar daughters, a prenatal glandular influence in the mother may be responsible. Diabetic women, for instance, may produce abnormally fat children.

HAND AND FEET ABNORMALITIES. These inherited types are of many kinds, almost all due to dominant or dominant-qualified genes. Thus, the conditions are markedly noticeable in families, since wherever a parent has one of these abnormalities, the odds are that half the children will have the same abnormality or some variation of it. Often the abnormality also appears in the feet or toes. Most common of these abnormalities (all usually dominant) are the following.

Stub Fingers (Brachyphalangy). Fingers are abnormally shortened or have middle joints missing (*hypophalangy*).

Extra Fingers. Usually extra fingers are on each hand, often extra toes also; sometimes this condition occurs as part of a syndrome.

"Claw" or "Split" Hand or Foot. The hand or foot looks like a lobster claw because several fingers (or toes) have grown together.

Webbed Fingers and/or Toes. The fingers are joined by a flap of skin. Sometimes only a slight webbing is present at base of two fingers.

"Spider" Hand. The fingers (and/or toes) are abnormally long.

Stiff Fingers. Joints of fingers are fused.

Other Inherited Conditions. There may be missing fingers or thumbs, paddle-shaped thumbs, misshapen toes. All these conditions are dominant. Double-jointed thumbs, capable of being bent

Inherited Hand Abnormalities

STUB FINGERS	"SPIDER" FINGERS	EXTRA FINGERS	SPLIT HAND ("Lobster claw")

Fingers abnormally shortened	Abnormally long and thin.	Usually one, but sometimes two.	Fingers fused.

NOTE: Any one of the above hand conditions may be accompanied by a similar condition in the feet of the individual. All are dominant or partly dominant in inheritance. (See text.)

back at an angle of 50 degrees, are quite common, and apparently inherited as a recessive.

Clubfoot. In some cases there is a possibility that congenital clubfoot is inherited, perhaps through multiple genes, but in a majority of cases prenatal accidents appear to be responsible.

Finger, Palm, and Sole Prints. In a number of genetic conditions, especially those due to chromosome abnormalities, there are characteristic peculiarities of the prints of fingers, palms, and soles (*dermatoglyphics*), which have proved useful in medical and genetic diagnoses. Most striking is the *simian crease*—a straight line across the palm—associated with mongolism (*Down's syndrome*), caused by trisomy (tripling) of the No. 21 chromosome. The simian crease may also go with trisomies of the No. 15 and No. 18 chromosomes, and in conditions with shortened hand bones (although these are sometimes also found in normal hands). The finger- and sole-print peculiarities include abnormalities in the proportions or types of loops, whorls, arches, and ridges. Some of these are among symptoms of sex-chromosome abnormalities, such as *Turner's* and *Klinefelter's* syndromes, or of chromosome abnormalities involving translocations or deletions (including the *cri du chat syndrome* [Chapter 17, p. 145]), and of a few gene-caused conditions, such as *Wilson's disease, Huntington's chorea,* and *neurofibromatosis.* Fingerprint peculiarities may also be among the nongenetic, prenatal effects of German measle infection, and occurred in the thalidomide babies.

SKELETAL DEFECTS. All the following conditions can be hereditary, although they are sometimes due to environmental factors or act only under certain conditions.

Brittle Bones (Blue Sclerotics). Accompanied by bluish eye-whites, deafness, defective teeth. Dom.-q.

Deformed Spine (Spina Bifida). Cleft or incompletely constructed spine, often with other effects (*anencephaly*). Variable (probably multiple-genic) inheritance, risks changing with family history.

Cobbler's ("Funnel") Chest. Dom.-q.

"Tower Skull" (Oxycephaly, Acrocephaly). Several types of high-pointed skull, sometimes with eye defects or mild mental defects. Dom.-q.

Marfan's Syndrome. Unusually long legs and fingers, often with deformities of the chest cage and eye lenses. Dom.-q. (Abraham Lincoln is believed to have had this condition in some degree.)

Bloom's Syndrome. Stunted growth, small, narrow face, skin lesions, sun sensitivity, and a blood defect, among other symptoms. Recessively inherited.

Crouzon's Disease (Craniofacial Dysostosis). Skull and jaw abnormalities. Dom.-q.

Congenital Hip Disease. Dislocation of one or both hips in newborn infants, with girls affected about six times as often as boys. Hereditary influences in some cases, but environmental in others.

TEETH AND MOUTH. Most ordinary teeth defects are undoubtedly due to improper tooth care, diet and faulty eating habits, water elements, etc. But under the same conditions heredity may play a part in giving people "good" or "bad" teeth, well formed or misshapen teeth. If under different conditions the same teeth defects or peculiarities have appeared in families, heredity may be suspected.

Missing Teeth. These may be molars, upper incisors, second bicuspids. Usually dom., but may also be rec. or sex-l.

Extra Teeth. These frequently occur with cleft-palate. Dom.-?

Teeth at Birth (Incisors). Dom.-q.

Defective Enamel. This may be brownish, pitted, transparent. Usually dom.; reddish enamel (*porphyrinuric*) is rec.

Malocclusion. This is improper adjustment of upper to lower teeth. It usually appears due to faulty chewing habits, but heredity may also be involved. Dom.-q.?

Cleft Palate and Harelip. Either condition may appear with or without the other, and they should not be mistaken as forms of the same condition. Although both result from the failure of the parts involved to fuse before birth, the causes—hereditary or environmental, or a combination of the two—may be different and not easily determined. Cleft palate by itself occurs more often in girls, but cleft lip together with cleft palate (in about 1 in 1,000 births) is more frequent in boys. Among identical twins, when one has harelip, with or without cleft palate, in 62 per cent of the cases the other does not. In a family where a parent has or had cleft palate, and a child with cleft palate alone has appeared, there is about a one-in-seven chance that it will reappear in another child. To the extent that heredity is involved, it may be through different types of genes or groups of genes, often governed in their action by adverse factors in the prenatal environment.

SKIN DEFECTS. When concerned about the heredity of any skin condition in yourself and/or a child, first establish through your doctor that it is not an *acquired* disorder, or due to an internal disease, which is usually the case. Less frequently, skin disorders and defects of many kinds are hereditary. Many have no serious effects other than on the person's appearance, but some are dangerous.

Albinism. (Previously discussed in Chapter 7.) This is mainly a skin-pigment defect, due to a recessively inherited metabolic error which blocks the normal processes of pigmentation. In the common type there may be accompanying defects of the eye (oscillating eyeballs, or *nystagmus*) and teeth. Albinism is found among all human beings, including Negroes and Mongoloid peoples. The highest incidence, up to 6 per 1,000, is among the San Blas Indians of central Panama, and there also are many albinos among American Indians in the Hopi, Navajo, and other Southwest tribes. Milder types of albinism include: *albinoidism*, moderate pigment in skin and hair, but eyes not affected (dom.-q.); *partial albinism* (*piebald*), with stripes on back, white patches elsewhere (dom. or dom.-q.); *white "blaze,"* or patch of white hair above center of forehead, usually from birth on (dom.). A wholly unrelated condition, W*aardenberg's syndrome*, includes a white forelock among various other effects (facial anomalies, eyes of different color, deafness), and is also dominant.

Birthmarks. The only birthmarks to be seriously concerned about are the rare types listed in Chapter 12 under "skin cancers." Among the common hereditary types, which are not harmful, is the *nevus of Unna*, on the nape of the neck, and many of those which are warty and hairy. But *whenever in doubt*, it is always well to check on birthmarks with a doctor.

Mongolian Spot. This is a temporary bluish patch near the base of the spine which appears in almost all infants of Mongolian stock (Chinese, Japanese, American Indians, Eskimos, etc.), in many Negro infants, and sometimes in darker-skinned white infants (Italian, Armenian, etc.). Mode of inheritance uncertain.

Blistering (Abnormal, Epidermolysis Bullosa). There are several types: blisters raised easily from childhood on (dom.-q. or sex-l.); severe birth-type, leaving scars (rec.-q.); rare extreme form, with bleeding, fatal in infancy (rec.); sunlight blistering, with scarring (*porphyria*); milder form, with reddish teeth (rec.); and severe form, with nervous disorders and other symptoms (dom.-?). (The latter condition is one that apparently afflicted King George III of England, who reigned during the American Revolution, and who was wrongly believed because of it to have been psychotic.)

Fatty Skin Growths (Xanthoma). These occur on eyelids or elsewhere (*xanthelasma*). Inc.-dom. Severe growths (*hyperlipemia* or *hypercholesterolemia*) also producing atherosclerosis. Inc.-dom. or dom.

Horny Skin, or Scaly or Fish Skin (Ichthyosis). There are various types: common, with skin shedding from infancy on (dom.-q. or sex-l.); *elephant skin*, a severe form of cracked skin, causing premature birth, early death (rec.).

Psoriasis. This is another scaly skin condition; may be inherited only as a tendency. Dom.-q.

Rubber Skin (Ehlers-Danlos Syndrome). This freak elastic skin can be greatly stretched and snapped back (as sometimes seen in circus side shows) with hyperextensibility of joints. Dom.-q.

Sweat-Gland Defects. The complete inability to sweat (with other defects, including missing teeth) is found mostly in males. A milder form is dom.-q. An opposite condition, *excessive sweating*, associated with eating, is dom.

Scarring (Abnormal). The tendency to form unusually thick scars (*keloids*) after cuts or operations is dom.

DEFECTIVE HAIR AND NAILS. There are several rare hereditary types of defective hair, among them a beady type of hair (*monilethrix*), present at birth and continuing to grow that way, and defective hair with abnormal nails, appearing at puberty and found mostly in some French Canadian families. The conditions described are either dom. or dom.-q.

Darier's Disease. This is a syndrome which may cause early hair-follicle defects, goose flesh, hair loss, stunted stature, sometimes mental deficiency; congenital or appearing in childhood. Dom.-q.

Graying, Premature. Unrelated to aging. Dom. (The belief that brunettes gray sooner than blonds is probably a visual impression, inasmuch as white hairs may stand out more clearly against a background of dark hair than of fair hair.)

Defective Nails. Since the nails and hair are fashioned of much the same substances, certain of the hereditary nail abnormalities accompany some of the hair conditions, such as the one afflicting certain French-Canadian families, mentioned above. But some other nail defects and abnormalities are inherited independently. These include absent nails, thick and protruding nails, spotted, bluish-white nails, milky-white nails, thickened nails (with also thick skins on palms and soles), and thin nails (small and soft, or flat). All the foregoing are usually dom. or dom.-q., but absent nails may also be rec.

BALDNESS. The common, widespread type of "pattern" baldness which comes to about two in five mature and older men is probably hereditary in the great majority of cases. In these, falling hair and sometimes its almost total loss appear to be unrelated to any disease, state of bodily health, or scalp disorder. Nor is there any truth in the old theory that men become bald and women do not because over the ages men have cut their hair or

Inherited Pattern Baldness

1.

2.

3.

Noticeable loss of hair at forehead, temples and sides. Also, in older men, small bald spot in crown.

Much of hair lost from the forehead to the crown.

Only sparse hair over ears, and in a fringe around the back.

NOTE: Different degrees of baldness, as shown, may run in families. Among women, hair loss rarely goes beyond stage No. 1. (See text.)

taken less care of it than have women. (As previously noted, the habits of ancestors could have no effect on their descendants' inherited traits. Further, many young men in recent years have been letting their hair grow to full length—and it will have no effect on whether they do or do not become bald.) The explanation for the sex differences in baldness, offered by geneticists, is that the baldness tendency results from a special kind of gene, called "sex-influenced" or "sex-limited" because the strength of its effects is governed, or limited, mostly by the sex of the person receiving it. Thus, only *one* of these baldness genes can produce baldness in a male, whereas in a female a single gene has virtually no effect, and even two of the genes may produce only a thinning of the hair or no more than mild baldness. One specific reason seems to be that the male hormones stimulate the baldness gene to do its work, whereas the female hormones counteract its effects. Backing up this theory are the findings that baldness rarely, if ever, develops in *eunuchs*—castrated males lacking the normal supply of male hormones—even if they have the inherited baldness genes. But if these same males are given doses of male hormones to make up for their deficiency, baldness develops in those with the inherited tendencies, though not in the others.

False Beliefs. The above facts should dispose of the old notion that a heavy head of hair in a man indicates virility and potency, while lack of hair suggests the contrary. Actually, once the baldness gene is present, it is the biologically more feminine and less virile man (deficient in male hormones) who is apt to retain his hair, whereas it is the biologically more masculine man (most abundant in male hormones) who is likely to become bald. But all of this applies only to the effects of hormones on the workings of the baldness gene. Otherwise, the fact that a man is or isn't bald proves nothing as to his "manliness."

Inheritance Workings. If a young man's father was, or is bald, there is at least an even chance he himself also will be. The threat is increased if there also was or is baldness on his mother's side (her father, brothers, etc.), since a son may have received a baldness gene from his mother, even though she herself has shown none of the effects. There are indications that the baldness genes and their effects in some families are stronger than in other families. Thus, degrees of hereditary baldness appear to range from almost total hair loss, beginning to develop in early maturity, to only partial hair loss or thinning in the older ages.

Race Differences. Baldness genes give evidence of being distributed differently among races and ethnic groups. The most baldness is found among Mediterranean peoples—Greeks, Italians, Turks, Egyptians, etc. Baldness is less common among Negroes than whites, and least common among Mongolians. (The latter, at the same time, also have less facial and body hair than whites. See Chapter 9, p. 67.)

Nonhereditary Baldness. In a minority of cases, baldness may result from such environmental causes as infectious diseases, glandular and nervous ailments, diabetes, or fevers, which may produce temporary or permanent hair loss. But medical authorities refute the claims of so-called baldness institutes that common baldness is caused by dandruff, oiliness of the scalp, or simple scalp disease, and that clearing up these disorders will cure or prevent baldness and restore hair growth. At this writing, no cure for ordinary, inherited baldness has been found, and advertising such a cure is forbidden by the United States Federal Trade Commission.

Patch Baldness. This is a rare type of premature baldness, unrelated to common baldness, in which a small bald area or patch appears on the scalp, at birth or at puberty, possibly increasing in size and spreading later. The condition may affect girls as well as boys, and may be dom.-q. in inheritance.

14

Sex Abnormalities

In infrequent instances the normal processes of sex determination and development (discussed in Chapter 4) can be upset or swerved so as to produce abnormalities of various types. These may include abnormalities (1) in the sex organs; (2) in the secondary sex characteristics (body form, hair growth, breasts, etc.); (3) in the stages of sexual development (greatly speeded up, or much retarded); and (4) in sexual and reproductive functioning. Many, if not most, of these abnormalities are caused in prenatal life, or in infancy or childhood, or purely environmental mishaps, glandular upsets, or diseases. But others may be directly due to genetic faults in the sex-determining processes, or to abnormalities in the sex chromosomes involving deviations from the XX or XY chromosome combinations which normally produce a girl or boy, respectively. These latter sex-chromosome abnormalities may occur in 2 to 3 per 1,000 births.

KLINEFELTER'S SYNDROME. The afflicted individuals are genetically abnormal males, usually with an XXY chromosome combination, which may be derived from a fertilized egg in which two Xs instead of the normal one X joined with the Y; or from an XY egg which split into XXY and OY, and only the XXY part continued to grow (the OY part not being viable). Although the Y itself swerves sex development toward maleness, the two Xs—which ordinarily result in a female—usually (1) keep the testes from developing fully and producing sperm, (2) cause deficiencies in male hormone production, (3) interfere with full development of other male physical traits, and (4) often produce mental defects as well. In rarer instances Klinefelter males may have XXXY, XXXXY, or XXYY combinations, with varying effects.

TURNER'S SYNDROME. Those afflicted are genetically

Chromosomally Caused Sex Abnormalities

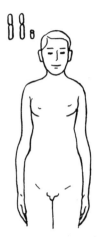

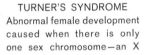

TURNER'S SYNDROME	KLINEFELTER'S SYNDROME
Abnormal female development caused when there is only one sex chromosome—an X	Abnormal male development caused when a Y chromosome is accompanied by two or more Xs

(For details about these syndromes see text.)

abnormal females with an XO sex chromosome combination—the unaccompanied, single X not making possible full female development. Such individuals develop from an X egg to which the fertilizing sperm failed to bring in another X, or a Y, or from which one sex chromosome was lost either at the outset or in the earliest stages of division. Even though the external sex organs of Turner females may take a female form, their sex glands remain undeveloped. They may have such other physical peculiarities as stunted growth and "webbed" neck, and do not develop breasts or menstruate in teenage unless given treatment with female hormones. (*Turner's syndrome* is only about one tenth as frequent in incidence as *Klinefelter's syndrome*.)

ADRENAL VIRILISM (ADRENAL HYPERPLASIA). This is an abnormality of sexual development, in either males or females, due to overproduction of male-type hormones triggered by a defect in the adrenal glands. A recessive gene is responsible. Affected males may be born with an enlarged sex organ and may grow abnormally fast. Affected girls may be born with abnormally developed outer sex organs—such as an enlarged, protruding clitoris—which may cause them to be mistakenly identified as boy infants. Early hormonal treatments with the adrenal hormone cortisone promotes normal sexual maturation in both affected boys and girls.

TESTICULAR FEMINIZATION. The transformation, prenatally, of a prospective male with an XY sex chromosome combination into an outwardly appearing female may be caused by a genetic defect (possibly recessive, probably sex-linked). In this condition, male development of the fetus is suppressed and the individual develops external female sex organs, and at puberty, outward female characteristics. However, the internal sex organs of a female do not develop, and there is no menstruation or possibility of childbearing. Nonetheless, these persons can have quite adequate lives as women, even without treatment, except in some cases where there is surgical lengthening of the vagina.

MASCULINIZED FEMALES. In certain rare instances girl fetuses have been masculinized during prenatal development by synthetic sex hormones given to the pregnant mother to prevent a miscarriage. These hormones may cause the little girl to be born with outward abnormalities which may create difficulties in properly identifying her sex. Surgical correction may be required and if so, should be done at birth.

TRUE HERMAPHRODITISM. Individuals with both male and female sex-gland tissues are extreme medical rarities (despite popular notions). Further, in no recorded cases have both the ovaries and testes, and the phallus and incomplete vagina of a human hermaphrodite, been so adequately developed as to permit the person to function sexually and reproductively as both a male and a female. Much more common, as previously noted, are the *pseudohermaphrodites*—individuals who in their sex glands are of one sex, with either ovaries or testes, but with some other anatomical details of the opposite sex, so that there may be uncertainty in classifying their sex at birth or later.

SEX-IDENTITY TESTS. In many cases of hermaphroditism the external organs are often the most sensible clue to a person's sex. There are, however, various tests that may help in making the determination. One is the *sex-chromatin* test, known also as the "Barr-body" test (after Dr. Murray L. Barr, who, with Dr. E. G. Bertram, devised it). In this test, cells scraped from inside the cheek will show on microscopic examination if an individual is genetically of the XX type (female) by the presence of a little clump of X chromosome material (*chromatin*) at the rim of the cells. (The clump may be caused by one of the Xs which has become inactivated.) If the person has only one X (true of either a normal XY male or an XO Turner female), this little clump will not appear. The "drumstick" test can also be useful. It involves the microscopic examination of a person's white blood cells at certain stages to see if there is a "drumstick" formation in the nuclear mass which appears only where there are two Xs characterizing the cells of a female. However, neither of the preceding tests alone can conclusively establish sex identity, inasmuch as the Barr body and the drumstick, ordinarily pointing to a female, may also be found in abnormal XXY male Klinefelter cells, and are missing from the cells of an abnormal Turner XO female.

The *direct sex chromosome* test, in which the sex chromosomes themselves are revealed by microscopic examination of the person's cells after the required processing, provides the most conclusive evidence of genetic sex. This test can show clearly if the individual has the normal female (XX) or male (XY) sex chromosome combination, or the Klinefelter, Turner, or other abnormal sex chromosome arrangements.

SEX-CHANGING. Sensational cases have been reported from time to time of "males transformed into females," or vice versa. In lower animals this is possible, and in some species occurs in the natural state. Thus, the oyster alternates from being a male one season to being a female the next. In poultry, where sex is not so strongly fixed as in humans, hormonal upsets sometimes may cause a hen to develop some characteristics of a rooster. However, these radical sex reversals have not been found possible in human beings. Most of the reported cases of human sex-changing have involved persons with sex abnormalities who were operated on and treated to bring them in line with their genetic sex. The more highly publicized cases of physically normal males who

claimed to have been turned into females involved plastic operations by which the outer male sex organs were removed and
female organs simulated, and female hormone treatments given to
induce breast development and skin-texture changes. Genetically
these individuals still remained males.

Females Changed into Males. Some of these cases have been
individuals who, through outward sex-organ abnormalities (previously discussed) were classified at birth as females and reared as
such, but later sought a change in sex or in sex identification.
In several publicized instances, winners in international women's
athletic contests were subsequently identified as genetically males
(their awards then being nullified), which led to the Olympic
games' stipulation in 1968 that entrants in the women's competi-
tions—either individuals or a sampling of teams—undergo prior
physical examinations and/or chromosome tests to remove any
doubt about their sex. Most of the other cases of "females changed
into males" have not been publicized, but the few which have been
included those of a celebrated Scottish "woman" physician, a
"woman" member of the Irish nobility, and a "woman" officer in
the British army auxiliary, all of whom were later reclassified as
males and married women friends. In some cases initial classification as female is due to a congenital abnormality in male infants
called *hypospadias*, in which a cleft beneath the penis and the
failure of the two sides of the scrotum to fuse cause the sex organs
to be mistaken for those of a female. This abnormality is in some
cases hereditary (dom.-q).

EXTRA NIPPLES (SUPERNUMERARY BREASTS). One,
two, or more additional pairs of nipples and/or breasts (usually
very small and rudimentary) in women, and occasionally in men,
may be hereditary in some cases, although how is not clear.

SEX MOSAICISM. A mosaic—something made of pieces of
different kinds—has its counterpart in certain rare individuals
whose bodies, or parts of their bodies, contain a mixture of two
kinds of cells with different sex chromosome combinations: perhaps
XY (male) cells interspersed with XO (Turner female) cells
which have lost their Y during some stage of cell multiplication,
or a combination of XX and XO cells which have lost one of the
Xs. In these mosaic individuals there may be various types of
partially abnormal sex development, such as (very rarely) a

female-type breast on one side and a small, male-type breast on the other, or normal male traits combined with some Turner female abnormalities.

PRECOCIOUS OR DELAYED PUBERTY. Marked deviations from the average time of puberty onset in certain families may be influenced by heredity as well as environment. In extremely abnormal cases precocious puberty (*pubertas praecox*) may begin in girls or boys as early as age three, or even at birth. These cases are usually due in boys to glandular upsets, often hypothalmic tumors, but where the condition has appeared in successive members of a family for several generations, the possibility of inheritance arises. As one example, a Texas boy who at age three achieved technical puberty and was producing fertile sperms had a father, grandfather, great-grandfather, and several other male relatives who also had shown extremely premature sexual development. The possibility of dominant inheritance, limited to the males, was suggested. In girls, precocious puberty may also run in families, usually without pathological causes. However, in average cases, the preponderant influence of environment on the timing of puberty is shown by its generally much earlier arrival in girls of many countries today—at ages of about twelve and a half to thirteen and a half compared with fourteen to fifteen or more in their grandmothers' days.

HOMOSEXUALITY AND TRANSEXUALISM. These are aspects of sexual *behavior*, which will be discussed in Chapter 24.

15

Defects in Senses and Body Functions

EYE DEFECTS. Heredity produces or helps to produce hundreds of eye defects, from very mild ones to those causing total blindness. Possibly one fifth of the blindness cases are hereditary, four fifths environmental. More than half the blindness in young people results from prenatal or later mishaps, such as diseases, infections, or dietary deficiencies. One condition, *retrolental fibroplasia*, which formerly blinded thousands of very premature infants, was found due to excessive oxygen in incubators. But about one eighth of the cases of congenital blindness are due to wayward genes which fail to construct properly some vital part of the eye mechanism—the iris, retina, eye nerves, etc. In addition, a considerable proportion of the cases of blindness which develop at later stages, in childhood, maturity, or old age, are also the result of wayward eye genes. One important feature of many inherited eye conditions is that they are sex-linked, afflicting males much more often than females (as explained in Chapter 11).

Color Blindness. This is the most common of the inherited eye defects and of the conditions which afflict males in particular (about eight times as many as females). Ordinary color blindness is the inability to distinguish the *color* differences between red and green, although, as with red and green traffic lights, the afflicted person might still recognize their differences in shade or intensity. About 4 per cent of white American males have the common form of color blindness, while another 4 per cent suffer from lesser deficiencies in red-green color vision, or other color vision. Among Negro males there is only about half this incidence of color blindness, and among American Indians only about one quarter. Whether any cases of red-green color blindness are due to environmental factors, such as possibly a vitamin-A deficiency, is uncertain. (It may be noted that virtually all lower animals, with the exception of monkeys and apes—man's closest animal relatives —are color-blind either wholly or to a great extent.)

Inheritance Workings. The inheritance of color blindness follows the principles of simple sex-linked inheritance (see Chapter 11), in which one color-blindness gene produces the defect in males, but two genes are needed to produce the defect in females. Since the color-blindness gene is in the X chromosome, and a male can receive this chromosome only from his mother, it is only by way of their mothers that males can inherit color blindness. For a female to be color-blind, both the Xs she receives—the one from her father and the one from her mother—must carry the color-blindness gene, which means that *her father must be color-blind* and her mother must at least be a carrier for the gene. Some women who are carriers, with a single such gene, may show it by a slight defect in red-green color vision. A possibility is that in some women carriers the X with the normal gene may be inactivated in part of their eye cells, permitting the X with the color-blindness gene to operate in other cells. (See "The Lyon Hypothesis" in Chapter 11.)

Other Visual Defects. *Astigmatism (defective focusing).* Its heredity is in doubt, but some authorities believe it may frequently be caused by complex genes. Dom.-q.?

Near-Sightedness (Extreme: High Myopia). This may be caused in different families by different types of genes. Rec.? Or sex-l.?

Far-Sightedness (Extreme and Congenital). This may be dom.-q. in inheritance. A serious type, with other eye defects, may be rec.

Night Blindness. This is the inability to see in dim light, possibly with other eye defects. There are various degrees of this condition and types of inheritance: dom., rec., sex-l. One form, *Oguchi's disease* (Japanese) is rec.

Day Blindness. Failing eyesight in bright daylight, and total inability to distinguish colors, is usually rec.

Eye Diseases. *Cataract.* Most cataracts in children, and many that develop in early maturity or middle age, are probably hereditary (usually dom., but with some types rec. or sex-l.). It should be clear that some congenital cataracts result from prenatal infections or acquired diseases, and that many cataracts of later life also may be due mainly to diseases and infections, as well as to aging effects. Before concluding that a cataract in any given case is hereditary, the family history must be known. In many families successive cataracts that are very similar in type, severity, and age of onset point strongly to the action of dominant-qualified genes. (Many hereditary cataracts are part of syndromes, such as pseudo-hypoparathyroidism and gargoylism.)

Glaucoma. When occurring in adults and linked with other eye defects, glaucoma may not be hereditary in most cases, but in many families there is considerable evidence that primary glaucoma (not linked to other eye diseases) is inherited possibly through dominant or recessive genes. Rarer inherited forms of glaucoma occur in infants and may be recessive.

Retinitis Pigmentosa. This is a very serious hereditary eye condition (sometimes a part of various syndromes) in which the retina fills with pigment. It has different forms and degrees of seriousness (sometimes with deafness, idiocy, etc.), developing at different stages of life. Inheritance may be dom., rec. or sex-l. Where the gene is sex-linked, women carrying it may sometimes be identified by optical examination.

Optic Atrophy. The optic nerve is withered, causing blindness. Different types exist: *congenital* (dom.); *childhood* (rec.?); *adult* (*Leber's disease*), with central nervous system effects (sex-l.?).

Cancer of the Retina (Retinoblastoma). This eye cancer is very rare, is congenital or occurs in early childhood, and requires eye removal to prevent death. It is usually dom., but the gene probably arises in many cases through mutation. When an afflicted person who survives has the condition in only one eye, the chances of transmission are greatly reduced.

Eye-Structure Defects. Among the various hereditary types of these defects are *corneas* that are clouded, or with an opaque ring, or enlarged, or cone-shaped; *displaced lenses*, sometimes with displaced pupils; *irises* with a segment missing, or almost closed, or wholly absent. These conditions are most often dom. in inheritance, but sometimes are rec. or sex-l.

Undersized Eyes (Microphthalmia). Extremely small eyes, often with other eye defects; can be dom., rec. or sex-l., or a chromosome abnormality. In a very rare type the eyes are completely absent. Rec.+? or chrom. abnormality.

Mirror Reading and Writing

An inherited oddity

Afflicted persons see and write upside down and backward. (To see what the boy above has written, hold illustration upside down before a mirror.)

Cross-Eyes (Strabismus). This common condition is sometimes hereditary, sometimes not. Where inherited, it is dom.-q.

Drooping Eyelids (Ptosis). The eyes always appear to be half closed. Sometimes acquired; when hereditary, dom.

Quivering Eyeballs (Nystagmus). This appears at birth, usually with weak eyesight. The common type (sex-l.) afflicts mostly males. A rarer type, with head twitching, is dom.

Eye-Muscle Paralysis. This inability to move the eyes, sometimes associated with one or several diseases, is dom. or sex-l. when hereditary.

Miscellaneous Eye and Vision Abnormalities. *Reading Difficulties.* Dyslexia, a condition which causes difficulty in reading and writing, is much more frequent in boys than in girls. Although there can be environmental causes, the disorder often appears to be hereditary (dom.-q?). *Mirror reading and writing,* in which persons from childhood on see in reverse and upside down, can also be hereditary. (Leonardo da Vinci was a "mirror writer.")

Pink-Eyes. Unpigmented eyes, as in albinos, but with no other albino effects, appear in babies, almost invariably boys. Rare, sex-l.

Dry-Eyes (Stenosis of Lachrymal Glands). Blockage or constriction of the tear glands, so they do not function properly or adequately, is believed to be dom.

HEARING AND EAR DEFECTS. Heredity may be involved in about half the cases of congenital deafness, close to three fourths of these being recessive, one fourth dominant, and about 3 per cent sex-linked. In adult deafness about one third of the cases may be hereditary. The exact facts are difficult to establish because diseases and accidents play such a large part in deafness, and there is often uncertainty about the causes in previous members of a family.

Congenital Deafness. This may be produced in babies prenatally by various diseases in the mother (German measles, syphilis, etc.) or, following birth, by meningitis, scarlet fever, mumps, and other conditions. But with the disease threats being increasingly reduced, heredity now may account for half the cases or more of congenital deafness in the United States, with the genes involved failing to properly control construction of the inner-ear mechanism. If a child is born deaf it is especially serious because inability to hear also interferes greatly with learning to speak. In former times this almost always doomed the congenitally deaf child to be a *mute* as well (hence the common use of the term "deaf-mute"), but today special training helps many deaf children to speak.

Inheritance. The manner in which congenital deafness is inherited is still uncertain, but it is believed generally due to *recessive* genes plus other factors—possibly additional wayward genes, or certain adverse influences in prenatal life. This is suggested by the fact that in many cases where both parents were congenitally deaf, children with normal hearing resulted. Generally, however, deaf parents whose condition has not been caused by accident or disease have a much greater than average risk of producing deaf children, especially if they are closely related and are carrying the same genes. Among identical twins studied, when one was totally deaf in infancy, the other was so in 60 per cent of the cases, and partially deaf in another 28 per cent.

Other Deafness Conditions. *Middle-Ear Deafness* (*Otosclerosis*). This is the most common of the serious hearing defects that develop in the more mature years, more often among women than men, and especially after childbirth. Some cases of adult deafness result from injuries and infections, but the hereditary type of middle-ear deafness is caused by a deposit of bony obstruction inside the ear. The genes responsible are possibly dominant with low penetrance, but in some instances are recessive. An operation to open the obstruction in the inner ear often greatly improves hearing.

Word Deafness. In this condition, hearing is normal, but the individual cannot interpret sounds and words, due to a brain defect. It appears in early life, most often affecting boys. Dom.-q.

Outer-Ear Defects. Various deformities in the structure of the outer ear, which do not affect hearing, may be inherited. Among them, appearing in babies at birth, are absence of one ear, cup-shaped ear (turned over at top), one or both ears "doubled," a gill-like opening near the ear passage, etc. All of these are dominant or partly so. Among recessive conditions are low-set ears, and ears with a thick, out-turned upper part (helix).

SPEECH DEFECTS. There is much uncertainty as to the hereditary factors in any of the common speech defects, such as stuttering or lisping (when not related to cleft palate or fo hereditary nerve and muscle disorders). Many psychologists maintain that stuttering or stammering in a child results mostly from some emotional or psychological disturbance. (Adults, too, may develop speech disorders under stress.) However, certain facts remain puzzling: (1) under the same conditions only some persons will develop the stuttering habit; (2) stuttering may run in families even when individual members have not been in contact with one another; (3) the incidences of speech defects among males is at least five times that among females, with no proof that this is all due to differences in emotional stresses; and (4) among identical twins, if one stutters, the other also does almost invariably, which is not so among fraternal twins. Some authorities believe, therefore, that heredity cannot be ruled out as a *predisposing* factor in speech defects. But if there are any genes involved, they have not yet been identified.

TASTE AND SMELL DEFECTS. Heredity undoubtedly has something to do with differences in the capacities of individuals to smell and taste substances of all kinds, or of particular kinds, but only limited facts on this point are as yet available. *Taste blindness,* with respect to the chemical "PTC" (phenylthiocarbamide), has been found inherited through simple recessive genes. About seven out of ten persons who taste paper impregnated with this chemical say it is "bitter," whereas the rest (those who carry two recessive "nontasting" genes) detect almost no taste. Possible hereditary differences have also been reported in tasting other chemical substances, which may be related to various foods.

Smelling defects, involving the inability to smell some substances, if not most substances, are usually due to nasal diseases, infections, or injuries. However, where total inability to smell runs in families, it may be the rare inherited condition of *anosmia,* which may be dominant or sex-linked.

MUSCLE AND NERVE DEFECTS. Doubt exists as to hereditary factors in the more common muscle and nerve disorders, such as multiple sclerosis, but inheritance of some of the special types has been well established. One must be extremely careful, however, not to confuse the hereditary muscular or nerve defects with similar types that are due solely to accidents, injuries, or diseases, whether before birth or after. In any case only after a given condition has been properly diagnosed by a competent specialist should the following facts about heredity be considered to apply.

Ataxias. These comprise a varied and complex group of disorders, many of which are associated with additional neurological defects. Hereditary types include *Friedreich's,* in childhood (rec.); *Marie's cerebellar,* in adults (dom.-q.); and *hereditary tremor,* with late onset (dom.).

Paralysis (Referring Only to Hereditary Types). *Spastic Paraplegia.* In childhood, boys are chiefly affected. Rec., dom., sex-l.

Familial Periodic Paralysis. This occurs in adults. Dom.

Wilson's Disease. This is a peculiar inherited defect in children, the result of an abnormality in copper metabolism. It is accompanied by facial distortions and jerky hand movements, sometimes also with mental defects. Rec.

Muscular Atrophies. Of these atrophies, *Peroneal*, in childhood is dom., rec., or sex-l.; in young adults, it is sex-l. or dom.; *spinal*, in infancy, is rec.; *progressive spinal*, in maturity (with cataract, sterility), is dom.-q.

Muscular Dystrophy, Progressive. There are various types; differing in age of onset, symptoms, and inheritance. The *Duchenne type*, severe, progressive, and attacking mainly young boys, is sex-l.; many women carriers can be identified by clinical tests. The *pre-adolescent type*, with onset about age eleven, is rec. The *young adult type*, with onset about age eighteen, is dom.

Multiple Sclerosis. Some evidence of hereditary predisposition is present, possibly rec.-q.

Myotonic Dystrophy. This condition involving slowed muscular relaxation occurs in early adult life. Dom.

Generalized Myotonia. The onset of this is at age four to five. Rec.

Myotonia Congenita (Thomsen's Disease). This is congenital. Dom.

Missing Muscles. In cases of various muscles being absent or left uncompleted, environmental and/or hereditary causes are unclear.

Dysautonomia, Familial (Riley-Day Syndrome). A severe congenital condition (rec.) affecting primarily the autonomic nervous system and its responses, this syndrome includes among its effects the inability to feel pain or to distinguish between hot and cold. It has been reported mainly in individuals descended from central European Jewish stock. (See also *Tay-Sachs disease*, in Chapter 17, under "Biochemical Mental Defects.")

EPILEPSY. Many authorities now believe that heredity is not involved in the majority of cases of common epilepsy, but that in a certain percentage of them (perhaps 25 per cent or more) heredity does produce some *predisposition* or *tendency*— that is, an inherent weakness in the brain or nervous system that can lead to epileptic symptoms under unfavorable conditions. These conditions may include various types of accidents and injuries (before birth or after), diseases, metabolic disorders, brain and nerve tumors, etc. The assumption might be, then, that some individuals start off with a nervous system sufficiently unbalanced, because of aberrant genes, to make them much more likely than average persons to become epileptic under a given environmental "push." There is evidence that persons carrying such genes may be identified through abnormal ("epileptoid") brain wave patterns. There is also the theory (not yet proved) that one or a pair of these genes may produce the abnormal brain waves without other effects, but that a double dose of the same genes may produce epilepsy or the tendency to it. However, only two *rare* conditions, both *myoclonic epilepsies* (differing in many ways from the ordinary types) have so far been proved directly hereditary, one of these being recessive, the other dominant.

Hereditary Evidence.   Various studies indicate that (1) among identical twins, if one is epileptic, the other will also show an abnormal brain wave pattern and will be epileptic in about 70 per cent of the cases, whereas among fraternal twins both are epileptic only a fourth as often; (2) among close relatives of epileptics the incidence of epilepsy is about five times that in the general population; (3) the abnormal epileptoid brain waves seem to run strongly in certain families, and if a child is epileptic, the epileptoid brain waves may appear in one parent if not both.

Epilepsy and Mental Defect.   In the large majority of cases there is no relationship between epilepsy and intelligence. About two thirds of the epileptics are average or above average in IQ; about 23 per cent are slightly below average, and only 10 per cent are retarded sufficiently to be placed in institutions. Epileptics most likely to be mentally defective are those whose condition results from brain injuries and not from any inherited tendencies.

CHEMICAL DISORDERS.   The more serious and common disorders resulting from possible hereditary defects in the body's chemical processes have been previously discussed (Chapter 12) or will be dealt with later (blood conditions, mental diseases and defects, etc.). Here we will discuss a few other conditions to which heredity may contribute.

Gout.   There has been a long-standing suspicion that this affliction has a hereditary basis, suggested by the finding that a susceptibility to gout results from an excess of uric acid in the blood (*hyperuricemia*) possibly caused by a dominant gene. Further, the much higher incidence of the disease among males is attributed to the fact that the male chemical make-up is particularly likely to promote the development of gout if the tendency is there, whereas the female chemical environment may help to suppress it. However, only about 10 per cent of males with hyperuricemia develop gouty arthritis. Conclusions about the genetic factors in gout therefore remain uncertain.

Urinary Disorders.   There are various hereditary types, identified by unusual amounts of different substances in the urine, and producing different effects: *porphyria* (with reddish teeth); *alcaptonuria* (darkish urine) sometimes with arthritis; *cystinuria*, occasionally with kidney stones; *pentosuria*, a sugar-assimilation defect, and *maple-syrup urine disease* (so named for the peculiar odor of the urine). These conditions are all usually recessive.

Fat-Metabolism Defects.   One of the more common conditions, *xanthoma*, was discussed under "Skin Defects," Chapter 13. Others fairly well known are *Niemann-Pick disease* (liver and spleen enlargement) and *Gaucher's disease*, both recessive and afflicting mostly children, with serious consequences. Inherited defects of fat metabolism also are involved in *essential familial hyperlipemia* (inc. dom.) and in *hypercholesterolemia* (dom. or inc. dom.).

Fabry's Disease.   This inborn error of glycosphingolipid metabolism has serious kidney effects. Sex-l.

Hurler's Syndrome, or "Gargoylism."   This is a defect in mucopolysaccharide metabolism, developing in infancy, which results in an unusual combination of abnormalities—facial, skeletal, and internal—and in stunted growth and mental defect. Fatal before puberty or maturity, it is recessive in inheritance. Somewhat similar but much milder conditions are the *Hunter* (sex-l.), *Sanfilippo* (rec.), and *Scheie* (rec.) syndromes.

Glycogen Storage Disease.   Due to enzyme defects of various types, this disease is usually serious. Rec.

Galactosemia.   This is an inability to metabolize properly the sugar galactose in milk. Its serious results if not treated make its detection important. Rec.

ALLERGIES.   Innumerable differences exist among human beings in the way they react to foods and drugs of all kinds, and very often heredity is involved. When the reaction produces unfavorable results because of an immunological sensitivity, it is called an "allergy." Probably every person is allergic to one or more things, which may be the fur of a particular animal, feathers, dust, ragweed pollen, or any of hundreds of foods (milk, cereals, berries, etc.), drinks, drugs, and chemical substances. Very often allergies result in or are linked with violent hay fever, asthma, or certain skin diseases or digestive disturbances, which in children may interfere with proper growth and development. Many authorities today believe that what causes an allergy to become acute is usually or often some emotional ("psychosomatic") disturbance in the individual which makes the chemical reactions of the body especially sensitive. However, the fact that individuals tend to be allergic only to *particular* substances, and that such allergies, often of a peculiar nature, tend to run in families, strongly suggests that heredity is also involved as an influence or direct cause, perhaps in three fourths of the cases. There is some evidence that allergy inheritance may be *dominant*. One theory is that there are two kinds of dominant allergy genes: if both kinds are inherited, allergic symptoms are likely to appear before puberty (in boys twice as often as girls); with one gene alone, a milder allergy will appear, after puberty. Another theory is that susceptibilities to *hay fever*, or *atopic asthma*, or *eczema*, are caused by variations of recessive hypersensitivity gene pairs.

Migraine Headache. This is sometimes viewed as an allergic condition and may be dominant in inheritance. Women are afflicted by migraine twice as often as men, the condition appearing to be aggravated by female hormones, and the worst attacks coming during menstrual periods.

Angioneurotic Edema. This is a rare, very serious allergic affliction in young people (twice as many boys as girls) which may produce sudden swellings in the skin, larynx, or vital organs, sometimes causing death. Dom.-q.

Collagen Diseases. This group involves allergies not only to certain foreign substances but to the body's own tissues, in which there is collagen, with effects on organs, nerves, muscles, and other parts. There are clear examples of familial appearances in these diseases, but no definite modes of inheritance have yet been established. Sometimes classed with these conditions is *rheumatoid arthritis.*

Cryopathies, Including Raynaud's Syndrome. This extreme sensitivity to cold air or cold water affects the hands and fingers. It may be genetically influenced.

The "Chinese Restaurant" Syndrome. Severe adverse reactions—headaches, burning sensations, chest pains, etc.—afflicting certain persons after eating in Chinese restaurants have been traced to extreme sensitivity to the food additive, monosodium glutamate (MSG), used in preparing wonton soup and other Chinese dishes. Suspicion of inheritance awaits confirmation.

Drug Sensitivity. Physicians have become increasingly alerted to the fact that in addition to allergic effects of foods and other substances on given individuals, there are a great many drugs each of which can produce adverse reactions in some persons because of specific inherited deficiencies or peculiarities in biochemical make-up and functioning. Among these drugs are *insulin* (used in treating diabetes), *isoniazid* (used in tuberculosis treatment), and *primaquine* (an antimalarial drug). The inherited adverse reaction to the latter drug is caused by a condition known as "G-6-P-D" deficiency, to be discussed in Chapter 18 under "Favism."

16

Mental Diseases

INSANITY. Fears of "inheriting insanity" are probably greater than those regarding any other type of affliction, and go back to earliest human history. First it should be clear that "insanity" is now only a popular term, applied to mental diseases without distinguishing one from the other. But actually, as modern psychiatry has shown, there are many types of mental diseases, different in their symptoms and causes. This is especially true with respect to *hereditary* factors or influences. In some conditions —mostly the rarer ones—heredity plays a direct and major role; in others it produces *tendencies* or *susceptibilities*, which will give way to insanity only if there is some strong, adverse environmental push. In any case, in each type of mental disease heredity may work in a different way and in a different degree. Accordingly, wherever persons fear that they or their children are threatened by insanity because it has appeared previously in their family, they must be careful to establish the type of mental disease with which they are concerned, and then note how heredity may be involved. But before taking up the mental diseases separately, a few special points should be made clear.

Insanity Incidence. Roughly, close to one in every twelve persons in the United States is, or will be at one time or another, afflicted by some mental disease requiring hospitalization. Does this mean that *every* person has an up to one-in-twelve risk of becoming insane? No. For some individuals there may be almost no risk; for others it may be considerably higher than one in twelve—in rare instances up to fifty-fifty. The risk in each case is determined by the nature of the mental disease, the relative influences of heredity and environment, the age at which the condition usually appears, and the individual's own make-up, habits, and experiences.

"Are People Becoming Crazier Because of Modern Pressures?" This question is hard to answer. Although there are now vastly more people in mental institutions than there formerly were, there are many reasons for this. Mental cases are diagnosed more quickly and expertly; the facilities for taking care of the mentally sick have enormously increased, so many more people can be put in mental hospitals; lengthening life spans have swelled the numbers of mentally ill old people; and the mental casualties of two terrible world wars have added thousands of others. Yet it also is possible that the complex conditions and pressures of modern life have made it more likely for mental disease to develop in unstable persons. One can only guess about this, since there are no accurate medical facts from former times with which to make comparisons. Similarly, one can draw no conclusions about the incidence of insanity in the United States as compared with other countries, or among those of one race or ethnic group compared with another, so long as the facilities for detecting and caring for the mentally ill differ so greatly. However, in most advanced countries, such as England, Sweden, and Denmark, the proportion of mentally ill is much the same as in the United States. Moreover, wherever psychiatrists have investigated, even among the most isolated primitive peoples living under the simplest conditions, they have found many cases of mental illness, which again strengthens the belief that the inborn tendencies are universal.

"Can Environmental Factors or Emotional Stresses Alone Produce Insanity?" Most authorities are now inclined to believe that except in very unusual cases, a person will not become insane *unless* he starts off with some inborn tendency. No more terrible, nerve-racking experiences can be imagined than those which vast numbers of soldiers and civilians underwent during World War II or in later wars. Yet only a relatively small proportion became mentally diseased. Evidence indicates strongly that those who did were especially *susceptible*. Further, there is considerable evidence that even *chronic alcoholism, syphilis,* or other acquired diseases do not ordinarily result in mental derangement unless there is some predisposition; and that in very old age, even though mental faculties may become weaker, actual insanity (*senile dementia*) tends to occur only in those persons who previously had some mental instability. Finally, there is no evidence that any one can ever "catch" insanity merely from contact with a mentally diseased person, no matter how close the relationship.

"How Can Heredity Produce Mental Disease or the Tendency?" Since the human brain is a very complex organ, or "mechanism," in whose construction and functioning many genes must take part, abnormalities in any of the "key" genes may upset, derange, or unbalance the mental workings at any given stage of life, especially when there is some severely jarring outside influence. Recent studies suggest that these abnormalities may include particular kinds of chemical or hormonal upsets or deficiencies which directly affect the brain cells and disturb or prevent their orderly workings. Supporting evidence comes from the great successes being achieved in treating mental diseases with various drugs such as reserpine, chlorpromazine, and lithium. Thus, if chemical treatments can control or reduce the symptoms of psychoses, it could be inferred that chemical imbalances or aberrations in individuals may also induce predispositions to psychoses or given diseases themselves.

"If a Person Inherits 'Insanity' Genes, Does This Doom Him to Insanity?" Not necessarily, and perhaps not at all in many cases. Mental disease need be no different from other diseases, whether inherited or acquired, in the possibilities for prevention and cure (as previously noted). Especially important has been the progress in detecting symptoms of mental disease in the early stages, through various behavior clues and tests, and in some cases through abnormal brain wave patterns. However, laymen are warned not to make judgments for themselves on the basis of any "peculiar" behavior, which may often stem from temporary emotional difficulties rather than from any mental disease.

"How Is 'Mental Disease' Different from 'Mental Defect'?" There are very important distinctions. "Mental disease" refers solely to a derangement of the mind, without regard to the person's intelligence, which may be of any level up to the highest. "Mental defect" refers to a *slow-working* or *inferior* mind, which prevents the person's intelligence from going above certain levels. The two conditions are entirely different in their causes and symptoms. Where in some cases a person is both mentally *diseased* and mentally *defective*, it is mostly coincidence. In this chapter we will deal only with mental diseases; in the next chapter, with mental defects.

SCHIZOPHRENIA. This is the most serious of the common mental diseases, because it starts earliest, is hardest to *cure*, and accounts for more than half the persons in mental institutions. The name of the disease comes from two Greek words, *schizo*, meaning "split," and *phrenia*, "mind," and is so called because the afflicted persons tend to have a mind or personality "split" between the normal and abnormal. The disease is sometimes also called *dementia praecox* (the "praecox" from the Latin for prematurity) because it often appears before or during adolescence, earlier than other common mental diseases. When one reads about demented little children, or high-school boys or girls with mental breakdowns (sometimes leading to suicide or acts of violence), the disease usually is schizophrenia. It first shows itself as a rule by extreme shyness, timidity, not mixing with others, indifference to outside things, etc., accompanied by hysterical periods and other symptoms. There are various types of schizophrenia each with special characteristics: quarrelsomeness and delusions of persecution (paranoia); pleasant stupor (hebephrenia); violent tantrums, obstinacy, or rigidity (catatonia). Milder types may show themselves only by occasional freakish or erratic behavior.

Hereditary Factors. On the basis of many studies, it is believed that schizophrenia is not likely to develop unless there is an inherited predisposition, probably produced through several defective genes—*a pair of recessives*, and perhaps other genes, or other biological factors. This would mean that a child cannot inherit schizophrenia (or the tendency) *from one parent alone*, but must receive one or more of the schizophrenia genes from *each* parent. In the unfortunate cases where couples do have a schizophrenic child, neither parent therefore has the slightest basis for saying, "It's all because of that insane streak running in *your* family." Any such inherited tendency in a child would have had to come equally through *both* parents. However, a bad emotional environment in the home, or exposure of the child to special strains, might cause the schizophrenic tendency to develop into the disease itself, and to that extent one parent might be more to blame than the other.

Evidence for Heredity. In the general population the average incidence of schizophrenia is about 0.8 per cent, or somewhat under 1 per cent. But wherever close relatives of a person have or had schizophrenia, the threat of developing the disease is very much higher than the average: twenty times the average if a parent was schizophrenic (with the risk rising to an almost two-in-three threat if both parents were so afflicted); fourteen times the average if a brother or sister was schizophrenic; and five times the average if a grandparent, uncle, or aunt had the disease. Among twins, if one of an identical pair is schizophrenic, there is a 40 per cent chance the other will also be or become so, whereas in fraternals the concordance is about 10 per cent—not much more than in two nontwin children of a family. But the fact that among identical twins one can be schizophrenic and the other not, although carrying the same hereditary factors, shows also how important environmental influences are.

Schizophrenia in Adopted Persons. A question often raised: "Cannot the fact that schizophrenics have high incidences of psychotic relatives be ascribed not to heredity but to similarities in disturbed family backgrounds and/or to close contact with psychotic parents?" In answer, recent studies have been made of individuals who had been adopted in early infancy and had later become schizophrenic or had schizophrenic-type symptoms. Investigation showed that an unduly high proportion of the true, biological parents of these persons had been psychotic, and that the schizophrenia of the offspring was correlated not with the environments in which they had been reared, or with the mental states of their foster parents or foster siblings, but far more with the occurrence of the disease in the true parents and other members of their *biological* families.

Biochemical Aspects. The belief that inherited biochemical abnormalities are involved in predisposing individuals to schizophrenia has been reinforced by reported findings among schizophrenics that their sweat may have a peculiar odor, that certain chemical substances excreted from their bodies may have powerful and sometimes hallucinatory effects on the mind, that there are chemical abnormalities in their muscle fibers, that they appear to have an excessive need for vitamin B-3, and that they may differ from normal persons in their tolerance to certain drugs.

Childhood Schizophrenia. Adding to the belief in the inheritance of the schizophrenic tendency are the increasing numbers of cases of this disease found in very young children, at age two or earlier. Often the disease appears spontaneously, with no evidence of anything wrong in the child's environment. Some psychiatrists believe that babies who are deprived of love and proper attention are most likely to become schizophrenic, but there is strong doubt as to whether any baby will develop the disease unless an inborn tendency is present. Strongly supporting this assumption are findings that children with schizophrenia have schizophrenic relatives in almost the same higher-than-average ratios as were given for afflicted mature persons. In any case, if a schizophrenic child appears, parents should not be blamed or assume any blame for themselves without full knowledge of the facts.

Infantile Autism. This peculiar condition developing in some children during infancy—withdrawal into themselves, general restlessness, and apathy often interspersed with violent outbursts— was formerly attributed to some environmentally caused psychological disorder (linked perhaps with parental neglect), but it is now believed that a biochemical abnormality may be involved. If so, what it is, and whether heredity is a factor, is not yet known.

MANIC-DEPRESSIVE INSANITY. This disease is so called because those afflicted may swing in periodic moods from mania (highly excitable and sometimes hilarious behavior) to extreme depression. As the disease progresses it may lead to violent outbursts. But on the whole, manic-depressive insanity is less serious than schizophrenia because (1) it takes less toll in years, most often appearing later in life, during maturity or in middle or old age (although cases are now also being recognized in young children), and (2) it is curable more often and more easily, many manic-depressives recovering after treatment of six months or so (although a dangerous part of the disease is that sometimes individuals who appear cured may suddenly crack up again and commit criminal acts or be suicides). As with schizophrenia, there are indications that this disease may be linked with biochemical abnormalities, it having been found that drugs can induce depressive symptoms as well as control them.

Hereditary Factors. There is a strong probability that a tendency to manic-depressive insanity is inherited, but differently and independently from schizophrenia. Although not certain, it is believed that the manic-depressive genes are *partly dominant*, or *irregularly dominant*, and that in addition to one or two key genes, certain others, plus some sort of special stresses or environmental influences, must be present. However, the major hereditary difference between this disease and schizophrenia is that in schizophrenia, the predisposition to which is caused mainly by *recessive* genes, inheritance must come equally from *both* parents; but in manic-depressive insanity, since the key genes are at least *partly dominant*, there is a considerably greater threat to a child if only one parent is afflicted. Thus, in schizophrenia, if one parent has the disease, there is an up to one-in-six risk the child will develop it; but in manic-depressive insanity, if one parent is afflicted, the risk may be up to one in three that a child will develop the condition. Also, because the manic-depressive condition usually comes on later in life, it may take a longer time to know if any tendency has been inherited. Finally, the fact that this disease is different in nature and inheritance from schizophrenia has a special significance. If only the one type of mental disease has appeared on one side of a family, and only the other type on the other side, the threat of insanity to offspring is very much less than if the same afflictions had appeared on both sides.

Depression without Manic Aspects. This condition, although classed with manic-depressive psychosis as an "affective disorder," is now regarded by some authorities as distinct in its causation and heredity. Inasmuch as it appears much more frequently in females than in males, one theory is that the condition is transmitted by an X-linked dominant gene.

Involutional Melancholia. This is another depressive condition that was formerly regarded as a form of manic-depressive psychosis (and which may also be related to schizophrenia). Generally developing in the older ages, it is sometimes accompanied by extreme anxiety, agitation, and delusions. Findings by the late Dr. Franz J. Kallmann were that among twins in whom the disease had appeared, if one of an identical pair was afflicted, so was the other in 60 per cent of the cases, whereas in fraternal pairs the double occurrence was in only 6 per cent of the cases.

HUNTINGTON'S CHOREA. This rare but terrible mental

disease, completely unrelated to any of the common types of insanity, is directly inherited through a *single dominant gene*. It is one of the most dreadful of all human afflictions, striking at a person in maturity—usually in the thirties or early forties—and from then on causing its victim literally to go to pieces in mind and body, with no known hope of cure, and ending in death after a few years. The worst feature of Huntington's chorea is that, since it is *dominant* in inheritance and comes on so far along in life, any child of a man or woman with the disease has a one-in-two chance of developing it, but may not know whether he will or will not until almost middle age. Tests may eventually make it possible to reveal before maturity those who have inherited this dreadful gene, which, if they could then be induced to forego having children of their own, would greatly reduce the chance of the gene's being passed along. As it is, there is the grim fact that more than a thousand of the cases of Huntington's chorea in the United States in the past three centuries had their origin in genes carried by three brothers who came from Suffolk, England, in 1630, settling in New England; and that during the past century, in Minnesota alone, more than a hundred cases of the disease have appeared or are on their way to appearing among descendants of one afflicted man born in 1831. Whether or not related to the aforementioned strains, the late noted folk singer, Woody Guthrie, was a victim of Huntington's chorea, and died of the disease in 1967 after years of degenerative illness. Each of his five children, among them Arlo, another noted folk singer, at this writing (1971) faces a fifty-fifty threat of developing the same disease.

Pick's Disease (Lobar Atrophy). This is another very rare degenerative affliction which, like Huntington's chorea, begins suddenly to cause deterioration of the brain and body in middle life, and is also inherited through a *single dominant gene.*

PSYCHOPATHIC (OR SOCIOPATHIC) PERSONALITY. This is a subtle and often not easily recognized type of mental disease which may cause great suffering, much more to the families of those afflicted and to society at large than to the diseased persons themselves. Psychopaths may often seem to be no more than "peculiar" persons—rather cold, selfish, and immature—given to lying, deception, and cheating, and to behavior which under certain conditions may lead to vicious and criminal acts. Fortunately, in other cases psychopaths with brilliant minds and talents may turn their energies into important and useful achievement. The fact that the true psychopath usually gives evidence of his peculiarities in early childhood, and often where there is little or nothing wrong in the environment, leads to the theory that some hereditary quirk is involved. The possibility of a brain disorder as one factor arises from reports that a majority of psychopaths have abnormal brain waves. (Lee Harvey Oswald, the assassin of President John F. Kennedy, had been diagnosed as psychopathic during his childhood, when he was a "problem case.")

Senile Psychoses. The fact that only a certain percentage of elderly people become mentally ill has led to the belief that a hereditary predisposition is involved in many of these cases. As evidence, (1) senile dementia appears to run in given families with much more than average frequency and (2) among twins in whom senile psychoses had developed its double incidence in identical pairs was 43 per cent, but in fraternal pairs, only 8 per cent.

Neuroses. These include many personality disorders and psychological disturbances found in people who can be classed as fully sane. There is much to indicate that ordinary neurotic behavior is largely the result of emotional stresses and difficult situations. But it is also not unlikely that heredity predisposes some persons more than others to become neurotic under given conditions. This is suggested by experiments with mice, rabbits, and other lower animals, which show that those of certain breeds are especially prone to develop neuroses when exposed to stresses and conflicts. Also, there is limited recent evidence of psychoneurotic traits (including pathological fears, anxieties, and hysteria) running so strongly in some human families that some investigators think a predisposition to such symptoms may be dominant in inheritance. In any case, since environment certainly and heredity probably are involved, a fair conclusion is that when parents are definitely of the neurotic type, there is a considerably above average chance that their offspring will become so.

ALCOHOLISM. Most authorities now regard this not as a crime or any ordinary form of wrongdoing but as a disease or personality disorder. At the same time, new theories have increased the possibility that heredity may be involved in *some* cases of alcoholism. That the condition is largely environmental is clearly shown by the enormous differences in the rate of alcoholism in various countries, nationalities, regions, and social groups, as governed by their habits, attitudes, and religious precepts; and by the great increase in alcoholism among women and young people since social codes became looser. However, to explain why in any group only *certain* individuals become alcoholics under the same conditions that leave others unaffected, recent studies indicate these possibilities: (1) that the chemical make-up of some individuals is such as either to induce an unusual craving for alcohol, perhaps because of certain dietary and vitamin deficiencies, or to cause them to react abnormally to its effects; and/or (2) that easily unbalanced mental and emotional states in some individuals predispose them to become alcoholics under little more than ordinary stresses. In either of these situations there could be hereditary factors producing or increasing the tendencies. For the present this is only theory. Until proved otherwise, one may assume that wherever alcoholism runs in a family (grandfather, father, son, mother, daughter, etc.), it is most likely that the members have *acquired* the habit from one another.

DRUG ADDICTION. The observations regarding alcoholism can be applied to drug addiction. Whatever the genetic factors that might make some individuals especially prone to becoming addicts, it is clear that the enormous increase in the drug habit among present-day young people is overwhelmingly a product of their environment.

SUICIDE. Although this is often a completely rational (if not justifiable) act, perhaps as many as half the suicides in the United States are linked with some kind of mental instability or disease (most often manic-depressive insanity, sometimes schizophrenia—particularly in young people). To the extent, then, that heredity may be involved in the mental condition, it may be playing a part in some suicides and the possible repetitions of the act in some families. However, there is much to prove that even if there might be any predisposition to suicide, the act itself is largely dependent on environmental factors. Thus, the suicide rate as a whole in any group, community, or country, or at different times, is directly related to (1) strains that make living less tolerable or bearable (as in depression periods, or during the horror reigns in

Europe); (2) the degree of social or religious approval of suicide (the rate being far lower where suicide is condemned, as in some religious groups, and in some countries); (3) the extent to which in any group individuals are isolated from others and, in periods of distress, can or cannot find help and understanding; and (4) the value that is placed on one's going on living. Changes in social and psychological environments in recent years may explain the increases in suicide rates in most advanced countries, including the United States (to a current rate of about 11 per 100,000) but a drop in the rate in Japan (to 17, from an earlier high of 28) and greater proportionate increases in the rates among women than among men, and among Negroes than among whites. (See below.)

Sex Differences. One of the most important facts about suicide is that almost everywhere in the world the rate among men is higher than among women—by about 3½ times in the United States, where among whites, 18 per 100,000 males and 6.7 per 100,000 females end their own lives (as of the mid-sixties). Among Negroes, even with marked increases in suicides in recent years, the rate remains much less than among whites—9.6 per 100,000 Negro males and 2.7 per 100,000 females. Chief reasons: (1) Men are under greater pressure to be successful, useful, physically active, and independent, and when they fail in these respects, are more impelled toward suicide. (2) By inheritance, as we have seen, males are much more likely to suffer from disease and defects. (3) There is some evidence that women inherently have better "shock absorbers," which can cushion them better against emotional upsets, disasters, and pain. Also, (4) psychoanalysts might maintain that insofar as self-destruction is aggression turned inwardly, males, being naturally more aggressive and given to violence than females, would more often commit suicide. (See also "Sex Differences in Crime" in Chapter 25.)

For other types of abnormal behavior, see also Chapters 22 ("Behavior"), 23 ("Personality and Temperament"), 24 ("Sex and Sexual Behavior"), 25 ("Criminal Behavior").

17

Mental Defects

WHO ARE THE "MENTAL DEFECTIVES"? When a person's mind is so slow-moving and retarded that he is unable to learn, think, work, and live in a normal way, he is classed as "feeble-minded" or "mentally retarded." (As explained in the preceding chapter, "mental defect" is entirely different from "mental disease" or "insanity.") About 3 per cent of the children born are in the mentally retarded group. Included are various grades and types of defectives which should not be confused with one another, and which may be due to quite different causes, particularly so far as heredity is concerned.

IQ Classification. Technically, the grades of mental defectives are decided by the levels of intelligence they can reach, as measured by their "IQs" on various tests (usually the Stanford-Binet). A person is not classed as feeble-minded unless his IQ falls below 70. In turn, the feeble-minded are graded as follows: *morons*, IQs of 69 down to 50; *imbeciles*, IQs of 50 down to 20; *idiots*, IQs of 20 or less. There also are important physical distinctions. The morons as a rule are defective only in intelligence, but with no physical abnormalities, injuries, or diseases to explain their condition. In the idiots and imbeciles, however, defects in bodily functions and physical make-up often go with and may be the cause of the defects in their minds. Moreover, whereas heredity may play a major part in producing many if not most of the morons, it is much less responsible for the idiots and imbeciles (except some of the rare types). Finally, as we shall see, the risk of having a moron child is closely related to the parents' intelligence (being least for parents with high IQs, and highest for those of low IQs), whereas the risk of having an idiot or imbecile child is almost the same for parents of high intelligence as for morons.

MORONS. These, with IQs as previously given, make up close to 90 per cent of the mental defectives. The great majority of morons are physically normal or average, and in only a minority can mental backwardness be traced to environmental causes, such as prenatal mishaps, premature birth, disease, lack of proper care and training, or learning difficulties unrelated to intelligence. However, in borderline cases mistakes are sometimes made in wrongly grading persons as morons, either because of errors in test scores or because the tests may fail to measure all phases of intelligence correctly. Thus, a child who may fall down badly on some or many parts of the standard intelligence tests especially those related to "school" learning, may be quite average or even above average with respect to certain mental capacities and skills. Many persons rated as morons by their IQs prove efficient at various jobs and make good social adjustments.

Hereditary Factors. Where no environmental causes are evident, many authorities believe that morons result mainly from inheritance of "slow-mind" genes that keep the brain from functioning beyond a certain degree of efficiency. The best theory is that these genes are *recessive-plus*—a pair of recessives *plus* perhaps a dominant gene or genes. Backing this up are these facts: (1) Moron children are very rare among parents of normal or superior intelligence, and very frequent among parents of low intelligence—more than three fourths of the morons coming from one tenth of the families. (2) If both parents are morons, the chance is anywhere from 60 to 75 per cent that a given child will be, whereas with parents of normal IQs it may be no more than 1 or 2 per cent, and with parents of above average IQs very much less. (3) Once a moron child has been born to two parents, the chance is about one in eight—five times the average—that they will have another retarded child. (4) Among identical twins, if one is a moron, so is the other in almost every case, whereas among fraternal twins this is true in less than half, and perhaps only one fourth of the cases.

"Pseudo Feeble-Mindedness." This refers to infrequent cases of children with normal intelligence who are wrongly classed as morons when parents and teachers are unaware that their backwardness is due to reading difficulties, speech or hearing defects, diseases, or emotional blocks. The mistake is most often made when difficulties of this nature are minor ones and not easily recognized. Careful tests by trained psychologists will easily distinguish the pseudo from the true feeble-minded children, and make corrective measures possible.

"Curing" Morons? Reports from time to time of phenomenal improvements or cures of feeble-minded children through this or that treatment must be accepted with extreme caution. In some cases a marked increase in a child's IQ or mental performance may follow if he was originally wrongly scored or if his backwardness was of the pseudo type just discussed. But once it is definitely known that the child's defect centers in a "slow" brain, the only thing that can be done (so far as science now knows) is to provide training which will make the most of his limited capacities. To date none of the much-publicized treatments or "cures," as with glutamic acid, thiamin, or other chemicals, have been proved effective.

IMBECILES AND IDIOTS. These, as previously noted, are defectives with IQs no higher than 50—from 50 down to 20 for imbeciles, and below 20 for idiots. Many in both groups also have physical abnormalities or peculiarities usually recognizable at birth, although in some in-between cases the symptoms may not be conclusive until the baby is several years old. Although prenatal mishaps, birth injuries, acquired diseases, and other environmental factors can account for many of the imbeciles and idiots, up to half or more of the cases are now traceable to gene defects or chromosome abnormalities. Among the stillborn or miscarried babies who are malformed and defective, it is probable that a considerable percentage would be idiots or imbeciles if they could survive. As it is, the death rates among the low-grade mental defectives, both prenatally and in the first years of life, are very high, so that those who live to puberty or beyond may represent only a minority.

MONGOLIAN IDIOCY (DOWN'S SYNDROME). With an incidence of 1 in 600 births, this condition accounts for the largest group—about 20 per cent—of all mental defectives below the moron level. Long a medical mystery, Mongolian idiocy was found in 1959 to be caused not by glandular abnormalities in the mother or prenatal accidents, as had been believed, but by a *chromosome abnormality*: an extra little chromosome—No. 21

(or No. 22?)—giving a child three instead of the normal two of this chromosome, and throwing development off the normal course in many peculiar ways. Among the odd effects are folds at the inner corners of the eyes, somewhat as in the Mongolian peoples, which had led to the mistaken notion that such babies had remote Mongolian ancestry. But there is no racial connection whatsoever: mongoloid children may be born to parents of all stocks. Going with the odd eyes are usually numerous other abnormalities in the nose, forehead, ears, tongue (fissured), voice, hands, palm prints (the "simian crease" across the middle of the palm), etc. Growth is stunted, and the combined abnormalities may make any two unrelated mongols resemble one another more than either does his or her own siblings. There may also be organic and functional defects (and a high risk of leukemia), which cause many mongoloid babies to die in infancy or childhood. If mongols survive and reach maturity, which most do not (only 20 per cent passing age thirty, and only 8 per cent going beyond forty), they usually are sexually undeveloped and sterile.

Parental Factors in Mongolism. The chromosome abnormality causing mongolism results in most cases from a mishap during the formation of an egg or sperm by which it receives two instead of the normal single one of a parent's No. 21 (or No. 22?) chromosomes, which, added to one from the other parent, makes an abnormal three (*trisomy*). However, the far greater likelihood that the abnormality comes from the mother's egg is shown by the fact that as mothers grow older (but not as father's grow older) there is an increasing incidence not only of mongoloid births, but of chromosomally caused abnormalities of other kinds (Klinefelter's and Turner's syndromes among them). Thus, half the mongoloid babies are born to mothers over forty; and whereas among mothers under thirty the incidence of mongoloid babies is less than 1 per 1,000, it rises among mothers over forty-five to 1 in every 35 to 40 births.

Heredity in Mongolism. Even though some unknown aberrant genes might perhaps increase the chances of the given chromosome abnormality occurring in an egg or sperm, in the vast majority of cases it is an accident not repeated in the same family, for if a mother has borne one mongoloid baby, the risk of her having another is only slightly greater than for an average woman of her age. The exceptions are in a very small percentage of the cases—no more than 2 or 3 per cent—where an outwardly normal woman may carry in her cells a *translocation* chromosome abnormality: in this instance a major, broken-off portion of her No. 21 having become stuck to another chromosome (No. 15?). If the mother passes this on to a child, together with her other, free No. 21, the child receives in effect two No. 21s from her, which together with the father's No. 21, produces the trisomy causing mongolism. Mothers with the translocation have a high probability of producing mongoloid babies, and may make up a large proportion of the *young* mothers who do. In addition, a third of their children, while normal, may be carriers like themselves of the translocated chromosome and potential parents of further defective offspring. (The "mongol-translocation" carriers can be identified by examining their chromosomes, and, if they are pregnant, an examination of fetal cells in the amniotic fluid can reveal whether the expected child will be mongoloid.) The translocation can also occur in a man, but the risk of a mongoloid child through him is much less than for a female carrier.

Other Chromosomally Caused Mental Defects. The *cri du chat syndrome* is named (the French term) for the peculiar cat-like cry of afflicted children, one of the effects of the syndrome (which includes other external and internal peculiarities) produced by an abnormal chromosome (No. 5). *De Lange syndrome* is a mental defect with grotesque features, such as bushy eyebrows, low forehead, and nasal and other peculiarities. Genetic factors are uncertain, but chromosome abnormalities are reported in affected children and some of their relatives. The *Klinefelter's syndrome* males (XXY), *Turner's syndrome* females (XO), and individuals with several other types of chromosomally caused sex abnormalities, are usually mentally retarded in some degree. (See Chapter 14.)

BIOCHEMICAL MENTAL DEFECTS. Various inherited "errors of metabolism" produce mental retardation among their effects. Included in this category are the following:

Amaurotic Family Idiocy. There are several types and degrees of this metabolic disorder, all inherited through recessive genes. The commonest and earliest-developing type is *Tay-Sachs disease*, which causes fatty swellings in the nerve cells of the brain and spinal cord, leading to idiocy, blindness, paralysis, and death in early childhood. The Tay-Sachs condition is largely confined to Jewish families of eastern Polish stock, among whom the mutated gene for the disease apparently arose centuries ago. A related affliction, *juvenile amaurotic idiocy*, occurs only rarely in Jewish families. (Another condition linked with Jewish families, *dysautonomia*, was discussed in Chapter 15.)

Phenylketonuria ("PKU"). This mental deficiency inherited through recessive genes, is due to failure to metabolize properly the amino acid *phenylalanine*, found in milk and certain other foods. Afflicted children tend to be blond and blue-eyed, with rough, dry, exzematous skins. Controlling the diet from early infancy on can reduce the degree of mental retardation. Tests of prospective parents can reveal if they are carriers of the "PKU" gene and the risk that any child of theirs will have the disease.

Lesch-Nyhan Syndrome. Resulting from another inherited metabolic error (sex-linked recessive, and afflicting mostly boys), this condition has mental retardation plus various other abnormalities among its effects, but is distinguished particularly by bizarre, aggressive, self-mutilating behavior such as the child's biting his lips or fingers, and banging his head, despite great pain.

Laurence-Moon-Biedl Syndrome. This combines a mental defect with obesity, and often eye defects, extra fingers. Rec.-Q.

Other Biochemical Disorders with Mental Defects. *Gargoylism* (*Hurler's syndrome*), *Gaucher's disease*, *Niemann-Pick disease*, and *maple-syrup urine disease* are all discussed in Chapter 15.

Cretinism. This type of mental defect is clearly caused in prenatal life by a thyroid deficiency in the mother (often if she is goiterous), which stunts the baby's mental and physical development and produces various other abnormalities. In maturity cretins still look like odd little children, with large heads, pot bellies, pug noses, thick lips, and protruding tongues. Cretinism sometimes runs in families, but whether heredity plays any part in this is uncertain. If it does, an unproved theory is that it is by way of recessive genes which produce either some thyroid deficiency in the mother or some special susceptibility in the child. (See also "Goiter" in Chapter 12.)

Microcephalic Idiocy. In this condition the individual has an abnormally small head ("pinhead"), which results from an early stoppage in the growth of the brain and the skull. Some cases of microcephaly are inherited through *recessive genes,* which may lead to several children of this type appearing in one family. But the condition may also be largely or entirely environmental, produced by various prenatal deficiencies or upsets. An occasional cause in recent years has been undue exposure of pregnant mothers to X rays, a factor likely to increase in menacing importance if there is atomic warfare.

Hydrocephaly ("Water Head"). In this condition the head is swollen abnormally by fluid in the brain, which often results in a mental defect but sometimes does not, especially if there is proper early treatment (including drainage of the fluid). The condition has been found inherited in certain lower animals, and there is a possibility that some (but not all) of the cases in humans may also be hereditary, perhaps through a dominant-qualified gene.

Epiloia. See under "Rare Skin Cancers," Chapter 12.

Epilepsy. Although previously discussed at length in Chapter 15, epilepsy is mentioned here because in about 10 per cent of the cases it is accompanied by some degree of mental retardation. This may happen only when the condition, which is primarily an ailment of the nervous system, affects the brain so as to retard its workings. In the great majority of cases, however, epilepsy has no such effect, and the afflicted persons are mentally completely normal and sometimes even brilliant. (Reported among epileptics were Muhammad, St. Paul, Julius Caesar, Peter the Great, Napoleon I, and Dostoevsky.)

Cerebral Palsy. As with epilepsy, only in a minority of cases is cerebral palsy accompanied by mental defects, if the prenatal or birth accident that caused the palsy also affected brain functioning. (This is especially likely in premature births, as of twins.) There is no evidence of heredity, except in occasional families where it appears to be recessive.

18

Blood Types
and Conditions

BLOOD INDIVIDUALITY. As the most vital fluid of
the body, blood has been given much careful study. Many important hereditary differences among individuals in their blood
elements and blood cells have been found. Some of these blood
differences involve abnormalities, deficiencies, or diseases with
varying consequences, ranging from mild defects to serious and
fatal results. Other differences have importance only in certain
situations, as in transfusions, when the blood of one individual
is mixed with that of another. Discoveries of the blood types and
of methods for "typing" persons have eliminated most of the grave
dangers that attended transfusions in former times.

Blood-Type Inheritance. The main blood type differences
among human beings, in the A, B, AB and O groups—involve
the presence or absence of certain chemicals in the red blood
cells. The A substance is determined by one *dominant* gene, the
B substance by another *dominant* gene. In addition there is an
O gene that determines neither substance, and is *recessive* to the
other two genes. Since a person must receive one of these three
blood genes from each parent, six paired combinations are possible. A blood will result from either an AA or an AO gene combination (the O gene being recessive). Similarly, B blood will
result from either a BB or a BO combination. But if a person
receives an A gene from one parent, a B gene from the other
parent, AB blood will result, because neither gene dominates the
other and both A and B substances are produced. Finally, O
blood will result only if an O gene is received from each parent.

"M-N" and Other Blood Types. In addition to the A-B-O
blood substances (and the "Rh," to be discussed later), there are
a number of less important inherited blood substances. Among

them are the M and N substances, inherited through mutually dominant genes, so that a person getting an M gene from one parent, an N gene from the other, would be the M-N type. Among other identified blood substances are the S, Kell, Duffy, Lutheran, Lewis, and Kidd. Many of these, especially the M-N substances (antigens), are of interest so far mainly in disputed paternity cases (Chapter 29) and in racial studies (Chapter 27).

Diseases and Blood Types. Limited evidence suggests that persons of some blood groups may be more prone to develop certain diseases than are persons of other blood groups. Such associations are claimed between blood group O and duodenal ulcer and between blood group A and cancer of the stomach.

TRANSFUSIONS. The most important application of the A-B-O blood type findings is in transfusions, for if a person is infused with blood of a type different from his own, there may be a clumping (agglutination) or disintegration of the introduced blood cells by incompatible antibodies in the recipient. This results from the fact that A blood and B blood each produces its characteristic chemical substance, or *antigen*, and with it, its serum carries an *antibody* to combat the incompatible blood of the other type (anti-B and anti-A, respectively). AB blood carries antigens of both types, but since they must live together, does not produce either of the antibodies. O blood, however, produces no antigens on the red cells and both anti-A and anti-B antibodies in the serum. Thus, the greatest danger arises if a type O person receives blood of any of the other three types; and then, in order of danger, if an A person is given B blood, or a B person A blood, or either A or B persons are given AB blood. An AB individual can more safely receive blood of the other three types. Contrariwise, O blood, being most neutral, can be transfused with least risk into persons of other blood types. But the term "universal donor," formerly applied to an O person, is frequently not valid, since any O donor might also be carrying powerful anti-A or anti-B substances which could be harmful if transfused to group A or B individuals.

Family Blood-Type Relationships. An important fact to keep in mind is that the blood types of two members of a family may differ through inheritance just as their hair color, eye color, or other traits may differ. Thus, where these differences occur, there may be precisely the same danger in transfusing a mother's blood into her own child, or the blood of one brother into another, as in transfusing blood from any unrelated person. On the other hand, the blood of an outsider, even of a different race, can be safely transfused into a person with the same blood type. The great majority of other blood factors are not important in immunization by transfusion or pregnancy. An exception to this is the *Rh blood factor* (Rh positive) in donor or fetal blood which induces the Rh-negative recipient or Rh-negative mother to produce Rh antibodies. The results are discussed in the section following.

THE "RH DISEASE." *Erythroblastosis fetalis,* a now widely known blood affliction of certain newborn babies, is produced in prenatal life by hereditary factors working in an indirect way to cause conflict between the baby's blood and the mother's. The disease itself is not inherited, but can develop *only* when the baby's blood carries an inherited chemical substance known as the "Rh factor," and the mother's blood lacks this substance, being of the inherited type known as "Rh negative." But even then, there is danger to the baby in only a very small percentage of the cases, for reasons which will become clear when we see the sequence of things which must happen.

1. In the course of prenatal development, some of the baby's red blood cells with the "Rh-positive" substances must break through the barriers of the placenta and filter into the mother's circulation. This generally occurs at the second or subsequent pregnancies.

2. The mother's body must respond by producing *antibodies,* or "anti-Rh" counteracting chemicals, to fight off the foreign Rh-positive red blood cells.

3. The Rh antibodies in turn must pass into the fetus in sufficient amounts to cause serious injury to its blood cells.

Altogether, there is serious danger in no more than *one in sixteen* of the *one in twelve* cases where the mother is Rh negative and the father Rh positive. If it is the mother's first pregnancy, and she has had no Rh-positive transfusion, she probably will not have enough of the anti-Rh antibodies to endanger the fetus or infant. But if she has previously borne an Rh-affected baby, and/or has had an Rh-positive transfusion, the initial level of

How an RH-Diseased Baby Is Produced

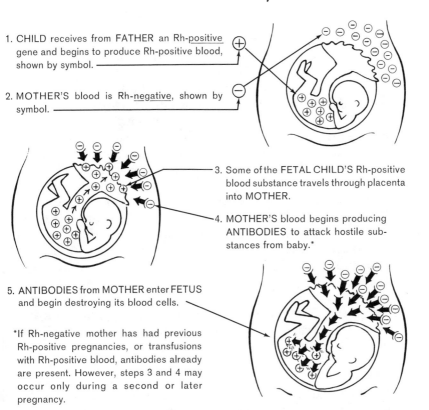

1. CHILD receives from FATHER an Rh-<u>positive</u> gene and begins to produce Rh-positive blood, shown by symbol. ———

2. MOTHER'S blood is Rh-<u>negative</u>, shown by symbol. ———

3. Some of the FETAL CHILD'S Rh-positive blood substance travels through placenta into MOTHER.

4. MOTHER'S blood begins producing ANTIBODIES to attack hostile substances from baby.*

5. ANTIBODIES from MOTHER enter FETUS and begin destroying its blood cells.

*If Rh-negative mother has had previous Rh-positive pregnancies, or transfusions with Rh-positive blood, antibodies already are present. However, steps 3 and 4 may occur only during a second or later pregnancy.

(Chart prepared with aid of Dr. Alexander Wiener and Dr. Philip Levine)

anti-Rh in her serum will have been greatly raised, and there is a decided risk that her next baby will develop Rh disease. In that case, should the child be born with gravely impaired blood cells, it may be saved by an immediate blood-exchange process whereby almost all of the infant's Rh-positive blood is replaced by fresh, healthy Rh-negative blood. However, advance precautions can be taken by vaccinating Rh-negative mothers against Rh-positive blood with injections of Rho-GAM (Rh-immunoglobulin) which will prevent them from thereafter producing menacing quantities of anti-Rh antibodies. (The injections are made within seventy-two hours after delivery of a normal Rh-positive infant.) The postnatal and prenatal precautions have greatly reduced the incidence of Rh deaths and injuries, although there still are thousands of Rh casualties in the United States and other countries annually.

The Rh Genes. The gene that gives rise to the Rh-positive type is *dominant*; the gene for Rh negative is *recessive*. Thus, to have Rh-positive blood a person need inherit only one Rh-positive gene. But to have Rh-negative blood a person must receive *two* Rh-negative genes, one from each parent. The relative proportion of positive and negative persons varies with racial groups. Among whites, about 85 per cent are Rh positive, 15 per cent negative. Among American Negroes only 5 or 6 per cent are Rh negative, which means the threat of the Rh disease for their babies is much less than for white babies. Going farther, among Chinese, Japanese, and other Mongolians, there are virtually no Rh-negative individuals, almost all being positive, so there is no Rh disease threat for Mongolian babies unless their parents carry some white genes.

Predicting Rh Threats. With the facts regarding Rh inheritance known, it is now relatively easy to establish in advance whether a given baby of a given couple is threatened by the Rh disease. There is no threat at all (with rare exceptions) if the mother is Rh positive. But if she is Rh negative, the father's blood must immediately be tested. Unless he is among the one in seven (whites) who are negative, one must go on the assumption that the baby will be positive and that there may be a blood clash with the mother. Thus, the mother must be tested further to see if her blood is already carrying anti-Rh antibodies which may menace a fetus or newborn child. What if the *father* is Rh negative and the mother Rh positive? In that case there can be no threat to a baby, for whether it is Rh positive, like the mother, or Rh negative, like the father (assuming it also received a recessive Rh-negative gene from the mother), it would not produce substances against which the mother's blood would react adversely.

Other Child-Mother Blood Conflicts. Additional conflicts may involve the *A*, *B*, and *O* blood-type substances, prenatal incompatibilities in which may cause abortions and jaundice—

mainly when the mother is type O.

The Rh Discoverers. Credit for the discovery of the Rh factor (in 1939), its method of inheritance, and its role in blood transfusion and the Rh disease, goes mainly to three Americans, Dr. Alexander Wiener and Dr. Philip Levine, and the late Dr. Karl Landsteiner, with whom they began their work. Many other experts have since helped in the researches which have led to the saving of thousands of babies yearly.

See also: "Blood-Type Differences" (racial) in Chapter 27; "Disputed Parentage Cases" in Chapter 29.

HEMOPHILIA. Although comparatively rare, hemophilia is the best known of the inherited blood diseases, mainly because of its appearance in European royal families. This in turn helped to draw attention to its inheritance as a *sex-linked* condition, confined almost exclusively to males, and passed along to sons through mothers. As is now clear, hemophilia (which is by no means confined to royalty, but is found in all social levels, nationalities, and races) results from a defect in a gene in the X chromosome concerned with blood clotting, or coagulation. (There are about five varieties of hemophilia, each with a deficiency of a particular compound.) Since the male receives only one X, and this from his mother, the defective gene will impair his blood-clotting process. But since a female receives two X chromosomes, her other, normal gene, will insure normal blood clotting. For a woman to receive *two* hemophilia genes, it would be necessary for her father to be a hemophiliac and her mother to be a carrier for the hemophilia gene—an extremely unlikely situation. One reason is that most male hemophiliacs have usually died in childhood or early maturity, before they reproduced; another probability is that if a girl baby did receive two hemophilia genes, the double dose would bring death before birth or soon thereafter. Nevertheless, a few cases of women presumably with hemophilia are in the medical records. (The disease has also been discovered in dogs, where it is inherited as in man. This fact has aided in experimental studies leading to remedies.)

Royal Hemophilia. The gene for hemophilia appears to have arisen in Queen Victoria, or in her mother, through a *mutation*— the way in which many other hemophilia genes are believed to arise. (Were it not for these new mutations, the hemophilia genes in circulation would previously have been greatly depleted by early deaths of the afflicted males. Today the new treatments are enabling many more hemophiliacs to survive into the reproductive ages. See further, Chapter 31.) Records indicate that Queen Victoria transmitted the gene to four, or possibly five, of nine children, including Leopold, who was a hemophiliac (and perhaps another son, who died in infancy), and three daughters, Victoria, Alice, and Beatrice. These last three carriers passed the gene on to various of their children and grandchildren. Luckily for the present British royal family, Queen Victoria's heir, Edward VII, did not receive the dreaded gene, so none of his descendants is threatened by the disease. (Prince Philip, husband of Queen Elizabeth II, is also a descendant of Queen Victoria, but he, too, is obviously also free of the hemophilia gene.)

Hemophilia B, or "Christmas Disease." Distinguished from the common hemophilia (and named after an English family in which it was first discovered), this is one of a number of hemophilia variants, occurring in about one in six hemophiliacs. Even though also sex-linked in inheritance, there are some differences from the common form in effects.

Pseudohemophilia (Von Willebrand's Disease). This is a much milder condition than hemophilia, and inherited through a dominant-qualified gene, thus afflicting females as well as males.

Afibrinogenemia. This is the absence of fibrinogen (clotting substance), causing abnormal bleeding but not as serious as hemophilia. Rec.

Bleeding under the Skin (Telangiectasis). Due to abnormally formed fragile blood vessels, this condition is inherited as an incomplete dominant. The most common symptom is frequent nasal bleeding (epistaxis), but different from ordinary nosebleed. A variant that mimics telangiectasis in some of its symptoms, but is not inherited, has been named the CRST *syndrome*.

ANEMIAS. Most of the common anemias, which involve deficiencies in the quantity or nature of the blood, result from diseases, infections, or malnutrition. However, a number of types are directly due to inherited abnormalities in the blood cells. Two of these widely known conditions, *Mediterranean (Cooley's) anemia,* and *sickle-cell anemia* (unrelated to each other), are of

Red Blood Cell Anemias

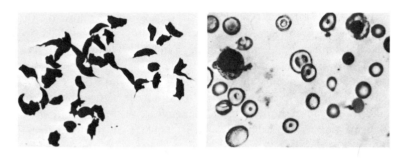

SICKLE-CELL ANEMIA. Cells shown in the severe double-gene condition. Usually fatal in childhood.

THALASSEMIA MAJOR (Cooley's or Mediterranean) anemia. Cells shown in the severe double-gene condition. Usually fatal.

(For details, see text.)

particular interest because each is largely confined to persons of specific racial groups, and because of their unusual method of inheritance. In both of these conditions *one incompletely dominant* gene produces certain mild effects; a double dose—two of the same genes—produces extremely serious effects. Fortunately, the mild effects caused by a single gene make it easy to identify the persons carrying it and to provide ample forwarning of the dangers to prospective children if two such carriers marry.

Mediterranean (Cooley's) Anemia. The disease is so called because it is found mostly among persons of Mediterranean stock—Greeks, Italians, Armenians, etc. (although it also occurs in Southeast Asia). The dominant gene responsible produces only mild blood abnormalities if inherited from just one parent. But if a child receives two of the genes, one from each parent, there will be very serious effects in the entire system, including skeletal abnormalities, mongoloid features, and disturbances that usually bring death in childhood.

Sicklemia and Sickle-Cell Anemia. These conditions, which afflict chiefly Negroes, are also inherited by the *incomplete dominant* method. A single gene, from one parent, will cause the mild condition of sicklemia, in which a small percentage of the red blood cells have a peculiar, twisted "sickle" shape, but with the individual otherwise quite normal. However, two of the same genes—one from each parent—will cause half or more of the red blood cells to have the abnormality, and to be so defective that fatal anemia may result by early adult life. The mild, one-gene sickle-cell trait was previously considered harmless, and is still so under most circumstances, but it has been found that exposure to high altitude pressures—as in paratroop service—subjects single sickle-gene carriers to severe damage to the spleen and other dangers. However, it has also been shown that the sickle gene provides *resistance to malaria*—one reason why the gene has survived through the ages. (The same antimalarial effect is associated with the *Cooley's anemia* gene.) The one-gene sickle trait occurs in about 8 per cent of American Negroes, the serious double-gene anemia in about 1 in 500, with the incidence of both conditions being far higher among Negroes of Africa.

Pernicious Anemia. This is a chronic, serious disease of maturity, due to a defect in the stomach cells which prevents the proper absorption of vitamin B-12 needed for normal blood production. Inheritance is possibly recessive or incompletely dominant. It is considerably more common among whites than among Negroes and Asian peoples.

Agammaglobulinemia. This, like hemophilia, is a blood deficiency inherited by males through a sex-linked recessive gene. Afflicted males lack *serum gamma globulin* and so cannot produce protective antibodies in their blood against various infections and diseases, especially pneumonia. Formerly they would usually die in childhood, but they are now able to survive with antibiotic and gamma globulin treatment.

Favism. In this unusual form of anemia, destruction of red blood cells occurs when the fava bean is eaten by genetically susceptible persons, mainly of Mediterranean stock. Sex-linked, its victims are mostly white males. A similar type of anemia, *primaquine sensitivity* (also sex-linked), afflicts certain Negro males when they take the antimalarial drug primaquine, or related oxidant drugs such as the sulfonamides. Both types of induced anemia are due to an inherited defect involving the enzyme glucose-6-phosphate-dehydrogenase (G-6-P-D) normally found in red blood cells.

Acholuric Family Jaundice (Spherocytosis). In this condition, the unusual fragility of the red blood cells (with a more spherical shape than usual) causes jaundice and anemia. It is inherited as a dominant. A preventive measure in threatened individuals is removal of the spleen.

Other Blood-Cell Abnormalities. *Acanthrocytosis* involves thorny-appearing red cells, associated with childhood intestinal and nervous disorders (rec.). *Elliptocytosis* has oval red cells, with somewhat increased red-cell destruction (rec.). *Pelger-Huet anomaly* involves undeveloped white blood cells, and is not harmful (dom.).

Leukemia. See under "Cancer," Chapter 12.

19

Length of Life

ONE'S "ALLOTTED" YEARS. Many people, past and present, have held to the belief that everyone has an allotted number of years of life. Thus, soldiers say, "You'll go when your number's up." This fatalistic view is hardly valid. What is true, however, is that human beings, first as a species—like all other species of animals—and second, as individuals, do have a "number" set by their heredity for the maximum years that they can live. This "number" for humans generally, so far as we know now, is greater than for any other living creatures, except the giant tortoises and turtles which may live to ages of 180 or more. The Bible speaks of humans who lived to much longer "years" (Adam, 930, Methuselah, 969, Cainan, 910, etc.), but authorities believe these pre-Flood Biblical "years" may have referred to periods little more than a tenth of our modern years. Also it is believed that the ages of post-Flood Biblical personages (Abraham, 175, Isaac, 180, etc.) were computed by systems different from those by which we reckon years today. It is significant that at a later state the Bible referred to man's allotted years as "three score and ten" (70), which—by coincidence or not—is almost exactly the average expectation of life in the United States today.

Modern Longevity Records. As in the past, reports continue to appear from time to time of persons supposedly living to the age of 130, 145, 150, etc. Almost invariably these persons are from remote backward regions or countries, with no authentic records to support their claims. Actually, proved human longevity records of modern times do not go beyond the age of 115. Moreover, despite the fact that we are living in the most favorable period for longevity in the world's history, only about 4 persons in 100,000 are reaching or passing the age of 100.

Increases in Longevity. Taking present life spans in the United States, from birth to death, people as a whole are now living almost a third longer than they did at the beginning of the century, and almost twice as long as in George Washington's time. The present average life expectancy at birth (of both sexes) is over 70 years, the average expectancy in 1900 was 48 years, and in Revolutionary times about 35 years. This tremendous gain has obviously not been because of any change in heredity, but solely because of the enormous improvement in health, living conditions, and medical care. Mainly this has brought greatly reduced death rates in infancy, childhood, and early maturity, enabling many more persons to live into the older ages. For people past middle life, however, the longevity chances are only a few years better than at the beginning of the century. As examples, an average man (white) today at age 50 has a further life expectancy of 23.3 years—only 2½ years more than the 20.8 years for a man the same age in 1900; at age 55, 2 years more (19.5 to 17.4); at age 60, 1.65 years more (16 to 14.35); and at age 65, 1.5 years more (13 to 11.5). In the ages from 70 on the longevity gain for men declines to not much more than a year over what it was in 1900. However, the increase for older women has been far more pronounced, with an advance at age 50 of almost 7 years over their expectancy in 1900 (28.7 years versus 21.9), and ranges down to an advance at age 70 of 3½ years over the one-time figure (13 to 9.6 years more of life expectancy). Among Negroes, who were far behind in life expectancy in 1900, the relative advances have been greater at all ages. (See "Race Differences," later.)

INDIVIDUAL LONGEVITY CHANCES. Whatever the average longevity limits for humans may be, there is little doubt that some individuals are geared by their hereditary makeup for longer "runs" or life spans than are others, given equal environmental conditions. Some of the ways in which longevity genes may work or be kept from working have been suggested in the chapters on diseases and defects. In certain conditions there are "killer" genes (technically called *lethals*), which bring death almost before a life is under way; in other hereditary conditions death may be set to occur at various more or less definite periods, in childhood, at puberty, in early maturity, or before middle age.

Less directly, there are various hereditary defects or weaknesses affecting the heart and arteries, kidneys and other vital organs, the nervous system, body tissues, etc., which may decrease individuals' survival chances. Predispositions to mental disease may also curtail longevity chances by adversely affecting the person's way of living, or inducing suicide. Finally, different gene combinations undoubtedly tend to construct the bodies and influence the general functioning of individuals in different ways, all of which have a bearing on the rates of wear and tear, disease resistance, aging, and risks of vital breakdowns. Thus, insofar as their genes may differ, no two individuals start out with exactly the same longevity chances. But the best of heredity can only give a person the possibility of living until such and such an age if the conditions are right. A sudden accident can cancel out all the effects of long-life genes.

Twin Studies. Some clues as to the relative effects of heredity and environment on human life spans were given in the studies by the late Dr. Franz J. Kallmann and his associates of the life courses of more than a thousand pairs of elderly (over sixty) identical and fraternal twins. The average time between the death of one aged identical twin and another was considerably less than in fraternal pairs—about two years less for the male identicals, a year less for the female identicals (who survived much longer and thus decreased the possible death interval). However, the fact that there was still an average difference of four to five years between the death of one identical twin and another showed the importance of environmental factors on longevity.

Long-Lived Families. As we have seen, we may make some guess about a person's longevity genes by knowing what hereditary defects he may or may not have. But also important may be the longevity records of his parents, grandparents, and other near relatives, because studies have shown that tendencies to longer or shorter life spans run in families under the same outside conditions. Mostly the differences are related to the incidences of death from major diseases. For instance, life insurance company studies show that persons in whose immediate family two or more members died from heart and related conditions under age sixty had about a 40 per cent higher than average death risk for their age. Family histories of diabetes, cancer, mental disease, and other conditions also may affect individuals' longevity chances, unless it is clear that they themselves are free of the conditions. In general, persons both of whose parents were long-lived (especially to ages of eighty-five or over) stand a much better chance of reaching a ripe old age than do those with only one long-lived parent, while the chances of long life are below average if both parents were short-lived (fifty-five to sixty-five, or less). In every case, however, one must establish the cause of the parents' deaths: If due only to accident, infectious diseases, or other purely environmental factors, their children's own longevity chances need obviously not be affected, unless they also were exposed to the same bad environmental factors. At the same time, even if hereditary conditions played a part in the parents' deaths, many such conditions may now (or presently) be checked, restrained, or cured by treatment. In either case, a family history of short life need not at all mean that any given member may not be long-lived. Especially important, allowances must always be made for a family's socioeconomic conditions. A higher income and social level usually goes with greater life expectancy; a lower income and social level with shortened life expectancy. The formula is most evident in the markedly different infant mortality rates of the most favored and the least favored groups.

SEX DIFFERENCES IN LONGEVITY. By far the most important general influence on any person's longevity chances is his or her sex. We have seen in earlier chapters how heredity works to make males much more likely than females to develop a great many diseases and defects that are sex-linked (with genes on the X chromosome), and also more vulnerable to many serious conditions that are not directly hereditary, but in which heredity may play a part, or to which the male system is particularly susceptible. This applies to virtually all major death-producing conditions except diabetes, exophthalmic goiter and gallstones, and, of course, the specifically female cancers. There also seem to be certain general factors in the female system that enable them to stand up better under environmental hazards of many kinds—accidents, shocks, infections, starvation, etc. Thus, as brought out in Chapter 11 ("Males and Females"), long before there are any environmental differences for the two sexes, in prenatal life and in infancy, the male death rate is about 30 per cent higher. (It is worth noting that among almost all lower animals there is also an excess of male deaths in early life.) In childhood and youth there is a drop to 12 per cent more male than female deaths, but in maturity the male death rate climbs again to a 30 per cent margin over that of females. However, after early childhood a considerable part (though far from all) of the excess male death rate is caused by the male's greater exposure to accidents, war, occupational diseases, and various other adverse factors. Throwing the longevity balance farther toward females is the fact that improvements in environment, medical care, and social conditions have benefited them relatively more than males. For one thing, deaths through childbearing have been cut to a small fraction of what they once were (now to about 1 in 3,600 births in the United States—or less than one twentieth the rate in 1914).

Male and Female Life Expectancies. The foregoing facts show up clearly in the present estimates of average American life expectancies, and of years remaining for males and females at given ages. (The different figures for whites and Negroes will be presented later.) At birth the average life expectation for males is 67, for females, 74.2. Further relative life expectancies for the two sexes are, at age 20, males, 49.6, females, 56.3; at age 30, for males, 40.5, females 46.7; at age 40, males, 31.4, females, 37.3; age 50, males, 23.1, females, 28.4; age 60, males, 16, females, 20.2. The margin declines with the older ages, but always continues in favor of women. Although these figures are for persons in the United States, they apply closely to those in other advanced countries, among a number of which—in particular the Netherlands and the Scandinavian countries—the life expectancies exceed the American averages. However, in less-favored countries where poor environments bring high death rates, particularly in childbearing, women have almost as low life expectancies as men. (Examples in recent years are Bolivia, Guatemala, India, Ceylon, Cambodia.) Thus, it cannot be argued that women are *by nature* "biologically superior" and equipped to greatly outlive males, for under fully natural conditions, with unlimited childbearing and many adversities shared equally with males, their life expectancies would be no greater. It is only under steadily improving modern conditions, and with relatively greater decreases in women's biological *disadvantages*, that there has been an opportunity for their inherent biological advantages to assert themselves in the much greater gains in life expectancies as compared with males.

Numbers of Men and Women. As stated in Chapter 4, the sexes start off at birth with about 105.5 boys to 100 girls. From then on the higher death rate of males steadily reduces their excess numbers, so that in early maturity the male excess is virtually wiped out, and by middle life there are about 20 per cent more women. In the seventies there are 30 per cent more women, in the eighties, about 60 per cent more, and from about eighty-five on there are twice as many women left as men. These figures are for the United States. The excess of women at the different ages is even greater in Ireland, England, Germany, France, and Russia, where the male ranks were reduced by emigration or wars.

Chances of Widowhood. In four out of five marriages now the husband is the first to die, whereas at the beginning of the century it was almost as likely to be the wife as the husband. The chances of widowhood for a woman increases, naturally, with the number of years that her husband is older; but because of the higher death rate of males, the husband must be more than five years younger than the wife before the odds are in favor of his surviving her.

GROUP DIFFERENCES IN LONGEVITY. Many mistakes were formerly made in comparing long-lived and short-lived stocks, races, groups, or classes of human beings, and ascribing their differences to "superior" or "inferior" hereditary make-up. As we have seen, heredity does tend to make many individuals and families longer lived than others, but this can be proved only when all the persons involved live under the same conditions. It is another matter when the environments differ greatly, for it may then be not the hereditary but the environmental factors that account for the differences in longevity. Thus, one finds today (as there has always been) a fairly close relationship between longevity averages and the conditions existing among different groups in the same city, state, or country, whatever their race or ethnic stock.

Race Differences. Although racial groups may differ to some extent in their inherited susceptibility to certain diseases and defects (as brought out in previous chapters), there is no evidence that when all factors are taken together, people of any race are destined by heredity to outlive others. There is much to indicate that such racial longevity differences as there are may be due mainly to environment. For instance, Negro life expectancies in the United States in 1900 were about fifteen years less than those of whites. But as conditions for Negroes improved, so did their life expectancies, until today their average longevity is only six to seven years less than that of whites: for white males now, 67.8 years, females 75.1 years; for Negro males, 61.1 years, females, 68.2 years. It should be noted that the Negro female life expectancy exceeds that of the white male, and that present American Negro life expectancies are already much higher than those of many white groups in other parts of the world today, or than the life expectancies of American whites a half century ago.

Ethnic Longevity Differences. Among European whites, and among foreign-born Americans and their children, those of different stocks show differences both in longevity and in death rates from specific causes. For example, Irish-Americans have a considerably higher death rate than Italian-Americans, and there also are differences in their cause of death. In turn, other longevity and death-rate differences for given causes appear among Americans of English, Russian, Polish, German, Jewish, and other ethnic origins. But since these groups differ from one another in living habits, diets, and occupations, it is difficult to tell whether environmental factors alone could account for their longevity differences, or whether—as some authorities believe—heredity also plays a part.

FACTORS IN INDIVIDUAL LONGEVITY. Within all groups—as classified by sex, family, race, ethnic origin, or living standards—the longevity chances for given individuals have been found related to the following factors in which hereditary tendencies may be involved.

Personal Health. The chief influences on one's longevity chances are the absence or presence of the major degenerative diseases—heart and artery, kidney and lung diseases, diabetes, cancer, etc. Apart from these and some of the less common conditions known to be fatal, one may be a chronic invalid and yet live a long life.

Body Build. Abnormal weight can have a bearing on life expectancy because it worsens the threats from many diseases.

Persons who are 25 per cent or more overweight for their age have a death rate about 75 per cent higher than those of average weight. Extreme underweight in young people also is a threat to life expectancy, but perhaps only because it often is a symptom of some disease or internal disorder. Among older people leanness may be an asset for longevity. Moderately tall persons also have better than average longevity chances—probably because those in the more favored groups tend to be above average in height. But heights over 6 feet 4 inches or so do not improve longevity chances and extreme tallness—well over 7 feet—is often a symptom of a glandular disorder and may carry the threat of a shortened life span.

Blood Pressure and Pulse. The higher one's blood pressure, the shorter the life expectancy, as a rule, because of the association with heart-arterial-kidney disease. Low blood pressure (if not extremely low) may be a longevity asset. Too rapid pulse (near or over 100 per minute), or very irregular pulse, may also decrease longevity chances, particularly if there is overweight or hypertension. Heart murmurs of certain types (functional—"inconstant apical" or "systolic pulmonic") are quite harmless, but other types of heart murmurs (organic) are symptomatic of various heart diseases, which are possible life shorteners.

Occupation. The more one's job affords opportunities for healthy and careful living, the better the longevity chances, from extra months to extra years. As groups, the longest lived are professional people—scientists, professors, teachers, social workers, engineers, and clergymen, with doctors, dentists, and lawyers somewhat lower on the longevity scale, as are artists and most business people. In the average longevity range are white-collar workers and craftsmen; somewhat below average, truck drivers, waiters, and writers and editors; still lower in life expectancy, laborers, policemen, firemen, taxi drivers, and musicians; and with the lowest life expectancies, miners, quarrymen, itinerant workers, and men in various dangerous occupations. Farmers are hard to classify because they are of different levels in work, income, and modes of living, but in general they are among the longest-lived persons, either because their work is more healthful or because they have to be healthy to be farmers.

Temperament and Habits. Persons who are excitable and

fast-living, and under constant stress, do not as a rule live as long as the placid and easygoing ones, and in this heredity may play some part. (In lower animals, too, the most active species and breeds, which burn up the most energy, tend to be the shorter lived. Compare rabbits and turtles.) Excessive smoking and drinking, to the extent that they go with tenseness and instability (hereditary or otherwise), may also be life shorteners; but medical evidence is that cigarette smoking by itself, or undue drinking, will increase the chances of developing degenerative diseases and thus of shortening one's life.

Diets. Granted that one's diet is nourishing and adequate in vitamins and other essentials, there is no proof that eating or eliminating specific foods, except in the case of certain diseases, will make one live longer. Ripe old age has come in different countries and periods with innumerable kinds of foods.

FUTURE HUMAN LIFE SPANS. How much farther longevity averages of human beings, or maximum longevity for some, can be extended is highly uncertain. Apart from the general improvements in environment and medical care which have greatly advanced life expectancies, no "life-prolonging" or "rejuvenating" methods have yet proved to be successful. This applies to gland transplants, hormone treatments, "rejuvenating serums," and other such methods. However, increases of at least a few more years in average life expectancy should lie ahead, particularly in the United States, which currently ranks well below many other advanced countries—notably the Netherlands and the Scandinavian countries—in longevity averages, and is about fifteenth on the list in its infant mortality rates (about 18 per 1,000 for white infants, 32 for nonwhites, as compared with about 12 to 14 in the Scandinavian countries). Reductions in the infant mortality rate can add considerably to the average life expectancies, and cures for or reductions in deaths from cancer and the heart diseases may add another two or three years more to longevity in the older ages. But in most advanced countries longevity seems to be approaching a plateau. Perhaps the average life expectancy in a generation or two may reach 70 or 71 for males, 78 or 79 for females. Whether it can go much beyond that, or whether any human individuals can be enabled to live to ages of 120 or over (and do so without becoming worthlessly senile), depends entirely on what limits have been set by heredity. As of now, one must assume that the life span of humans—as that of every species of animal—is set for a certain maximum, with individual genetic differences set at different points short of that along the way.

20

Intelligence

HOW MUCH IS INHERITED? If heredity produces different degrees of abnormal and low intelligence (Chapters 16, 17), should it not also produce different degrees of *normal* and *superior* intelligence? Undoubtedly it does, for variations in intelligence are no less subject to the workings of genes than are variations in size or stature, or in physical functions. We see this most clearly in comparing the mental capacities of human beings and of lower animals and, often, the responses of various breeds within a given species, such as dogs. There can be no argument that these differences are overwhelmingly due to heredity. What is at issue is only whether—or to what extent—the relatively small differences in normal intelligence among human beings themselves are also produced by heredity. This, as we shall see, is extremely hard to establish, because human intelligence is far more complex than it was formerly thought to be and is so greatly subject to environmental influences. Nevertheless, even the limited evidence available is sufficient to refute many wrong beliefs about human minds and to make clear how heredity and environment interact to influence them.

Judging Intelligence. In everyday life we rate people as "brilliant," "bright," "ordinary," "stupid," etc. But even if these offhand ratings are correct, psychologists are well aware that the intelligence *shown* by an individual does not necessarily reflect the true quality of his mind. Many persons never had or have the chance to develop their mental capacities fully, and are frequently misjudged because of the common tendency to confuse intelligence with *education*. Thus, before we can tell what role heredity plays in human mentality, we must have scientific standards for measuring it.

What Is Intelligence? There is increasing awareness that intelligence is not a single trait, as was formerly thought, but a combination of a great many traits and capacities. Among them are abstract thinking, quickness of learning, memory, word fluency, language comprehension, arithmetical ability, speed of judgment, ability to visualize shapes and spaces, ability to "sense" people, "intuition," etc. The different elements of intelligence may not go together in the same person, which helps to explain why some are bright or capable in certain ways and not in others. (For special talents, see Chapter 21.)

Brain Genes. Since intelligence is compounded of many capacities, a great many genes undoubtedly contribute to its quality and type. Most probably there are, first, a large number of genes, in different orders of importance, which govern the general construction of the brain and brain cells, their functioning, and their "hookups" with the sensory organs and other parts of the nervous system. Second, there are additional genes involved with particular processes relating to specific mental traits and abilities. For example, there is strong evidence that *mathematical ability* is inherited (to be discussed in the next chapter), and studies of twins have suggested that verbal reasoning and spatial visualization also may be under the influence of hereditary factors controlled by certain genes.

INTELLIGENCE TESTS. The various widely used intelligence tests are extremely helpful in measuring the relative mental *performances* of individuals. But how far the tests also dig beneath environmental influences and measure inborn mental *capacities* is a question. Actually, the standard tests (such as the Stanford-Binet) measure mainly the "academic" abilities, required for mastering the usual school subjects. Other tests also help to measure special abilities needed for given tasks, jobs, and professions. Where the tests so far are weakest is (1) in measurements of (*a*) "social intelligence," involved in understanding other people and getting along with them; (*b*) traits such as "drive," curiosity, sense of humor, shrewdness, or "intuition"; (*c*) unusual qualities of the mind involved in "creativeness," "originality," or mechanical ability, needed in many fields (Chapter 21); and (2) in comparisons among groups—social, ethnic, or racial—which have differed greatly in environments, training, and opportunities.

IQ Scores. These are derived from two kinds of tests, one for children, one for adults. The IQs of children, through age sixteen, are determined by how well or poorly a child does in comparison with the average for his age. In Chapter 18 there were given the subnormal IQ ratings under 70, for idiots, imbeciles, and morons. IQs of 70 to 80 are in the "borderline" group. Beyond these, individuals are classified by IQs as follows: 80 to 90, "dull-normal"; 90 to 110, "normal"; 110 to 120, "superior"; 120 to 140, "very superior"; 140 or over, "genius" (only in the technical IQ sense, but not as applied to the true and extremely rare geniuses to be dealt with in Chapter 21).

Adult IQs. Psychologists long proceeded on the assumption that intelligence becomes "set" toward the end of adolescence. For this reason, the intelligence tests for persons of all ages after sixteen made little allowance for age. Any advantages of younger adults on some parts of the tests, because of quicker minds and better memory, were considered offset on other parts of the tests by older persons' greater store of acquired knowledge and experience. In general the IQ averages of older individuals do correlate quite closely with their scores in earlier years. However, Dr. David Wechsler, after preparing his now widely used tests for adults, concluded that intelligence (as measured by test performance), increases from adolescence until age twenty-five or even age thirty, and then declines slightly from year to year. The Wechsler Adult Intelligence Scales (WAIS) therefore make allowances for age differences. But as with children's IQs, there is still much uncertainty as to how closely adult test scores reflect basic or all-round intelligence. Particular caution must be exercised with respect to possible brain disease or deterioration in aging persons, which may influence specific types of mental performances (memory, verbal ability, abstract reasoning, spatial analysis), depending on which area of the brain is affected.

Variations in IQs. The same person's IQ may sometimes be given as different by several points (up to ten or more) on tests in successive years, or even within a few weeks or on different days. This may be because of differences in the tests or test methods, or in the examiners, or in the person's state of health, energy, and degrees of application. In very young normal children (under five), IQs are not too easily or reliably determined. (Unrecognized reading or hearing difficulties, emotional and psychological blocks, and sometimes physical factors may occasionally impede a young child's mental performance or cause it to vary greatly from one year to another.) But at older ages an individual's IQ ordinarily tends to remain fairly constant from year to year.

IQs and Achievement. To the extent that IQs are not always true measures of mental capacities, they may also not be accurate forecasts of future success or failure. Nevertheless, IQs (plus school marks) are still very important in determining how children will be educated, and which students will be admitted to the more selective colleges and accepted for medical and other professional schools. IQs and other test scores are also being used in engaging workers for various jobs in industries and by the armed forces in choosing men for special training and advancement. Thus, IQs and the opportunities for achievement, if not achievement itself, are becoming more closely related. As one example, the celebrated group of 1,500 gifted individuals with IQs ranging from 140 to 200, first studied as children by the late Prof. Lewis M. Terman and his associates, and then followed up for thirty-five years, turned out to be exceptionally outstanding in achievement, on the average, with a large proportion becoming prominent in professions, the arts, and industry. But emphasizing that a high IQ alone does not ensure success, about 5 to 6 per cent of this gifted group failed of even moderate achievement (through ill health, emotional instability, lack of drive, bad luck, or other factors), some of them failing in college and ending up in lowly jobs. (See also "Prodigies" in Chapter 21.)

Creativity. That persons who do not rank high in IQ or in school marks may still have the capacity for great achievement in creative fields—the arts, invention, public life, and various professions—is being increasingly recognized. In fact, such qualities as imagination, enterprise, and nonconformity, essential in creativity, may often be in conflict with academic requirements. Thus, about 20 per cent of the National Merit Scholarship awards in the United States, formerly based on high IQs and school records, have in recent years gone to students who showed unusual creative ability and other special qualities. (See also next chapter.)

IQS AND INHERITANCE. The brain, like every other organ and part of the body, is a *chemically functioning* mechanism;

and inasmuch as "biochemical individuality" characterizes every aspect of human make-up and functioning, one must assume that there would be inherited differences among individuals in the structure, workings, and degrees of efficiency of their brains, and hence in their intelligence and capacity for mental performance of different kinds. But to prove just how and to what extent these differences are inherited presents many problems. So far the studies of the inheritance of human intelligence have depended mainly on comparisons of the IQs of parents and children, and of identical and fraternal twins in relation to nontwin brothers and sisters.

Parents' and Children's IQs. There is much evidence that IQs of children, on the average, are fairly close to those of their parents. In individual instances this may not be so, but taking families collectively, parents with high IQs tend to have children of well-above-average brightness, and rarely a dull child (except for the defective cases discussed in Chapter 17). In the opposite direction, parents with low IQs, as a group, tend to have low-IQ children, and only very rarely a brilliant child. (See also concluding section of this chapter.) Further, IQs of children of men engaged in the "brainier" jobs tend to be higher than those of men in jobs requiring less mental expression. Thus, children of professional men have been found to have IQs averaging 116; of semiprofessional men and business executives, 112; of upper white-collar men, most businessmen and skilled workers, 107; of clerks, minor business people, and semiskilled workers, 105; of slightly skilled, 98; and of day laborers and rural farmers, 96. (The figures are for the United States, but are closely paralleled in England and other countries, including the Soviet Union.)

Bias in the Studies? How far the facts presented prove inheritance of intelligence depends on the fairness of the tests for the different groups. There is some evidence that the IQ tests may indeed be slanted toward the kind of learning acquired by children from the more educated and more privileged homes. Therefore these children would tend to score higher IQs than less-privileged children, even if hereditary factors were equal. Yet it cannot be ignored that the mental environments provided for children are in themselves considerably influenced by how basically intelligent or unintelligent their parents are. Allowing for all biases, then, the relationships between parents' and children's

IQs very likely reflect the influence of both heredity and environment.

Twin and Sibling IQs. Added proof of the role of heredity in intelligence is seen in findings that the IQ differences between identical (one-egg) twins are quite small (5.9 points), and even when *reared apart* average 7.7 points, whereas the IQ differences between fraternal (two-egg) twins *reared together* average 8.4 points, and between nontwin siblings (brothers or sisters) reared together, 14.5 points. However, about one in twenty identical twins (including some reared together) differ in IQ by 15 points or more, indicating how much environment can affect intelligence test scores.

Orphaned Brothers and Sisters. Studies made in orphanages some years ago showed a much closer relationship between the IQs of brothers and/or sisters in the same institution than between unrelated children, even though all were in the same environments, and regardless of how long they had been there.

Adopted Children. There is uncertainty as to the degree to which the IQs of adopted children tend to follow those of their true parents or of their foster parents. Conflicting findings are due to special difficulties in making this type of study. One can hardly doubt that an adopted child's IQ will be influenced by the care, training, and education he or she receives. But perhaps the majority of experts would hold that if two adopted children were reared in the same home in the same way, a child whose true parents were mentally superior would be considerably more likely to show high intelligence than would a child whose true parents were mentally only average, or below average.

BODY AND MIND. Among normal individuals in general, there is little indication that the "mental" genes are linked with genes for physical traits, or that under ordinary circumstances the bodily condition affects the IQ by more than a few points either way. Even though the children who are bigger and healthier for their age than others tend also to have higher IQs, they generally come from better environments, with more cultural and educational advantages. Further, although almost all present-day children are bigger and healthier, and achieve puberty earlier, than those of past generations, there is little to indicate that they are any brighter. Nor did persons in Europe today who as children during World War II suffered the most extreme hardships and the scantiest diets, turn out to be any less intelligent than those reared under the best conditions elsewhere. Going still further back, the cave men of fifty thousand years ago, scientists believe, had as much brain power as modern human beings, despite enormous differences in health, diet, and physical make-up. Altogether, apart from mentally retarding diseases previously mentioned, and severe and prolonged dietary deprivation, there is little evidence that physical deficiencies have any profound effect on human intelligence.

Head or Brain Size and IQ. Popular notions that the size of the head, forehead, or brain offers a good clue to a person's intelligence have little scientific support. Between lower animals and human beings the very great differences in brain size and structure (particularly in the forepart, the *cerebral cortex*), do go with their relative mental capacities. But among human beings themselves the sizes of brains (other than in abnormal cases, such as microcephalic or "pinhead" idiots) are of little significance compared with their qualitative structure and functioning. Whites, for instance, have smaller brains on the average than Eskimos; some geniuses have had big heads, some small heads; and many prehistoric men had bigger brains than modern men. As it is, no brain specialist can yet tell from the size, shape, or convolutions of a normal brain how intelligent an individual might be or was.

MALE AND FEMALE INTELLIGENCE. Where bodily factors working in a highly complex way may possibly affect intelligence in the *direction* it takes, if not its *quantity*, is in the sexes. Within any group, anywhere, one can find important differences in mental qualities and performances between boys and girls, men and women. But since the environments, rearing, objectives, and roles of the two sexes are not and never can be completely the same, one cannot expect to measure accurately their mental capacities on the same scale or to prove that either sex is superior, inferior, or even precisely equal in total intelligence to the other. Only in their performances on specific mental tasks can the sexes be properly compared. Here are some findings:

Girls from the earliest ages are consistently better in finger dexterity (lacing shoes, dressing themselves, etc.), in tests involving language (little girls begin to talk earlier than do boys, as a rule, and far fewer girls have speech difficulties), reading and writing, memory (of songs and of what they have read), esthetic responses (matching shapes and colors), and "sensing" people and noting details about them. In high school and college, girls continue to be superior in verbal tests and modern foreign languages and also—or on jobs—in perception of details, clerical skills, verbal fluency, and rote memory.

Boys are consistently superior as a group in abstract reasoning, mathematics, mechanical ability, problem solving, spatial perception, structural and motor skills, and curiosity about the way things are put together or what is happening outside of them. As they go on into college, boys excel in the sciences, mathematics, history, civics, and economics. Also, in groups starting out with the same high IQs or scholarship levels, more boys continue at the high levels, more girls drop behind (as was true in the Terman gifted group previously mentioned).

What Causes These Sex Differences? Theories that all the sex differences in mental performance and professional achievement are entirely due to social and cultural conditioning, or to disparities in training and opportunity, are open to doubt. As we saw in previous discussions, the XX and XY chromosome mechanisms set off the development of numerous differences between the sexes in biological make-up and functioning (Chapter 9, "The Features"; Chapter 10, "Shape and Stature"; Chapters 11 to 18, on defects, diseases, and abnormalities; Chapter 19, "Length of Life.") Thus, whatever may be the imposed differences in the *external* environments of human males and females, there also are inherent differences in their *internal* environments that would inevitably influence their mental functioning, conditioning, and performances in many areas, although precisely how or to what extent awaits proof. One fact should not be overlooked: As education and training of women have more closely approached that of men, and their opportunities for jobs and service have been extended, they have shown capacities in many fields—the professions, science, politics, business—for which their "minds" were previously thought unfitted. Not until all the conditions affecting the training, attitudes toward, and opportunities for achievement of the two sexes could be completely equalized—which in the fullest extent may never be possible—can they be weighed mentally on precisely the same scales, or can firm judgments be drawn as to how women's *inherent* mental capacities compare with those of men. (See also discussions on sex differences in Chapter 21.)

RACE DIFFERENCES IN INTELLIGENCE. Whatever differences might currently be found in the thinking and mental achievements of persons of different races and nationalities, there is no way yet of proving that these are inborn. The chief reason, as already indicated, is that the available intelligence tests cannot be fairly and equally applied to groups of people reared, educated, and living under markedly different conditions. Further, since the standard tests were mainly devised by and for white Europeans and Americans, they may discriminate against individuals of other races and nationalities.

Negro and White Intelligence. The foregoing observations apply particularly to any findings that average IQs of Negroes are below those of whites. An unquestioned fact is that environments and learning opportunities of Negroes have for generations been inferior to those of whites and, despite great advances in recent years, still are. Wherever Negroes enjoy relatively more equality and more opportunity for education, their IQs average considerably higher than in areas where they are repressed. In fact, among American Army draftees in World War II, Negroes from some Northern states had considerably lower rejection rates for substandard intelligence than had whites from some Southern states. There also has been a marked increase in the relative numbers of Negro children with high IQs (140 to 150 or over), and in Negro individuals reaching top professional ranks. Most authorities feel that until environments are fully equalized, no valid conclusions can be drawn about the relative IQs or mental capacities of whites and Negroes, or those of other races.

The Jensen and Other Reports. Despite the evidence cited in the preceding paragraph, several investigators have claimed that the major differences in mental performance between Negroes and whites may be due more to hereditary than environmental factors. Most widely publicized has been the report by Dr. Arthur R. Jensen, a California psychologist. He has interpreted the available data as suggesting (though not proving) that heredity may account not only for the lower average IQs of Negroes but also for their relatively lower scores on abstract thinking and problem-solving.

Another investigator, Dr. William Shockley, a Nobel prize-winning physicist, has theorized that up to 80 per cent of the lower Negro IQ averages may be ascribed to heredity. Both reports have been severely criticized by almost all geneticists, and by most social scientists, as having paid far too little attention to the great cultural, educational, economic, occupational, and psychological disadvantages of Negroes, past and present, which could seriously affect their mental performances. Specifically, a committee of the National Academy of Sciences asserted (1967):

> There is no scientific basis for a statement that there are or that there are not substantial hereditary differences in intelligence between Negro and white populations. In the absence of some now-unforeseen way of equalizing all aspects of the environment, answers to this question can hardly be more than reasonable guesses. Such guesses can easily be biased, consciously or unconsciously, by political and social views.

In short, while not dismissing the possibility that there may be some racial differences in genes affecting the complex mental processes, just as there are genetic racial differences affecting physical traits and diseases, such genes still remain wholly unidentified, and until—and if—they are identified, and until all environmental disparities are eliminated, there can be no conclusive proof that given racial groups are superior, inferior, or precisely the same in their inherited mental potentialities. (See also Chapter 28.)

CONCLUSIONS. Despite the uncertainties dealt with in this chapter, these conclusions are justified:

1. The intelligence any person shows is always the combined result of his heredity and his environment.

2. *Physical* influences (health, diet, climate, comforts, etc.) are less likely to affect a person's mental performance than are *psychological* influences and opportunities for learning.

3. The inherited mental factors are so numerous, of so many kinds, work in such complex ways, and are so difficult to determine and measure, that no precise predictions can be made about the transmission of intelligence from parents to children according to any such ratios or formulas as are possible with respect to many simpler traits.

4. What can only be said is that high intelligence, judged by

both high IQ and achievement, signifies the presence of superior mental genes. If both parents are of this type, the children are more likely to start off with superior mental equipment than if only one parent shows high intelligence, and much more so than if neither parent is mentally outstanding. However, where parents are exceptionally brilliant, the odds are that the children will not quite approach their mental levels. (See "The 'Genius' Genes" in Chapter 21.) On the other hand, parents of below-average IQs may well have children with IQs averaging considerably higher than theirs, particularly if the parents had lacked opportunities for adequate mental development.

5. It may never be possible to draw conclusions about the inheritance of a person's *whole* intelligence. But it may eventually be quite possible to measure and predict the inheritance of separate elements of intelligence, or of different mental abilities and capacities, each of which may be influenced by different genes. (Further discussions are in the next chapter.)

21

Talent and Genius

DIFFERENCES IN ABILITY. Most people find out in the course of time that they are good at certain things and not at others. Alert parents will notice children showing special talents at early ages, and will also be aware that one child may differ markedly from another in given abilities. What causes these differences? A first important fact is that special aptitudes or talents need not be related to intelligence. A person may be good at music, painting, writing, knitting, pie-baking, or what not, and yet be much less bright than someone who is a bungler at the same specialty. Again, different abilities may or may not be related to one another. Some persons are good at many things, others seem to be good at only one thing. And for any given ability, there may be a range from up to "phenomenal" down to nearly zero. All this would suggest that just as there are genes which govern a person's capacity to develop physically and mentally in various ways, there may be genes which govern or influence his capacity to develop special abilities. However, we are just beginning to identify particular "talent" genes and to evolve theories as to how they work—always keeping in mind that the expression of any talent can be much influenced by environment.

MUSICAL TALENT. Of all human talents, musical ability gives the clearest evidence of heredity because it reveals itself most spontaneously, at the earliest ages, and in all sorts of environments, and because there is abundant evidence that it runs brilliantly in particular families. Further, in musical *performance*, the talent of one individual can be much more easily compared with that of another than is the case in other arts and fields of achievement. (Many of the facts that follow are derived from the author's own study of the talent backgrounds of large groups of outstanding musical virtuosi and opera singers. The study was reported in detail in the author's book *You and Heredity* [1939] and summarized in his *Your Heredity and Environment* [1965].)

Precociousness. In almost every case great musical talent expresses itself before the age of five or six, and often as early as age two or three. This has been true of virtually every great musical artist, past and present. The talent may appear without any training, being revealed through singing, humming, or response to music, sometimes in a baby who has not yet learned to talk. Many authorities believe that if marked musical ability is not definitely revealed, or cannot be detected, in the very early years, there is little likelihood that it will be developed later.

Family Backgrounds. Usually there is marked talent in parents and/or near relatives of great musicians. But as proof that a musical home is not of itself the determining factor, some of the greatest virtuosi came from untalented families, and many brilliant musicians have found regretfully that their children, despite the finest musical environment, failed to develop talent.

How Musical Talent Is Produced. The basic equipment must be superiority in the musical aptitudes—the senses of pitch, time, intensity (loudness and softness), harmony, rhythm, and musical memory—which can be measured by standard tests. Degrees of capacity with respect to each of these senses *separately*, and not as a group, appear to be inborn: First, because one sense may be present without the other, so that a person can have a keen sense of time, but not of harmony, or may have a fine sense of rhythm and harmony, but poor musical memory, etc. Second, training cannot be shown to "create" any of these senses, or (say authorities) to improve them much beyond the degree that the inborn capacity for development is there. All of this would suggest that there are separate genes for each musical sense, working with different degrees of intensity.

Absolute Pitch. This is the keenest sense of pitch—the ability to "hit" or judge any note correctly by ear alone. Even though absolute pitch is found in many virtuosi and is usually revealed in childhood, the great majority of outstanding musicians fail to develop it despite years of practice. On the other hand, many persons without musical training have absolute pitch from the start, and many have it with little else in the way of musical aptitude. Strengthening belief in its inheritance (possibly through a dominant gene) is the fact that absolute pitch may run in families for successive generations, as it did in the great dramatic soprano, Kirsten Flagstad, her mother, maternal grandmother, and maternal granduncle.

Musical Memory. A phenomenal musical memory appears to be an almost indispensable ingredient of musical virtuosity, having been evidenced by the great musicians from Beethoven through Toscanini and on to the present-day virtuosi, among them the conductors Leonard Bernstein, Lukas Foss, Lorin Maazel, and Zubin Mehta. Although training undoubtedly contributes to it, there is every indication that a strong hereditary potential is a major factor in exceptional musical memory. However, many persons who are not otherwise distinguished musically may display this capacity from childhood on by singing or whistling complex melodies.

"Tune Deafness" or "Tone Deafness." The inability to carry a tune, or to recognize tunes, which afflicts some individuals, is believed due to heredity in many if not most cases. In families in which it appears, there is evidence that the condition may be caused by a dominant gene. If true, such a gene could completely block the appearance of musical aptitude or musical development, regardless of how superior the afflicted person's other musical genes might be.

"Musicians' Hands." Music experts belittle the popular notion regarding "piano hands" or "violin hands"—that particular shapes of hands or fingers destine a child to become a good musician, and failure to have them means that he won't be. Even though some hands are unquestionably better constructed than others for developing performing technique, varied types of hands and fingers are found among top musicians, and some have anything but "long, tapering fingers." Any special "sensitivity" in musicians' hands is mostly the result of the way they have been used.

How Musical Virtuosity Might Be Inherited. A good assumption is that although a great many genes contribute to musical talent, the majority are in wide circulation; anyone who can carry a tune or learn to play a musical instrument must have many of them. But the special key genes required for great talent are rare. However, the fact that great musical talent can persist through three or four generations would indicate that these key genes are limited in number, and are probably dominant, since otherwise the needed combination could not be long maintained.

The "Music Gene" Theory. Let us suppose (and this is only a *theory*) that there are five of the superior or "virtuoso" key genes for the basic musical senses, which we will designate in this way: "M*U*S*I*C*." Next, the ordinary genes for the same senses could be designated in this way (without the stars): "M-U-S-I-C." Finally, the inferior or defective genes are represented with small letters: "m-u-s-i-c." Since each person receives a pair of genes of every type—one gene from each parent— any combination of superior, ordinary, and inferior talent genes could be inherited: (M*M-Uu-S*S-I*i-CC), or (Mm-U*U-S*S-II-C*C), or (mm-uu-Ss-II-C*c), etc., producing talent or aptitude in various degrees. Only with at least one virtuoso (starred) gene *of each type* in every pair would great talent result: (M*M-U*U-S*S-I*I-C*C). This could explain a number of hitherto puzzling situations.

Untalented Parents, Talented Child. If each parent carried only part of the needed gene combination, neither parent alone would show much talent. But between them they could contribute all the genes required to produce a highly talented (M*U*S*I*C*) child.

Talented Parents, Untalented Children. Even the most musically talented persons are undoubtedly carrying—in addition to their superior genes—some "hidden" genes which are ordinary and possibly inferior, so it is quite likely that the new gene combination received by any child will not be as talent-producing as that of the parent. This would be particularly so if the other parent was not talented.

Talented Parents, Talented Children. Although an untalented child may also appear, as explained above, the more talent there is in both parents, the greater is the chance that a child will receive the needed "talent gene" combination. Thus, the author's study of virtuosi musicians and singers showed that where both their parents were talented, there was also talent in about 70 per cent of their brothers and sisters; where one parent was talented, in about 60 per cent; where neither parent was talented, in only 15 per cent.

The Extra Talent Requirement. A great deal more than musical aptitude is required if the musician is to reach the heights in his field. Also essential are such qualities as feeling, sensitivity, powers of concentration, drive and stamina, plus "personality." How much heredity may contribute to these qualities is still unknown. At any rate, deficiencies in these traits, as well as unfavorable turns in the environment, may help to explain why so many musical prodigies peter out in later years. Further, with so many complex factors, hereditary, environmental, and psychological, involved in the development and manifestation of great musical virtuosity, it is only in exceptional instances that it is achieved by a parent and child successively, or by two or more siblings in a family (classic examples being the Bachs and Mozarts). Coming closest to this in recent years have been Artur Schnabel and his son, Karl Ulrich; Rudolf Serkin and his son, Peter; David Oistrakh and his son, Igor; and Yehudi Menuhin and his son, Jeremy, and sister, Hephzibah (both pianists). Of special interest has been the remarkable Fishberg musical family stemming from an immigrant flutist in New York, Isaac Fishberg (who died in 1951 at age 103), all of whose twelve children were highly musical—seven of them professional musicians, including the late concertmaster, Mischa Mischakoff—with the continuing line of descendants to date numbering scores of other professional and amateur musicians.

Composing Talent. While the highest degree of musicality is required for the great composer, as for the great musical performer, the special talents needed for one do not necessarily go with those for the other. Many great composers have been undistinguished performers, and many virtuosi musicians have shown no talent for composition. Whatever the special composing gifts may be, they also appear to have a hereditary basis and to reveal themselves through precociousness and spontaneity. Thus Handel was composing church services at eleven; Mozart at fourteen had a score of symphonies and short operas to his credit; and Mendelssohn and Schubert by age seventeen or eighteen were already notable composers. More specific knowledge regarding the role played by heredity in composing talent is lacking mainly because there are as yet no reliable tests for identifying and measuring its basic elements. This is true of all the arts involving creativity, as we shall explain later.

Why No Women among Great Composers? The striking absence of women among the top composers is one of the great mysteries. Many women have shown outstanding talent as musicians, and some have been recognized as among the most gifted composers of songs and études. (One woman, Nadia Boulanger, while only moderately successful as a composer herself, was an outstanding teacher of composition, with her pupils at various times having included George Gershwin, Aaron Copland, Virgil Thomson and Roy Harris.) But no woman has ever been credited with producing a great symphony or other musical work of the highest type. Possible reasons for this will be discussed toward the end of this chapter.

"Popular" Music. Virtually all the musical talent studies to date have been of musicians in the classical field. But there is every possibility that most of the general facts brought out here also apply to outstanding composers and performers of semi-classical and popular music. For instance, George Gershwin showed mastery in both the popular and classical forms, while Leonard Bernstein has varied his classical career with immensely popular composition, as in the score for *West Side Story*.

VOCAL TALENT. A common mistake is to suppose that to be a great singer, one need only be born with a great voice. But the voice is only an instrument—like the pianist's piano or the violinist's violin. To be an outstanding singer also requires great musical talent, so that the vocal equipment can be developed and used properly. Thus, much of what has been said about the inheritance of musical talent in instrumentalists also applies to singers. The important differences stem from the fact that the singer's instrument is part of himself and that he is at all times at the mercy of its condition. Also, because the permanent quality of the voice cannot be determined until puberty, intensive vocal training usually doesn't begin until then or later. Finally, such external factors as the singer's looks, personality, and dramatic ability, plus the whims of the public, play a much greater role in the vocal than in the instrumental fields. Nevertheless, the records of the great singers all point to a high degree of inborn musicality, and their family backgrounds reveal almost as much talent as do those of the virtuosi musicians. (*Note:* For complete details, see the author's *You and Heredity*, 1939, pp. 245 to 255.)

Voice Types. Limited evidence of inheritance indicates that *bass* voices in men and *soprano* voices in women are determined by one type of "voice" genes; that a different type of gene produces *tenor* in men, *alto* in women; and that a mixed pair of genes—one of each type—produces *baritone* in men, *mezzo-soprano* in women. The author's own study further suggests that where both parents have high voices (father, tenor; mother, soprano) the children's voices will tend to be in the high range; whereas baritone or bass fathers tend to produce a marked majority of low-voiced sons. Among European whites, the highest incidence of bassos and sopranos, 61 per cent, is in northwest Germany, the lowest, 12 per cent, in Sicily.

RACE DIFFERENCES IN MUSICALITY. People of some races or nationalities undoubtedly *show* more talent for music, or for particular forms of musical expression, than do others. One must be struck by the preponderance of Italian opera composers, conductors, and singers; of Jewish violinists, pianists, and composers of both classical and popular music; of Negroes among jazz musicians, composers, and singers; and of the special musical characteristics of various other racial or ethnic groups. Most authorities feel that these can be explained largely by differences in musical atmosphere and environment, although hereditary factors are not entirely ruled out.

Jewish Virtuosi. There has been speculation as to what accounts for the preponderance of Jewish musicians among the violin virtuosi (such as, currently, Jascha Heifetz, Isaac Stern, Yehudi Menuhin, Nathan Milstein, Leonid Kogan, and David Oistrakh). It has been theorized that there was something in the Jewish ghetto culture that especially favored the production of violinists. However, Jewish virtuosi have also been and continue to be found in remarkably high proportions in most other areas of music—notably among pianists, conductors, and composers. Whatever may be the cultural common denominator responsible for Jewish musical virtuosity—manifested in many environments and countries (including the Soviet Union)—it is still to be pinpointed.

Negro Music. The social and psychological environments of American Negroes may explain why they have expressed themselves so strikingly in "blues," in particular types of rhythm, and in their special folk songs and "spirituals"; at the same time, with limited chance for training in classical music, their musicians, singers, and composers have turned largely to the popular fields. (The first American Negro to have achieved eminence as a classical conductor to date has been Dean Dixon—incidentally, one of the group of former Juilliard students who, in 1938, filled out questionnaires for the author's musical talent study.) Tests so far made of the basic musical senses of rhythm, time, harmony, etc. have shown no significant differences between Negro and white children, nor of these as compared with other racial and ethnic groups.

Japanese and Other Musicians. As another clear illustration of the influence of cultural environment on the nature of musical expression, Western music was not introduced into Japan until just before the turn of the century, but in growing numbers Japanese have been rising to the fore in rendering classical and modern European and American music as instrumentalists and conductors (among the latter being Seiji Ozawa). In short, while special types of music-talent genes may possibly be distributed differently among the peoples of the world, it seems well to conclude that musical talent is found plentifully among all peoples, and that the degree and manner in which it is expressed has so far been largely dependent upon training and opportunity.

ARTS, SCIENCES, CREATIVITY. The talent for music is undoubtedly not alone in requiring special hereditary capacities. Particular inborn endowments may be equally necessary for high achievement in painting, sculpture, writing, acting, dancing, and other arts, as well as in science and invention. But in these other fields any inherited factors are harder to identify because of the greater and more complex role played by environment.

"Born Artists." This term is often rather loosely applied to anyone having characteristics supposed to go with persons engaged in the various arts. It has meaning so far as it relates to individuals with sensitivity, imagination, creativeness, and other essentials for artistic achievement. But it is an error to assume that "artistry" is linked with a particular type of face, hair, hand, or body. If people who are artistic do show it in any way in their looks, it is only because in the course of time they have developed certain physical traits through their ways of working, thinking, and living. In the cases of any child, however, there is no way one can tell from his physical characteristics that he is or isn't a "born" artist.

Elements of Artistry. In all the arts the basic components are much the same: The feeling for composition, form, rhythm, shadings of expression (nuances), and the more elusive aforementioned qualities of "creativeness," "sensitiveness," and "imagination." It is not improbable that these elements are much influenced by some general hereditary endowment, which may explain why artistic or creative persons usually show talents of various kinds, and often excel in several fields simultaneously. But proficiency in a specific art demands additional special abilities, and therefore special supplementary genes (as we have already seen in the case of music). The great painter must have a keen eye for color, which would rule out the color-blind person (although he would not be prevented, if he had great artistic ability, from being an etcher, lithographer, pen-and-ink artist, or sculptor). So, too, great fiction-writing, drama, poetry, and other arts undoubtedly demand special sensory and personality factors, all of which may be conditioned by heredity as well as environment. Thus, a general "artistic heredity," plus an "artistic environment," may explain families in which many members for successive generations were outstanding in one or another of the arts. At the same time, added specific requirements may explain why some members excelled in one art form, some in another form, and some (lacking necessary key genes) showed talent in none of the arts.

GENIUS. The clearest indications that great talents are inborn come from studying the backgrounds and histories of true "geniuses": the rare individuals, arising once or twice in a century, who reach the topmost levels of human achievement. Socrates, Leonardo da Vinci, Michelangelo, Shakespeare, Newton, Beethoven, Franklin, Lincoln, Edison, Einstein—these have

How Genius May Be Produced

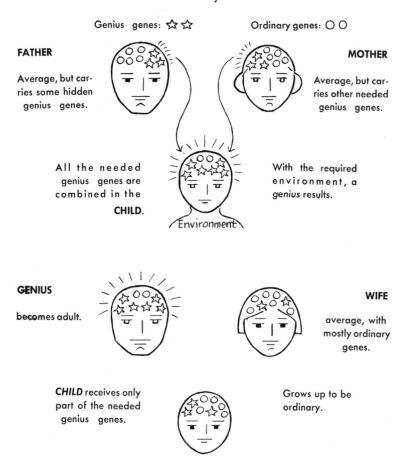

Genius genes: ☆ ☆   Ordinary genes: ○ ○

FATHER

Average, but carries some hidden genius genes.

MOTHER

Average, but carries other needed genius genes.

All the needed genius genes are combined in the **CHILD**.

With the required environment, a *genius* results.

Environment

GENIUS

becomes adult.

WIFE

average, with mostly ordinary genes.

CHILD receives only part of the needed genius genes.

Grows up to be ordinary.

been among them. In former times geniuses were awesomely regarded as products of supernatural and mysterious forces. Today science sees the genius as someone initially endowed with a *rare and unusual combination of superior genes*. Obviously, environment also plays a part in permitting the seeds of genius to take root and flourish. But the belief that geniuses are the products primarily of unusual heredity rests on the fact that no special type of environment can be shown to have produced them, and that geniuses have arisen in many types of environment.

Leonardo and Shakespeare. Perhaps the most amazing genius of all time was Leonardo da Vinci. The illegitimate son of a Florentine peasant girl and a minor official of the fifteenth century, Leonardo as a child spontaneously displayed a bewildering variety of talents. These he proceeded to develop—many of them without training or precedent—until eventually he led his world in sculpture, painting, science, mathematics, engineering, and invention, and was also notable as a musician and a poet. There seems to be no other explanation for Leonardo except phenomenal inborn endowment. Nor can any environment explain the incredible literary and dramatic powers of Shakespeare, who, too, came from an obscure background, with little schooling and nothing exceptional in the way of opportunity.

The "Genius" Genes. Having already dealt with various talent genes, we may now seek the answer to genius in the most potent and the rarest of human "achievement" genes which make possible the maximum development of human senses and mental powers. Most persons would probably not be carrying any of these genes, some persons might carry one or two; but only once in many millions of times would a couple in any generation be carrying between them all the genes required to produce a genius. The parents themselves, each lacking some of the essential "genius" genes, might be nobodies—which explains why geniuses so often seem to arise suddenly out of nowhere. Again, the chance that a child of a genius would receive exactly the same, or an equally remarkable, combination of genes is exceedingly remote, which could explain why successive geniuses do not follow in the same family.

Are Geniuses "Abnormal"? There is a long-standing belief that geniuses must be mentally or physically abnormal in some way. To back this up, lists have been compiled of geniuses and near geniuses who suffered from various mental or physical disorders: Socrates, Molière, Nietzsche, Caesar, Napoleon, Van Gogh, etc. Also true is that an unusually high proportion of the great writers and artists of our time were alcoholic, or mentally unstable, or extremely eccentric, or sexually deviate. On the other hand, it has been pointed out that many other persons of genius caliber were fully normal in every ordinary sense. As examples, of men close to our own time, and of whom we can speak with accuracy: Benjamin Franklin, Thomas Jefferson, Lincoln, Shaw, Churchill, Einstein. It remains possible that the incidence of physical and mental abnormalities may have been, and may now be, higher than average among geniuses and other highly creative persons, not because abnormality goes with their genius genes, but for these reasons: (1) A person with unusual talent, who is not physically or mentally average or "normal," may be especially likely to think in unconventional ways and do unusual things; (2) talented persons who are maladjusted, sickly, or otherwise "different," may have an exceptional drive to "compensate" by working feverishly toward their goals; (3) persons far in advance of their times in their thinking or creations are likely to be considered "queer" by their contemporaries, and if this leads to added social and financial stresses, they may have an above-average chance of cracking up. Today the better understanding of the nature of genius and improved methods of educating and rearing exceptionally talented children may very well diminish such relationship as there has been between genius and "queerness."

Longevity of Geniuses. Another popular belief, that geniuses tend to be short-lived, is not supported by evidence. Many geniuses in the past did die young, but this was when average life spans were short. On the other hand, many geniuses (especially in the arts) lived to very ripe old ages: Michelangelo, Titian, Rubens, Newton, Shaw, Sibelius, Matisse, Roualt, Picasso. A recent analysis shows that the average longevity of thousands of geniuses and near geniuses was no less than that of their respective generations.

PRODIGIES. Even though most geniuses were prodigies—children with exceptional mental powers or talents—it does not follow that every prodigy is a potential genius. Some prodigies may be "incomplete" geniuses, endowed with only some of the required "genius" genes (or with other mental stimuli) which may start them off in a remarkable way but not carry them too far. In other cases a prodigy is equipped with only a phenomenal memory, or quick reading and learning ability, which enables him to go through school studies by leaps and bounds. In still other cases clever and ambitious parents may succeed, by intensive training, to induce precociousness in a child. But whenever a child's reasoning ability or innate talents are also not exceptional, as is very often the case, a letdown in achievement generally results at maturity. Parents and teachers should therefore be extremely cautious about overestimating the importance of seemingly precocious mental powers or other gifts in children, and trying to force their development.

Mathematical Prodigies. As with musical genius (to which it appears to be related in some ways), phenomenal mathematical ability usually appears spontaneously at very early ages, many of the greatest mathematicians—Galois and Leibnitz, and more recently, Norbert Wiener and Julius Schwinger—having been prodigies. Murray Gell-Mann, Nobel-prize physicist, started out as a prodigy mathematician. Whereas great mathematical achievement requires great intellect, mathematical aptitude by itself (again as with musical aptitude) need not be related to intelligence. Many phenomenal mental calculators had or have mediocre minds in all other respects, and some have been found among the feeble-minded, these being known as *idiot savants*. (Remarkable examples were two mentally retarded identical twins, studied at the New York State Psychiatric Institute in 1966, who at age twenty-six were able to solve many complex mathematical problems and to give the day of the week for dates going back several thousand years, but failed on some simple problems of arithmetic.) Because unusual mathematical ability has run in families for as many as five generations, some authorities believe it may be produced by a simple genetic mechanism, possibly a single dominant (or dom.-q.) gene.

Chess Talent. Chess-playing ability appears to be a specialized offshoot of mathematical ability, in which the traits of phenomenal memory and of visualizing complicated arrangements are principal factors. Some hereditary basis is also indicated. Thus, as with musical and mathematical aptitude, phenomenal chess-playing aptitude appears in childhood, almost every chess master on record having been a child prodigy in the field. (Samuel Reshevsky, former chess champion of the United States, was giving chess-playing exhibitions at the age of six, and Bobby Fischer, a late starter at age twelve, became the national chess champion at age fifteen.)

SEX DIFFERENCES IN ACHIEVEMENT. Earlier in this

chapter we touched upon the puzzling absence of women among the great composers. Equally puzzling is the fact that while women are among the fine painters and sculptors, none has achieved ranking with the very best, that is of the caliber of the top old masters, or of Cézanne, Picasso, Matisse, Jacob Epstein, etc. In literature, poetry, and drama, despite the many women who have made outstanding contributions, it can hardly be said that any have approached the status of Shakespeare, Molière, or Shaw. Nor in science, with full recognition of the achievements of Mme. Curie, Lisa Meitner, and several others, have there as yet been any women Newtons or Einsteins. As for *inventors*, one finds virtually no women among them. How is this explained? Unquestionably, women's creative potentials have never had—and certainly still do not have—full opportunity for expression. But allowing for all adverse environmental factors, the possibility must be considered that inherent differences between the sexes could affect the ways in which their talents might be expressed and developed. We have seen that the same genes for many physical traits—body form, stature, disease, etc.—work quite differently in the two sexes and produce different results. With the same stature genes a brother will grow to be several inches taller than a sister; with the same muscle genes he will become very much stronger. Might this possibly be true of the genes for various talents? Or, at least, might not the achievement *trends* of women be inherently different from those of men? There is little evidence on this point, except as offered by aptitude tests of little boys and girls before their environments have become too different. These tests (discussed in Chapter 20) show little girls to be superior in learning to speak, read, and acquire vocabularies, in noticing details, and in sensing people's reactions. Could this explain why among all the arts, women are relatively best in fiction and poetry? Little boys show superiority in mathematical, structural, and abstract reasoning tests. Since such aptitudes are highly important in musical composition, painting, sculpture, and drama, as well as in science and invention, could this not help to explain male pre-eminence in these fields?

Conclusions.   Whatever the present arguments or limited facts, it is not likely that with women constituted differently from men by inborn factors, and with the probability that they will also continue to be reared, trained, and employed differently in many ways, we will ever have complete answers as to what their relative abilities may be. As new opportunities have opened up for them, it is already evident that ever-increasing numbers of women have been forging ahead in all creative fields, with many of them excelling a large proportion of men in the same fields. Thus, challenging the Freudian theory that "anatomy is destiny," many women today strongly contend that, given greater equality with men, their sex will be producing large numbers of geniuses and greatly reducing the gap between the two sexes in high achievement in every conceivable area.

22

Behavior

BEHAVIOR DIFFERENCES. The most important thing about human individuals in relation to one another is how they *behave*. Is a person pleasant or unpleasant? Calm or hot-tempered? Kind or cruel? Decent or viciously criminal? Lazy or enterprising? Timid or aggressive? And so on. We have seen that heredity governs people's looks, and to a great extent their body functioning and intelligence. Does heredity also destine or incline individuals to behave in specific ways? An immediate difficulty in answering is that we know human behavior differs greatly in different environments, and that even the behavior of the same person varies considerably at different stages of life and under different conditions. Nevertheless, as we shall see, beneath the layer of outside influences there quite probably are differences in people's behavior "machinery" which may strongly affect their acts, personalities, and reactions to others.

Instincts. If there are any inherited behavior tendencies in human beings, these must be similar to what we call "instincts" in lower animals. "Instinct" refers to an *inborn* tendency to do things or behave in certain ways without training. Some psychologists dislike using the term on the ground that the behavior of lower animals even in a natural state may be considerably influenced by experience, learning from their elders, and changes in environment. In place of "instincts," terms such as "conditioned reflexes," "stimuli," "drives," etc. are suggested. But this may be quibbling. For most authorities, and for the general reader, it is clear that each species throughout its long history had and has its own spontaneous (unlearned) ways of courting and mating, building nests or shelters, seeking and selecting food, caring for young, getting along with its own kind, reacting to enemies, etc. Whether we think of bees, beavers, bears, bunnies, bulls, bullfinches, bluefish, boas, baboons, billy goats, or butterflies, we can identify with each species particular types of *inborn* behavior tendencies, which are almost as much a part of them as are the shapes of their heads and bodies.

Behavior Programming. In terms of computers, it could be said that nature has "programmed" each species with a different input of inherited behavioral instructions to respond to specific stimuli and needs in characteristic ways. This inherited programming—with variations among individuals of each species— could be continually subjected to modification or alteration by training and experiences. For example, the instinct of a newborn duckling would be to follow the first moving body it saw—normally its mother; but ducklings have been conditioned to follow, instead, a man, or even a man's moving boot; and monkey infants, taken immediately from their natural mothers, have been conditioned to regard as their mothers contrivances made of wire and cloth. This process of conditioning an infant away from its normal behavior—which must be done in the early formative or "critical period"—is called *imprinting*.

Are There "Human" Instincts? People constantly speak of their instincts: "He has the 'right' instinct"; "Her instinct told her"; "They instinctively liked each other," etc. And in a general way, we refer to "human" or "inhuman instincts." In the earliest stages of mankind the behavior of humans undoubtedly was governed by as many, if not more instincts, as those in lower animals. We can be sure that humans, too, started off with inborn behavior patterns which directed mating, caring for their young, selecting and securing food, fighting or avoiding enemies, etc. Otherwise they could not have gone far on the road to survival. Any genes governing such instincts that human beings had we probably still have in great measure today. But the biggest difference between human beings and lower animals is that, going with our superior brains, we also have the capacity to control, modify, and train our instincts, and at the same time to change and improve our environments so that the need for our instincts would be lessened. Thus, as civilization has progressed and as life and training have become increasingly complex, the human instincts have been pushed farther into the background as only *starting points* or "potentialities" for behavior.

Dependency Period. Aiding the environmental influences on human behavior is the fact that the period of dependency—before offspring become mature and can lead their own lives—is greater for humans than for other animals, giving parents much more opportunity to train their children. Among apes, however, the period of "childhood" is almost as great (chimpanzees and gorillas not reaching puberty until the age of about nine or ten). So for the most part, it is still the inherited flexibility of the human mind and its capacity for being molded that permits training and experience to greatly influence our behavior.

Infant Behavior. Evidence that the "instinct" genes have not been bred out of us can be seen when we watch infants. As babies come into the world, inborn tendencies to behave in definite ways show themselves in the way they feed, move, grab, smile, etc. Moreover, there seems to be an inherited "time-clock" mechanism which sets off given types of behavior at given stages: when the baby will first begin to babble, coo; turn over, sit up; observe and grab things; recognize faces and identify with its parents and family members; walk; respond to language, talk; be ready for toilet training, etc. This behavior is common to babies among all peoples, civilized and primitive. It is taken so much for granted that when babies anywhere fail to react in the expected ways at the appropriate stages, parents rightfully worry. At the same time, it is also expected and noted that (within the prescribed limits) particular babies will behave in particular ways. In fact, any two babies of the same mother are apt to be no more alike in what they do and when they do it than in their looks. But we know that the individual behavior patterns of infants are much more conditioned than are their looks by their experiences in the womb, and by many subtle influences after they are born. So we can be far less sure of the part that heredity may play in producing these individual differences than of its effects either on infants' looks or on their general patterns of behavior. (Further discussion on this is in the chapter following, under "Infant Personality.")

"Wolf Children." To support the theory of how completely human behavior can be distorted by conditioning, accounts have been cited of children reputedly reared from infancy among wolves, baboons, or other wild animals, and who, when found, behaved like these animals. When several such reported cases (always in remote regions of India or Africa) were actually studied by trained investigators in recent decades, the supposedly "feral" children proved to be mentally diseased or defective individuals who, shortly before, had strayed from or been abandoned by ignorant, poverty-stricken parents; and the "wild animal" traits ascribed to the hapless youngsters were usually identified as symptoms of conditions such as *infantile autism* (described in Chapter 16, p. 135).*

SOCIAL INSTINCTS. As in infancy, so in later ages and among peoples of all kinds, we can see certain similar patterns of behavior: mothers nursing and fondling their babies, and protecting them with their lives if need be; fathers (or mothers, where there is no male) providing for their families; males rallying to defend their families and territory against enemies; males strutting or performing to impress females or fighting to possess them, and females acting coyly or enticingly in the presence of males; groups of individuals trustingly following a dominant leader; and so on. All such behavior, although more strongly conditioned in human beings, is paralleled in lower animals. More important, scientific studies and experiments have linked social behavior patterns in lower animals with biological factors found to be hereditary.

Further, animals have been bred in which one or another of these social traits is expressed in greater or lesser degree. Also, marked changes in such types of behavior can be produced in individual animals by causing an increase or decrease in the production of certain hormones, or administering drugs, or operating on or electrically stimulating certain brain and nerve centers. Some of these procedures and their effects have been found applicable to human beings; and to the extent that hormonal or other biochemical agencies may induce behavior changes, inherited normal or abnormal biochemical variations among human

* One much publicized "wolf boy," known as "Ramu," died in 1968 at the age of about twenty-seven, in Lucknow, India (where he had been found fourteen years before). An autopsy showed that his brain had been severely damaged at birth, which could account for his mental retardation and the odd, presumably "wolflike" behavior he had manifested as a child.

individuals could conceivably produce results not too different from what has been achieved in experiments with lower animals.

Parental Behavior. As is well known, many different forms and degrees of parental instincts appear among lower animals. In humans we also speak of "natural-born" mothers and fathers, or "motherly" and "fatherly" types, and their opposites. But whereas in lower animals it is clear that parental behavior is largely governed by hormonal stimuli and other biological factors, among human beings individual differences in this respect appear to be conditioned mainly by social and psychological influences. However, some authorities report that degrees of "motherliness" among women tend to go with certain physical factors which show themselves in breast types, hip forms, menstrual functioning, etc., as well as with certain kinds of behavior recognizable even in young girls.

Dominance. Are some human beings born to be "bossed" and others to be leaders (irrespective of intelligence)? Among various animal species individuals in any group can be graded according to degrees of "dominance" or "submissiveness." In most flocks of birds or poultry a "peck order" can be observed: a given bird pecks at another which submits, but which in turn can peck submissive birds lower in the scale. In groups of apes, mice, and perhaps even dogs, similar rankings of dominance and submissiveness have been found. However, it has been shown experimentally that an animal's standing in the dominance or pecking order can be completely changed by altering its hormonal make-up, or through a brain operation. It may be guessed that in human beings, too, hormonal states or deviations in the brain structure—hereditary or environmental—could influence the dominance feelings and behavior of individuals toward others. But how far the biochemistry, rather than the conditioned psychology of given individuals, is involved in most of their relationships would be difficult to determine.

Aggressiveness. As with dominance, degrees of aggressiveness or lack of it have been found conditioned in lower animals by their hormonal workings and brain functioning, with hereditary factors playing a part. Among dogs, for example, the adrenal glands—which strongly affect emotional states—are relatively much larger in the aggressive wire-haired fox terriers than in the less aggressive beagles or cocker spaniels. There also may be individual differences in the way the areas of the brain which control aggressiveness react to certain stimuli—as suggested by experiments with lower animals in which these areas can be electrically controlled to turn cats, monkeys, or bulls into either violently aggressive or very docile animals, as desired. Although human beings have not yet been subjected to such extreme experiments, drugs used in treating mental disorders have proved capable of inciting or suppressing aggressive behavior; and it is obvious that normal variations in the internal states of people can contribute to their feeling "high" or "low," pugnacious or docile. But again, since psychological factors can produce the same results, it may be very difficult in any given cases to show that these traits in persons have a hereditary basis.

Fear. Tendencies to special types of fears are inherited by each lower animal species and help to protect it against its natural enemies or hazards. One can only assume that buried deep in the human unconscious there also are inherited fear tendencies that aided our remote ancestors. For example, it has been shown that babies from only two weeks on respond with fear to looming shadows of unidentified moving objects. This would indicate that very young human beings, like the young of other animals, have an inborn protective instinct to recoil from or get out of the path of any strange menacing object or individual. Other findings are that crawling infants will stop instinctively at the brink of a precipitous drop. But in people as they grow, most fears have been shown to be conditioned by past personal experiences. Even women's fears of mice or snakes, which were once considered instinctive, appear to be mostly psychological and easily overcome by training, as is proved in many college laboratories where girl students work unconcernedly with these animals.

SENSORY REACTIONS. The responses of persons to particular tastes, smells, sounds and colors, or to pain, affect their everyday behavior and social relationships in many ways, and for this reason are extensively studied by psychologists. That heredity plays an important part in sensory reactions is obvious, most clearly so in the case of the lower animals, each species of which is characterized by its own special sensory equipment. Among human beings, inheritance of individual sensory differences has been established mainly with respect to deficiencies in color vision, sound, taste, smell and reaction to cold (Chapter 15), and in the musical senses (Chapter 21). While a considerable range of differences is also apparent among individuals in preferences for or aversions to particular foods, odors, or colors, the role of heredity with respect to these differences remains to be clarified. Such investigation is not easy, because the development of the human senses in given directions, and the degrees to which tastes express themselves, are much influenced by training and individual psychological factors.

Extrasensory Perception. The belief that there is an innate "sixth sense"—the capacity to read other people's thoughts, or to know what is happening to loved ones far away—is reported by some psychologists to have been borne out by their experiments with "extrasensory perception" (ESP). However, most scientists are skeptical of the findings to date, regarding them as statistical artifacts, although not denying the *possibility* that the phenomenon may exist and that some individuals, through inheritance or otherwise, may have something of this ability in a more than average degree. One special reason for doubt is that paired identical twins, who presumably should be especially attuned to each other's thoughts (in keeping with popular beliefs), have not been found in the experiments to do any better in ESP communication than any average nontwin siblings, or even two friends.

23

Personality
and Temperament

WHAT PERSONALITY MEANS. First, "personality" refers to all a human individual's behavior traits (discussed in the last chapter), *plus* all the other special qualities of mind, body, sex, and social adjustment that distinguish him as a particular *person*. Second, personality refers to qualities developed by one person in relation to other persons. Strictly speaking, then, only human beings can be considered as having personalities. Although we might like to think that cats, dogs, and other animals also have personalities, scientists prefer to speak of their traits as "behavior patterns." A distinction is that behavior traits are simpler and, as we have seen, can be almost directly inherited in lower animals in the form of instincts. It is far less certain whether any personality traits are ever directly inherited.

Infant Personality. Human infants, like other little animals, come into the world with inherited behavior patterns, as noted in the last chapter. But from the moment they begin to be trained and influenced by their parents, older children, nurses, and other human beings, they cease to be merely instinctive creatures, and any inborn tendencies become only the raw materials from which the forces outside of them mold their personalities. How far the inherited tendencies can push their way through the conditioning forces, and stay on top, is a question. Some studies (Dr. M. M. Shirley, Dr. Patricia Neilon), which have followed the same individuals from infancy through adolescence, indicate that in most cases those who were especially good-natured, alert, aggressive, difficult, etc. (or the opposite) tended to have the same personality traits in later years. Many mothers will confirm this in their children. Another study, made prenatally at the Fels Research Institute, showed that children who as fetuses had been most sensitive to jolts, loud sounds, and other stimuli generally turned out later to be the most timid, submissive, and anxiety-ridden individuals. Dr. Lester W. Sontag of the Institute concluded that the reactions of fetuses to given aspects of the prenatal environment, which foreshadowed later behavior, may be conditioned by genetic factors.

Child-Rearing Theories. The beliefs that children's personalities are greatly and permanently affected by whether they are breast-fed or bottle-fed, weaned early or late, given or denied adequate "mother-love," diaper-trained and toilet-trained one way or another have been much debated. The conclusions to be drawn from reports by various authoritative investigators who have analyzed the literature and made studies of their own are that (1) none of the theories to date warrants general acceptance as a scientific prescription for a child's proper personality development, and (2) how a child's personality ultimately evolves depends more on inherent tendencies, the good sense of the parents, individual circumstances, and external environmental factors than on any child-rearing method.

Physical Influences. In addition to the obvious mental and nervous disorders, a great many inherited diseases, defects, and organic weaknesses or peculiarities have characteristic effects on personality. Persons suffering from migraine headaches, for example, have been reported as tending to show "intolerance, perfectionism, sexual difficulties, etc." Particular personality patterns may also go with glandular disorders, allergies, vitamin deficiencies, digestive disturbances, and other conditions in which heredity may play a part. Changes in the body's chemical state or functioning by means of various drugs (particularly the psychedelic drugs such as LSD and mescaline), and operations on the brain and nervous system (as mentioned in Chapter 22), have been shown to affect personality in many ways. One may assume, then, that any inherited differences—large or small—in the workings of the glands and other organs would account for some degree of difference in the personalities of individuals. The body's chemical transitions at adolescence, during the menopause in women, and in aging also have their definite effects on personality. But very probably, beneath the outer personality-layers of individuals which can be much affected by changes in health or other factors, there is always an *inner core* of personality which persists through life. And it is this "inner personality" which may be strongly directed by inherited tendencies.

Adolescent Development. Boys whose growth and puberty came first in their group have been found, as a rule, to be the most admired, poised, and good-natured, whereas those who matured later were apt to be more talkative, self-conscious, and anxious to get attention; also, even though the physical differences usually straightened out after a few years, the personality patterns tended to differentiate the early and late maturers well into their adult lives. Among girls, likewise, those who reached puberty and developed earliest tended to be regarded as more grown-up and "womanlike" than the late maturers, to be most admired and looked up to by their girl classmates, and (obviously) to attract boys sooner and to date oftener, all with impacts on personality formation. To the extent that heredity affects the onset of puberty (Chapter 10, p. 71), it may play an indirect part in this personality differentiation.

Birth Order. The position of birth in a family has been considered as having an important influence on one's personality. In particular, first-born members, as compared with later-born, have been reported as most likely to go to college and achieve eminence, to be drawn to others, and to be more dependent and more susceptible to social pressure. Oddly enough, order of birth *can* have genetic effects on individuals with respect to being a twin or having a chromosome abnormality—such as Mongolian idiocy or the Klinefelter and Turner syndromes—the chances for which are least for first-born, and greatest for the late-born of a mother as she grows older. (Chapter 5, p. 37; Chapter 17, p. 144.) However, birth order can have no effect on the distribution of any specific *genes*, so whatever influence it may have on personality or achievement must be caused solely by subsequent social and psychological factors.

LOOKS AND PERSONALITY. People have alway believed that certain looks go with certain personalities. From Shakespeare's plays through to modern novels, dramas, movies, comic strips, and TV shows, one will find people with given types of faces and bodies cast as characters with given personality traits: heroines, fair, slim, and lovely; heroes, tall, straight, and handsome; villains, lean and

Looks and Personality

All of these notions are wrong!

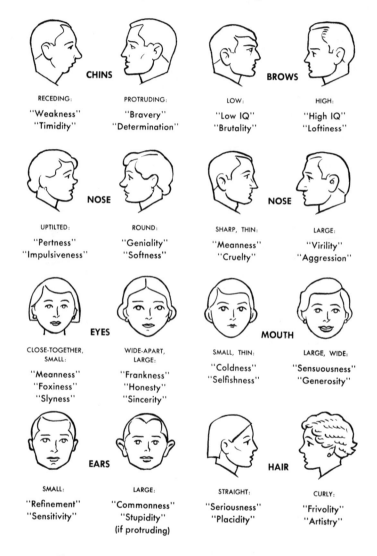

CHINS

RECEDING:
"Weakness"
"Timidity"

PROTRUDING:
"Bravery"
"Determination"

BROWS

LOW:
"Low IQ"
"Brutality"

HIGH:
"High IQ"
"Loftiness"

NOSE

UPTILTED:
"Pertness"
"Impulsiveness"

ROUND:
"Geniality"
"Softness"

NOSE

SHARP, THIN:
"Meanness"
"Cruelty"

LARGE:
"Virility"
"Aggression"

EYES

CLOSE-TOGETHER, SMALL:
"Meanness"
"Foxiness"
"Slyness"

WIDE-APART, LARGE:
"Frankness"
"Honesty"
"Sincerity"

MOUTH

SMALL, THIN:
"Coldness"
"Selfishness"

LARGE, WIDE:
"Sensuousness"
"Generosity"

EARS

SMALL:
"Refinement"
"Sensitivity"

LARGE:
"Commonness"
"Stupidity"
(if protruding)

HAIR

STRAIGHT:
"Seriousness"
"Placidity"

CURLY:
"Frivolity"
"Artistry"

The genes that determine physical traits need not at all be related
to the genes that affect personality traits. (See text.)

swarthy; redheads, fiery natures. Bold men are depicted with jutting jaws, weaklings with receding chins, sneaky people with warped bodies, etc. Science has found no such connection between genes for looks and genes for personality, character, or temperament. The only exceptions are in certain inherited diseases and abnormal conditions (discussed in earlier chapters) which may together affect both outward appearance and behavior. Otherwise almost any kind of nose, eyes, mouth, complexion, coloring, or other bodily detail can go with any kind of inborn personality tendency. However, *facial expressions* involve something else. The way a person has used and uses his mouth and eyes may offer real clues to his personality, as may also movements of the head, body, hands, etc.

Body Build (Somatotypes). There have been various theories that given types of body build do in a general way go with given types of personality and temperament, presumably because the same glandular and other factors which affect body build also may produce certain behavior tendencies. (This would in turn bring heredity into the picture so far as it governs these glandular and other workings.) One of the first to claim this relationship was Dr. E. Kretschmer, who classified people as "pyknic" (fat), "aesthetic" (lean), and "athletic" types, ascribing certain general personality characteristics to each. Subsequently, Dr. W. H. Sheldon devised these classifications: *endomorphs* (soft, round physiques, tending to obesity)—"inclined to be home-loving, placid, sociable"; *mesomorphs* (athletic, muscular, heavy-boned)—"likely to be fighters, leaders, heroes, lovers of thrills and action"; *ectomorphs* (slim, flat-chested, stringy-muscled)—"inclined to be 'mental' and alert, but not too aggressive, forward, or at ease with people." Various gradations and in-between types of physiques are rated by how much of each "morph" component there is in an individual's body build. Many psychiatrists consider these classifications helpful in diagnoses (if used with other evidence). But authorities differ as to their dependability and, especially, as to whether they can be related to *inherited* personality traits. (See also "Criminal 'Looks' and Somatotypes" in Chapter 25.)

Physiognomy and Phrenology. Still persisting and taken seriously are old notions that different "areas" or parts of the face and head are in some way tied up with specific mental traits, and therefore can reveal character. For instance, that "development of various areas of the nose reflect capacity for observation, imagination, etc."; or that in the areas of the temple and eyebrows one can read such and such other traits. To this, as to "phrenology," which purports to read character through bumps on the head, reputable scientists say, simply, "Bunk."

Effects of Looks. While heredity may couple any kind of feature or looks with any kind of personality trait, people themselves tend to ignore this fact. As a result, personalities can be much affected by how looks are regarded. If a little girl is drooled over because she's "so pretty," she certainly won't develop the same personality as will a homely sister. Similarly, to the extent that people react differently to tall or short persons, slender or fat ones, blonds and brunettes, the fair-skinned or dark-skinned, or to this or that kind of mouth or nose, the individuals' personalities will also develop differently. But it is important to remember that attitudes toward the very same types of looks—nose size, hip size, leg shape, skin color—may differ greatly in different groups, and when they do, so do the effects on personalities. Fat women in the United States are made to feel inferior, and slim women feel superior; but in some parts of the Orient and Africa the plumpest women are the glamour girls, and the slim ones are the wallflowers. A few decades ago girls with small bosoms were most approved among Americans (as they still are among Japanese), and those with large bosoms self-consciously tried to strap them down. As need hardly be said, there's been a change. So, too, the small, cupid's-bow mouth has currently yielded in desirability to the full, large mouth, and increases in stature have revised the scale by which persons are rated and feel themselves "too tall" or "too short." The genes for looks remain the same generation after generation, but their effects on personalities may be almost anything that people wish to make them.

HANDS, FEET, ANKLES. The notion that thick, large hands and ankles betoken peasant or common ancestry and a coarse personality, whereas slim hands and ankles go with aristocratic or genteel ancestry and inherent refinement, has no scientific support. It is true that people who do heavy manual work in time develop thicker hands and ankles than those who do not, but these effects cannot be passed on through inheritance; and if the descendants themselves no longer do heavy work, they may have just as slim hands or ankles as those of "aristocratic" blood. Apart from the direct effects of work and living habits, the sizes, shapes, or textures of hands and feet have no relationship to personality factors. (For "Musicians' Hands," see Chapter 21.)

Palmistry. Despite claims of "palmists" and their writings (and the enormous number of people who believe them), science has found absolutely no relationship between specific lines in palms and any inborn traits of personality, mental qualities, success tendencies, or what not. (The only exceptions are those associated with a few genetic abnormalities, such as Mongolian idiocy, described in Chapter 13 under "Finger, Palm, and Sole Prints.") Even more, the belief that anyone can predict future events (whom one will marry, how long one will live, or how many children one will have) by "reading" palm lines is pure superstition. Clever palmists may sometimes make good guesses, but only as any keen observer might do, not by looking at the palms but by noting details of a person's general appearance, behavior, and speech.

Mannerisms. Characteristic movements of the mouth, eyes, hands, and head, or ways of walking, praying, etc., observed in groups of people from the same stocks, countries, or localities, almost invariably result from formed habits, and are no more hereditary than are their languages or accents. Likewise, those in given occupations (farmers, policemen, sailors, actresses, etc.) develop distinctive ways of gesturing and moving. Children, in turn, tend consciously or unconsciously to imitate their parents, so it is not surprising to find certain mannerisms running in families. However, there are cases where some odd or unusual gesture or movement or a facial "tic" of a parent seems to appear spontaneously in a child (as in a son who has never seen his father). This leaves open the possibility that such mannerisms may arise through inherited muscular reflexes. Adding to the theory are findings that different breeds of dogs have their characteristic involuntary movements.

Hand Movements. When characteristic of individuals, these can provide clues to personality: "sensitive," "nervous," "expressive," "placid," "rigid" hands, etc. While such movements may be cultivated, they often are outward evidences of various hereditary tendencies, and sometimes symptoms of neurological and mental disorders, hereditary or otherwise. Where the pathological symptoms can be detected through handwriting, they provide the basis for the medical specialty of *graphodiagnosis*. But how far handwriting in normal individuals can reveal personality traits, or whether the principles of graphology are scientific, has been questioned. Nor is evidence available of what part heredity might play in handwriting styles. While there often are similarities in the handwriting of family members, this could be the result of conditioning. For one thing, the handwriting of identical twins may be quite different, and graphologists may fail to distinguish from samples that they were written by twins.

Handedness. Being a "leftie" among preponderantly right-handed persons may affect personality only to the extent that it attracts attention or presents difficulties. The possible role of heredity in producing left-handedness is not clear, for one reason because its simultaneous appearance in identical twins is scarcely more frequent than in fraternal twins. (See Chapter 5, p. 37).

Voices. People's voices have long been identified with personality traits: "sweet," "kind," "gentle," "gruff," "timid," "strong," "cultured," "coarse," etc. Family similarities in voice qualities have been noted, but there has yet been no study of inheritance in this regard (other than studies of voice *types*, reported in Chapter 22). The likelihood that such studies will be made has been increased by the development of the new techniques whereby the distinctive *voice prints* of individuals can be recorded.

Tongue Twisting. Geneticists have long been intrigued with certain inherited oddities in the control of the tongue muscles, such as the ability to turn up the side edges of the tongue (very common—in about two out of three persons), or to fold the extended tongue tip up and in, or to roll up the tongue in the mouth, or to curl up the tongue in a "clover-leaf" form. These abilities are inherited, usually as qualified-dominants.

ASTROLOGY. This is mentioned here only because so many millions of people who read astrology books and consult astrologers or "astrological horoscopes" sincerely believe that their personalities were and are dictated, and their fortunes governed by, the stars they were "born under." It may shock or anger them to be told that true scientists regard astrology as no science at all, but,

Tongue Tricks

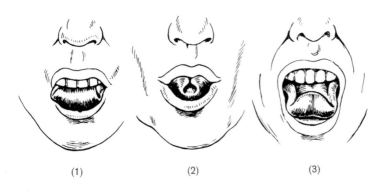

(1) (2) (3)

Certain persons have the inherited ability to fold up their tongues in one of the ways shown above: (1) folding the extended tongue tip up and in; (2) rolling up the tongue in mouth; (3) folding the extended tongue tip up, also curling in the sides. (In the rarest instances persons can curl up their tongues in "clover-leaf" form.)

like palmistry, as mere superstition. Incidentally, one should not confuse astrology with astronomy (although in ancient times the two were linked). Astronomy is now the recognized science that deals with the stars and planets, and their movements. But astronomers reject all the hocus-pocus going with astrology, and some years ago one of their official committees (headed by Harvard professor Bart J. Bok) flatly stated that "astrology is a magical practice which has no shred of justification in fact." Note, for example, that among twins (discussed next) the fact that they were "born under the same star" by no means makes their personalities or fortunes the same—particularly if they are fraternal twins, who may be as different in personality as any two children of a family born under different stars.

TWIN STUDIES. Although difficult, if not impossible, to prove inheritance of personality as a whole, significant evidence has come through analyses of separate traits as shown by identical and fraternal twins. In major respects many personality traits of identical twins are usually much alike, whereas those of fraternal twins are not. It is true that identical twins are reared more closely together. However, remarkable similarities in traits have also developed in identical twins separated in early infancy and reared widely apart in different localities and types of homes.

Specific Findings. Many studies, in which traits of paired identical twins have been compared with those of fraternals, have tended to strengthen theories of the inheritance of personality components. Drs. Raymond B. Cattell, Duncan B. Blewett, and John R. Beloff concluded from their twin studies that heredity may play a leading role in making some persons more easygoing, sociable, and warmhearted, or bolder and more outgoing, than others. Dr. Steven G. Vandenberg found much more similarity between the identicals than the fraternals in tastes for music, art, clothes, and color, and in degrees of self-confidence and stubbornness. Drs. D. G. Freedman and Barbara Keller, studying twins in infancy, reported that the fraternals differed considerably more than the identicals in mental and motor abilities and personality development.

Twins Reared Apart. The argument that merely being reared closely together and treated alike would tend to make identical twins more similar in personality has often been cited. Accordingly, the most important studies of identical twins have been of those separated in early infancy and reared apart in different environments, and then brought together years later (as a rule through the coincidence of being mistaken for one another). Scores of such cases have been studied, and in numerous instances the long-separated twins were found to be remarkably alike in many aspects of personality. Some of the best findings have come from Denmark, where a dozen pairs of long-separated adult identical twins were studied by Dr. N. Jule-Nielsen. Striking similarities in personality—including neurotic traits, marital maladjustments, and antisocial tendencies—were revealed by some of the twins. (Also of interest was the finding that the brain wave recordings of the two members of each identical pair were almost completely alike in significant details.) However, many of the reunited Danish identicals showed certain differences in personality which reflected their different home environments and training. Bearing on this point have been the findings regarding two long-separated American identical twins, named Tony Milasi and Roger Brooks by the respective families who had adopted them, one Catholic Italian, the other Jewish. Although, when reunited as young men, psychological tests showed them to have nearly the same IQs and basic aptitudes, Tony proved to be more "extroverted and self-assured," while Roger (who had had a disturbed childhood after his foster parents separated) was "more sensitive and impressionable." (A book about these twins, by Bard Lindemann, with a foreword by Amram Scheinfeld, was published in 1969, by Morrow.)

Effects of Twinship. Being a twin may have variable effects, with degrees depending on the closeness of the members and the type of twinship: the most for identicals, less for fraternals of the same sex, least for twins of opposite sex. Attitudes toward twins, and of one toward the other, may influence their psychological and social development, sometimes negatively, but often for the better. (Whereas some psychologists have stressed confusion or loss of "ego identity" in twins, others have noted that twins are less likely than singly born to feel isolated, and, being linked from birth with another child, are more likely to have a sense of "belonging." However, there is no proof for the popular belief in a "mystic bond" between twins. See "Extrasensory Perception" in Chapter 22, p. 200.) The average incidence of maladjustment, homosexuality, emotional disturbance, or psychosis in twins is no greater than in singletons and, where occurring in twins, can be traced much more to adverse factors in the home or social environment than to twinship per se. (Detailed discussions of this subject will be found in the author's book, *Twins and Supertwins*, published in 1967 by J. B. Lippincott Company.)

The Dionne Quintuplets. Personality studies of this famous all-identical set (discussed in Chapter 5) were made only in their early years. Certain differences in their personalities were observed, but these were for the most part no greater than those which parents recognize between any two identical twins. However, some of the differences persisted and became strongly marked in the later ages, particularly with respect to the two who have died to date, Emilie (at age twenty, in 1954) and Marie (at age thirty-five in 1969). As noted in Chapter 5, these two were almost like a pair of twins within the set of five, probably having been the last to develop from the same final subdivision of the egg. Marie was the weakest, sickliest, and shyest, while Emilie was epileptic, and both were less poised and less well adjusted than the other three. The two, also, had entered convents, then given up the plan to become nuns.

Yvonne, however, did become a nun. Annette, Marie, and Cecile married, but only Annette's marriage endured, the other two having ended in separation. Whatever the genetic makeup of the Dionnes might have portended for them, the extraordinary pressures of being in the world's spotlight from birth on must have enormously influenced their personalities and the turns taken in their lives.

GENERAL CONCLUSIONS. The facts about personality brought out in this and preceding chapters can refute the earlier theories of "behaviorists" that a normal child comes into the world with a "clean slate" so far as behavioral and personality traits are concerned, and that the development of such traits is governed almost entirely by conditioning and experiences. As has been shown, there is growing evidence that inherited differences incline individuals from birth onward to develop traits of behavior and personality in given directions, or to respond to similar environmental influences in different ways. Any personality genes that there may be, however, are far less direct, definite, or forceful in their workings, and much more likely to be modified in their effects by environmental forces, than are the genes for the physical traits or mental capacities. In sum, heredity provides the *raw materials* or potentialities for personality development; and these same raw materials can be processed, shaped, and packaged in a great many different ways as determined by the outside influences to which a person is subjected.

See also "Psychopathic (or Sociopathic) Personality" in Chapter 16; "Sex Traits" in Chapter 24; "Temperamental Factors" (in criminal behavior) in Chapter 25; "Racial Stereotypes" in Chapter 28.

24

Sex and
Sexual Behavior

THE SEX DIFFERENCES. Of all influences on behavior, none is more important than a person's sex. Just as among lower animals the male and female of each species differ in their behavior in many ways, so do they also among human beings. These human behavior differences may be classed under two headings: (1) *sex* behavior, referring to distinguishing traits of males as compared with females in actions, mannerisms, speech, movements, attitudes, etc.; (2) *sexual* behavior, directly involving the sexual impulses, feelings, and acts, as they reveal themselves in love-making, intercourse, and other sexual outlets. Both types of behavior are the extremely complex results of an interplay between inborn tendencies and environmental influences. Our purpose in this chapter will be mainly to look for possible hereditary factors.

The Two Roads. At the moment of conception, as reported in Chapter 4, the XY sex chromosome combination in males and the XX combination in females start them off immediately on different developmental roads. Further, as reported in other chapters, with succeeding stages of development the sexes show marked differences in their growth rates, body form and functioning, onset of puberty, physical capacities, sexual organs, reproductive and parental roles, susceptibility to diseases and defects, aging effects, and other biological manifestations. Not the least of these are the processes peculiar to women: menstruation, childbearing, childnursing, and the menopause. Even if every effort were made to equalize the external environments for both sexes, each of the factors mentioned would tend to produce some differences in the behavior of females generally as compared with males. However, one must not ignore the fact that environment may continually work to intensify and sometimes distort these differences through training, moral and religious codes, courtship patterns, marriage roles, jobs, styles, etc.

Hormonal Factors. Among the biological factors most directly affecting male and female behavior are the differences in the sex hormones—not in type, but in quantity. Males produce about twenty times as much as females of the so-called male hormone—*androgen*; females produce much more of the so-called female hormone—*estrogen*. In lower animals the sex hormone effects on behavior are striking. In poultry, when young female chicks are dosed with male hormones, they begin to act like little roosters, showing sudden aggressiveness and trying to crow; grown hens, if deprived of female hormones, also take on rooster characteristics; and very young roosters, if castrated and deprived of male hormones, lose their "cockiness" and become feminized. In dogs, female puppies if dosed with male hormones before birth, later assume the male position in urinating (one hind leg raised, where female dogs otherwise squat). Also, in rats and guinea pigs, as well as poultry, individual animals that are aggressive and dominant over others can be made submissive by decreasing the balance of male hormones with respect to female hormones; or by the reverse process, submissive animals can be made more aggressive and dominant.

Sex Hormone Changes in Humans. Experiments such as those just mentioned have not, of course, been performed on human beings. However, certain diseases or defects that disturb and greatly change the balance of the sex hormones in either boys or girls can swerve their behavior patterns from what is usual for their sex. Most pronounced are the feminizing effects of castration on boys *before puberty*. Castration in maturity, when the masculine physical and behavior traits have already been set, may produce only limited and gradual effects on behavior. As men age, and their output of male hormones decreases, they become progressively less masculine in behavior, and very old men may behave not too differently from very old women. As for females, what corresponds to castration—removal of the ovaries—before puberty, prevents proper physical and psychological adolescence, and if done after puberty, induces premature menopause, with effects on the individual's mood and sense of well-being.

The Menopause. This is also called the "change of life" because it marks the natural end of the woman's reproductive or possible further childbearing phase, although she may still be otherwise vigorous and healthy, and often quite young—sometimes well under forty. Although behavior changes often accompany the menopause, and may result from the biological changes and transitions, the effects may be considerably intensified by the psychological state of the woman. As a rule, women who have previously been emotionally well balanced show little behavior change during and after the menopause.

Male Change of Life.   There is little to show that men have anything equivalent to the female menopause. There is no abrupt stoppage in men of hormonal secretion and reproductive capacity, but rather a gradual diminution which is part of the general aging process. Any marked behavior changes that might also occur in a man during his late forties or in his fifties are quite likely to be almost entirely psychological, the results of his feeling that he is "losing his grip."

Abnormal Sex Development.   Many of the sex abnormalities discussed in Chapter 14—the chromosomally caused Klinefelter or Turner syndromes, the sex hormone defects, the hermaphroditic conditions, and retarded or accelerated sex development—in which genetic factors may play a part, obviously affect sex behavior. However, the direct effect on sex behavior of these abnormalities may often depend on how they are regarded by the individual, the family, or outsiders. This applies particularly to the cases in which an outwardly appearing female has the sex chromosomes of a male, or a genetic male has the outward appearance of a female, or a child with outward sex abnormalities has been mistakenly reared in the nongenetic sex pattern. Specialists at the Johns Hopkins Hospital, Dr. John Money and associates, have made extensive psychological studies of such intersexual individuals. They have reported that the gender identity and sexual behavior of hermaphrodites is not preordained by their genetic sex, nor even by their gonadal or hormonal sex, per se, but follows, rather, in the pathway of their assigned sex and the sex pattern in which they had been reared. However, there is still a question whether human beings—either biologically normal or abnormal as to sex—are started off in a sexually *neutral* state (which is not true of other animals) or whether training can ever fully suppress the effects of the individual's genetic sex make-up on his or her sex behavior. (Further discussions on this point follow.)

SEX TRAITS. How far the many significant psychological, social, and behavioral differences observable between little boys and girls are due to inborn factors or to the way they are trained cannot be easily determined. As parents have observed, little boys as a rule tend to be more restless, active, aggressive, destructive, and somewhat harder to manage. Little girls usually are more restrained, more self-sufficient, and quieter, less interested than boys in mechanical toys and rough play, but given more to sedentary diversions; and after the age of two or three, they tend to be more aware of people, shyer, and perhaps more nervous (with more nail-biting and thumb-sucking) than boys. Also, as noted in Chapter 20, little girls show greater hand dexterity and independence in dressing themselves. Some of these early differences have been regarded as influenced by natural tendencies, because even among lower animals young males and females act differently in various respects. For example, psychologist Harry F. Harlow, noted for his studies of primates, reported that "male and female infant monkeys show differences in sex behavior from the second month of life onward." The little males threaten others, but the little girl monkeys do so much less often and tend to be more passive, to groom more frequently than males, and to engage less frequently in rough-and-tumble play. Dr. Harlow concluded that these secondary sex differences are found equally in young humans and "are innately determined biological differences, regardless of any cultural overlay." But undoubtedly, as childhood progresses, the ways in which boys and girls are reared can heavily accentuate and more strongly differentiate any of their inborn behavior tendencies.

Tomboyism. Pertinent to the foregoing are findings by Drs. Anke A. Ehrhardt and John Money (1967) that "tomboy" behavior developed in nine out of ten girls whose mothers during pregnancy were given a synthetic pregnancy hormone or progestin (a miscarriage preventive) which sometimes leads to masculinization of female offspring. These girls, when studied at ages three to fourteen, showed preferences for boys' toys, athletic activities, and outdoor pursuits, and "a minimal concern for feminine frills, doll play, baby care and household chores." However, this tomboyishness did not exclude their having feminine thoughts of future romance, marriage, childbearing, and homemaking. (Also important, the IQs of these girls averaged an unusually high 125, consistent with other findings that prenatally masculinized girls tended to have elevated IQs.)

Masculinity and Femininity Criteria. Almost everywhere in the world the traits linked with males and most admired in them are strength, virility, bravery, aggressiveness, dominance, enterprise, adventurousness, interest in outdoor activity, and ability to *do* things (particularly of a mechanical nature). Linked with and most admired in females are interest and proficiency in domestic activities (cooking, sewing, homemaking, child-rearing), tenderness, affection, sentimentality, sensitivity, etc. But as indicated previously, there is much question as to the relationship between these ascribed traits and the biological sex traits. One could argue that greater strength, aggressiveness, dominance, and bravery in a physical sense could more naturally characteristic of men, as they are of males among many other species (bulls, roosters, stags, etc.). And again, traits such as tenderness and domesticity might also develop more naturally among women through their childbearing and child-rearing functions. Yet in a psychological sense there is no evidence at all that women cannot be and are not as brave, aggressive, enterprising, and venturesome as men. If they reveal these qualities less, it could be much more because of social influences than of their gene workings.

SEXUAL BEHAVIOR. As explained at the beginning of this chapter, *sexual* behavior refers specifically to the impulses, feelings, and acts in any way connected with the sex organs and sexual outlets. This is an enormous subject. We must limit ourselves here to the possible hereditary aspects as they relate to individual differences in sexual behavior, and to those types of behavior which are markedly unusual and nonaverage, or "abnormal."

Sociosexual Development. This refers to a human being's sexual behavior as it develops in relationship to other persons. In average individuals such sexual development proceeds through quite definite stages, as listed below; and it is when these stages are not properly experienced or completed that cause for concern, or suspicion of "abnormality," may arise.

1. Infancy and babyhood: Interest only in one's own sex organs and feelings. Individuals stopping at this stage are the *narcissists* who cannot show sexual feeling for anyone but themselves, and derive satisfaction only from their own bodies. Causes are probably psychological.

2. Early childhood: Play with members of the opposite sex, but with little active sex interest. Those who do not outgrow this stage remain undeveloped in the sexual feelings and responses, and very low in sex drive. While again the causes may be psychological, sometimes they are traceable to deficiencies or defects in the sex glands and organs, which may or may not have a hereditary basis. (See Chapter 14.)

3. Ages six to ten (approximately): Interest primarily in those of one's own sex, and indifference or antagonism to the opposite sex. Those remaining at this stage after puberty and into maturity may be in danger of developing into *homosexuals*. (See later discussion.)

4. Adolescence: Marked interest in the opposite sex, and an urge for sexual relationships, but with little desire yet for permanency (except as to "going steady" for a while). Those who do not pass beyond this stage may include persons constantly seeking new and frequent sexual partners because they lack mature sex feeling and never can obtain full satisfaction with anyone. In most cases the causes are chiefly or entirely psychological.

5. Maturity: Selection (where there is opportunity) of one individual of the opposite sex as a permanent mate, not only for sexual union, but for marriage and establishing a home, family, and social life. This is considered as the final—and socially approved (or "normal")—stage of sexual development and mature sexual behavior in most civilizations.

THE SEX STUDIES. Many investigators have thrown light on the incidences and degrees of various forms of normal and deviant human sexual behavior. Most extensive and most often cited have been the studies of Dr. Alfred C. Kinsey and his associates, based on data from about 15,000 men and women who volunteered to give their sex histories. Among the Kinsey findings: The sex life of average males is more extensive and continuous than that of females; male sexual responsiveness and performance develops much sooner on the average but reaches its peak much earlier than that of females (at age eighteen or so in males, close to age thirty in females); and no male can rival some females in frequency of sexual performance and response, although a far higher proportion of females—up to 30 per cent—are and remain sexually unresponsive throughout life. Major criticisms of the Kinsey studies were based on the fact that (1) the *volunteer* interviewees were probably not representative of the general population, so the precise percentages reported for this or that sexual activity, or for individual and group differences, were statistically questionable; (2) the same criteria (orgasm frequency, for example, no matter how arrived at), were arbitrarily used for evaluating the relative sexual performances of males and females, despite their great differences anatomically, functionally, and psychologically; and (3) the reported sexual *performance* of individuals, or of males compared with females, was equated with sexual *capacity*.

Inheritance Theories.   No evidence emerged from the Kinsey reports regarding inherited differences among human beings in degrees or patterns of normal sexual behavior (nor have any other studies to date offered such evidence). However, the Kinsey group did conclude that psychological factors or social conditioning certainly could not account for all the great differences in erotic capacities throughout the population, and that genetic factors must contribute to them. Theoretically, there could be "sexual genes" governing the construction and functioning of the sex organs and mechanisms, sensory organs, and the amounts and types of hormones, which would predispose individuals toward different amounts and forms of sexual activity. Such inherited factors have been found in lower animals. At the same time, the great importance of psychological and social factors in repressing, inciting, and directing human sexual activity, whatever the inherent tendencies, has been made evident by the recent changes in sexual behavior with regard to populations and generations.

HOMOSEXUALITY. Male.   This condition has many puzzling and debatable aspects, particularly as related to *overt* homosexuals—those who consistently and preferably turn for their sexual relationships to their own sex and who may have distinctive and easily recognizable mannerisms, "feminine" or otherwise. (Some overt homosexuals are outwardly extremely masculine in appearance and actions.) The incidence of homosexuality is uncertain, partly because of the different standards for appraising it. Most estimates are that up to 3 per cent of American males may be exclusively homosexual, and a considerable number of others sporadically so. It is quite likely that different types and degrees of homosexuality may arise through different factors—psychological, social, and biological. Although most authorities stress the psychological influences, there is some possibility that inborn quirks are involved in male homosexuality of the most feminized types. As reasons: (1) Overt homosexuals have appeared among human beings throughout history and in the most diverse environments. (2) Many homosexuals everywhere, whether in the most primitive or the most civilized societies, show similarities in movements, mannerisms, vocal inflections, and various other behavior traits. (3) They often seem to arise spontaneously, with tendencies shown in childhood, and no recognizable conditioning factors that can explain them. (4) Studies of twins, by Dr. Franz J. Kallmann and others, indicated that in the great majority of cases where one of a pair of identical twins was homosexual, so was the other, but that this was not necessarily true of fraternal twins. However, the argument that homosexuality is an entirely "natural" and "normal" variant of human sexual activity because it also appears in lower animals is diminished by this fact: in other animal species it is not a *preferred* form of sexual behavior when members of the opposite sex are available.

The Intersex Theory. A few scientists have maintained that male homosexuals of the extreme "invert" type (with "feminine" physical traits) may represent an in-between sex. In certain lower species one does find individuals in whom the sex chromosomes are out of balance, so that they are neither completely male nor completely female. But there is no proof that this happens in human beings. Another theory is that overt male homosexuals tend to be deficient in male sex hormones. But tests have not proved this to be so as a rule, nor have hormonal treatments been found to change homosexual impulses. Nevertheless, the belief that there is an inborn biological cause of homosexuality, and that homosexuals constitute a "third sex," is still widespread and is held by many homosexuals themselves.

Conditioning Factors. Whether or not inborn tendencies or susceptibilities are involved in homosexuality, there is considerable evidence that specific environmental factors can do much to turn a person toward this behavior. Most often held responsible for male homosexuality are neurotic, sexually frustrated, dominant, or clinging mothers, who seek to raise their boys unmasculinely and implant in them fear or distaste of opposite-sex relationships. However, there are many cases where such influences are lacking, and where it would be highly unfair to blame the parent. Further, the apparent marked general increase in the *manifestation* of homosexuality as social and legal barriers have eased (and assuming that the predisposition to it has remained the same) would suggest that its overt expression may be much influenced by factors outside the home. In any case, when the homosexually inclined individual is still young, or in an indecisive stage, there is the best chance of conditioning him toward normal (i.e., wholly heterosexual) behavior. But in an adult, once the homosexual pattern has been strongly set, the possibility of a "cure" is minimal— although it has been reported in some cases—and many psychoanalysts believe the best procedure is to adjust the individual to his preferred way of life.

The Arts and Homosexuals. The apparent disproportionate numbers of homosexuals in the arts, past and present (literature, decoration, the ballet, music, the theater) has prompted the assumption that such inherent tendencies as may make for homosexuality also produce artistic talent, and vice versa. For lack of any such evidence, a more tenable theory might be that men with homosexual tendencies have traditionally gravitated toward the arts because they have found in these pursuits and in the artistic milieu readier acceptance, employment, and outlets for their special traits and interests.

Transvestism and Transsexualism. Transvestism is an uncontrollable urge to dress and behave like one of the opposite sex. Transsexualism, occurring more often in males than in females, is the desire to change one's sex—in the extreme cases *anatomically*, and achieved to some extent by a considerable number of men who have undergone operations. (These "sex-changing" operations, involving surgical alterations of the external sex organs, plus hormonal induction of breast development, cannot change the person's genetic sex.) Transvestism and transsexualism may be independent of one another, and sometimes may be independent

of homosexuality. Many individuals display transvestite or trans-
sexual traits early in childhood, and even though these traits appear
to be largely psychological quirks, where no environmental explanation can be found it is considered *possible* that some hereditary
predisposition may be involved.

Female Homosexuality.   The problem of female homosexuality
is not so serious as that of male homosexuality because the incidence is much lower (probably under 1 per cent), it is much less
on the surface, and its social effects are not as adverse. (All the
foregoing statements may require modification in view of the
recent greater emergence of female homosexuals into the open,
and their demands—supported by the "women's liberation" movement [see below]—that they be recognized and respected as a
minority group.) The greater need and desire of women to marry
and have children may suppress homosexual tendencies in them
more than in males. Otherwise most of the basic facts given for
male homosexuality apply to the corresponding behavior in the
female. Thus, although some female homosexuals are masculine
in outward appearance and behavior, many others are completely
feminine in all respects save their sexual inclinations (although
they may have relationships with males as well as females). Again,
some female homosexuals appear to be products solely of warped
emotional or psychological conditioning, but others seem to have
started with strong inner tendencies toward abnormal sexual
behavior, which may or may not have had a biological basis.
Finally, as with males, the chance for conditioning a homosexually
inclined female toward normalcy depends largely on whether she
is in the young and/or indecisive stage or is adult and has already
been strongly set in the homosexual pattern.

"Women's Liberation."   The movement to achieve for women
"complete equality with men" has brought to the fore a summing
up and re-evaluation of all the questions regarding sex differences
discussed in this and preceding chapters. Traditional roles and
behavior for many women have already been greatly changed by
the breakdown of many pre-existing barriers between the sexes in
their work, social lives, and habits. Undoubtedly the changes can
and will go farther, but how much more so will ultimately be
governed by the degree to which the effects of basic, inherent
biological sex differences can be minimized. First, while the neutral

area in employment—that in which physical sex differences are
not a factor—has been greatly widened, there still remain many
important activities, in jobs, sports (professional and college),
everyday chores, and social and personal relationships—in which
the male's greater strength and other special physical capacities—
will continue to discriminate between the sexes; and, as related to
women, the differences in sexual activity and their consequences,
and the effects of menstruation, childbearing, and the menopause,
will continue to influence the female psychology and behavior in
considerable degree. Further, the evidence cannot be ignored that
many of the sex differences in behavior begin to be manifested at
a very early age, independent of conditioning (as previously
brought out), and that even some of the socially imposed codes
governing the relationship between the sexes may have some
genetic basis: for example, while "chivalry" has been denounced
by feminists as no more than an "artifice of chauvinistic males to
keep women in subjection," its counterpart is found widely in the
mammalian kingdom, where males in many species usually refrain
from using their greater strength against females; and "women
and children first" has its parallel among apes and other group or
herd animals, within whose ranks, when an enemy threatens, adult
males range themselves as a protective barrier in front of the
females and young. (Detailed evidence on the foregoing and
related points appeared in the author's book *Women and Men*,
1944). But whatever part the genetic and other biological sex
differences will have to play in differentiating the roles and
relationships of men and women, it must always be kept in mind
that we are speaking in terms of averages. In any given area there
must be a place for every human individual, female or male, to
live, behave, and achieve in keeping with his or her capacities and
inclinations.

25

Criminal
Behavior

"**CRIMINAL TAINTS.**" It is an old belief that "evil streaks" or "criminal taints" run in certain families, and also that some human groups, nationalities, or races are more "criminal" by nature than others. No scientific evidence for this has yet been produced. Further, there are only guesses or suppositions about the extent to which individuals in any group may inherit tendencies toward criminality. On the other hand, we can now refute or question many of the earlier theories about criminal inheritance. It is these *disproofs* regarding criminality which are perhaps most important.

What Is the "Criminal Type"? Our first difficulty in trying to find out whether criminality is inborn is to decide what we mean by it. Legal and social definitions of "criminality" vary and have varied enormously, depending on places or periods. Nor can we distinguish between "criminals" and "noncriminals" merely on the basis of those who have or haven't been convicted of wrongdoing, since law and justice are far from always the same. But even when a person's acts are so consistently vicious and antisocial as to clearly stamp him a criminal, we still have to dig deeply into his background, make-up, and thinking before we can assume that his heredity may be in any way responsible. Finally, the many types of crime—murder, robbery, rape, drug addiction, tax evasion, fraud, etc.—may often be completely unrelated; and even the same crimes (as murders, or sex offenses) may be of many different types in nature and motive. To find genes causing criminality in general might be as impossible as to find genes for disease in general. Only when we examine separately each form of crime and those committing it can we begin to see what causative forces might be at work.

HEREDITARY FACTORS IN CRIME. Keeping in mind the foregoing reservations, it is nonetheless true that no matter what the crime rates or types of crime are in given groups, or what the existing conditions are that breed crime, only *some* individuals—and often only one or two in a family—become criminals. There is therefore a basis for believing that certain persons may be innately predisposed to commit crimes of various or specific kinds, just as there are inborn predispositions toward other types of behavior. The evidence in support of this, however, is only circumstantial or inferential, except possibly with regard to the XYY condition described below.

The XYY Chromosome Abnormality. The Y chromosome being the determinant of maleness (Chapter 4), and maleness being in turn associated with greater proneness toward criminal behavior, special significance has been attached to reports that males with the abnormal chromosome combination of *two* Ys (instead of the normal one) in their cells, coupled with an X, were in disproportionate numbers among prisoners charged with serious crimes. In addition, studies (the first made in Scottish prisons in 1965), showed that the XYY individuals tended to be unusually tall, aggressive, emotionally disturbed, erratic, of low intelligence, and often with genital abnormalities. Thus, in a number of cases in which XYY individuals were charged with murder or other crimes, it was argued that because of the inborn abnormalities they were not legally responsible for their acts. On this basis one XYY man was acquitted of murder in Australia in 1968, but in a similar case in France that year, the XYY plea was rejected, as it was in several later cases in the United States. Subsequently, new studies showed that the XYY abnormality may occur in up to 1 in 300 males at birth (indicating that the XYY criminals were not nearly as disproportionate as had been thought originally), and that the large majority of these turned out to be noncriminal, or quite normal in behavior. Thus, the special relationship of the XYY abnormality to crime at this writing is uncertain. In any event, the abnormality has not been found transmitted by any XYY man to a son, which rules out inheritance of criminal behavior by this means at least.

Twin Criminals. Studies of crime among twins have shown that where they were identicals (with the same hereditary factors) if one was criminal, so was the other in three out of four cases, whereas in fraternal twins (with different heredity) this was true for only one in four. But in weighing this evidence it must be remembered that identical twins are usually reared more closely together, and one influences the other more than is true of fraternal twins.

Mental Disease and Crime. Where acts of violence or other crimes arise through mental diseases, such as schizophrenia, manic-depressive insanity, or psychopathic personality, heredity obviously is involved to the extent that it plays a part in these conditions (Chapter 17). There also is limited evidence that a disproportionate number of criminals have abnormal brain-wave patterns, the findings being clearest in the case of those who have committed murder, violence, arson, or acts of cruelty on sudden impulses and without rational motivation. However, the majority of criminals show no symptoms of diseased minds and appear to be no more than warped products of unfortunate conditioning, experiences, and circumstances.

Feeble-Mindedness and Crime. Authorities are also finding decreasing connection between low intelligence and crime. A generation or so ago about 35 per cent of the prison inmates were feeble-minded and (as with insanity), where heredity could be blamed for the mental defect, it might also be blamed for the criminal acts. Today, with better care and training, and more good institutional homes, fewer of the mentally retarded get into trouble or reach prisons. In some prisons IQs of inmates may continue to be below average if the least intelligent are the ones most likely to be arrested and convicted.

Criminal "Looks" and Somatotypes. Various theories have been advanced that criminals as a group tend to differ from non-criminals in features (ears, eyes, foreheads, mouths, etc.) or in *somatotypes* (body build). But as was stated in Chapter 23, there is no evidence that any inherited facial or bodily detail goes with any particular inherited behavioral trait (other than in cases where defective genes or chromosome abnormalities produce both physical and mental aberrations). Where there is any recognizable "criminal" look, it may be only that acquired through the person's habits. As to the "body-build" theories, it is possible that since some types of crime tend to be committed more often in some groups than in others, differences among these groups in body build would be reflected in the criminal population. Whatever the reasons, Dr. William H. Sheldon found that delinquent youths tended to be more than ordinarily short and stocky. Also, Drs. Sheldon and Eleanor Glueck, Harvard criminologists, after studying large numbers of youths, reported that the solid, muscular, energetic type much more often characterized the delinquents, while the nondelinquents had proportionately more of the longish, fragile, less vigorous type. But the Gluecks concluded that many other influences—socioeconomic, cultural, and psychological—played a part in delinquency, and combined their findings in constructing a "delinquency-prediction" scale which social agencies have found useful. However, the recent tremendous increase in crime among young people of all types has led to a minimizing of the biological factors. (See next section.)

ENVIRONMENT AND CRIME. Whatever part heredity was once believed to play in crime has now been dwarfed by the growing evidence of the overwhelming effects of environment. This is most clearly proved by the recent great increases in crime rates in the United States and other advanced countries as conditions and behavior patterns have changed. Thus, in the decade from 1959 to 1969 (according to FBI reports) the rate of major crimes—murders, robberies, burglaries, aggravated assaults, and forcible rape—among Americans jumped 120 per cent. Most ominous was the enormous increase in crime among young people of all groups, many from families of "good stock" and substantial social, economic, and educational levels where criminal delinquency had previously been rare or unknown. As a general rule, however, crime rates continue to be markedly higher wherever social and psychological conditions are worst—as in slum areas—or where government, the courts, and police are most lax and corrupt and the public is most tolerant toward wrongdoing.

Racial and Ethnic Differences. Geneticists have found no evidence that heredity is accountable for differences in racial and ethnic crime rates. On the other hand, the environmental explanation is solidly based. In the United States, for instance, the crime rates of persons of its various ethnic stocks have generally been far higher than those of their kindred abroad. Further, the crime rates of persons of the same stock have varied greatly in different regions and areas of the country. In Europe, too, within given countries, crime rates have changed radically—mainly toward higher levels—from the past to the present. (Nor need it be noted that in once law-abiding Germany masses of people reached terrible peaks of barbaric criminality under the Nazis, and then, almost at once, quieted down to normal behavior patterns.) There are times when people may feel ashamed or disturbed because given types of crime seem unduly prevalent among those of their own race, religion, or ethnic group. But this may have no more to do with their genes than corned beef and cabbage has to do with Irish genes, chitlings and corn pone with Negro genes, spaghetti with Italian genes, or kosher salami with Jewish genes. Thus, crime differences among Americans of all origins have tended to diminish or disappear as their ways of living and habits have become more the same. (See also "Racial Stereotypes," Chapter 28.)

Negro-White Crime Differences. Consistent with what was said previously, the present high crime rate among Negroes is ascribed by authorities in no wise to heredity, but largely to the following factors: (1) The inferior conditions under which Negroes have lived and most still live, on the average; (2) discriminations against them, and less chance to get adequate legal aid, which makes them more likely than whites to run afoul of laws, be arrested, convicted, and sentenced; (3) various other environmental factors which work adversely against Negro family life, proper child-rearing, and individual adjustment. Wherever economic, educational, and social conditions for Negroes have improved, and they have been enabled to live, work, earn, and be accepted on a level closer to that of whites, their crime rates have dropped greatly. (The foregoing observations apply equally to the current crime rates of Puerto Ricans in the States.)

SEX DIFFERENCES IN CRIME. Both heredity and environment are peculiarly interrelated in producing the vastly higher rate of crime among males than among females everywhere, and the differences in types of crime, as measured by arrests and convictions. However, many recent changes in the psychological, social, and workaday environments which have affected women and their behavior, have brought sharp increases in the female crime rate and decreased the sex differences in this regard. Thus, where in 1953 male arrests outnumbered female eight to one in the United States, by 1969 the ratio was six to one. But the sex difference in major crimes continued to be marked: In arrests for murders, men outnumbered women six to one; in burglary, twenty-five to one; in robbery, seven to one. The female offenses were relatively highest in the less violent crimes—fraud, embezzlement, bad checks, shoplifting, forgery—where they accounted for from one fourth to one third of the arrests.

Biological Factors. Although the excess of male over female crime has diminished as women have had more freedom to adopt men's habits and practices, the question remains whether training, moral codes, and other conditioning factors can entirely account for the sex differences in crime. The theory that men by nature are more inclined to commit crimes of violence than are women, everything being equal, rests on these facts: (1) among other animals—all mammals and most birds—males are inherently more aggressive, more given to violent behavior, and harder to train or domesticate; (2) experiments with lower animals have shown a direct relationship between male hormones and aggressiveness; treating females (rats, hens, etc.) with male hormones makes them develop male aggressive and fighting qualities, whereas in males, subtracting male hormones through castration, or adding female hormones, tends to make them more passive and submissive; (3) in the youngest children one can note a greater tendency of boys to be aggressive, unruly, and destructive; (4) superior strength and physical capacities of men lead them more into occupations inducing violence and familiarity with weapons; (5) differences in sexual functioning, in their natural parental roles, and in the consequences of loose conduct tend to make women more restrained than males in their behavior, and further differentiate their activities, opportunities, and inclinations with respect to crime.

Temperamental Factors. The foregoing points, as noted, apply mainly to crimes involving physical acts. There is no evidence that nature or heredity have made women any more moral or "angelic" than men. The crimes of women almost always have tended to be more subtle, veiled, and personal, and more likely to evade the meshes of the law, than those of men. But as their opportunities for open wrongdoing have increased, women's crime rates have shot upward. Thus, the introduction of firearms, eliminating the strength disadvantages, has caused a marked rise in murders by women; and occupational changes have greatly increased the convictions of women for theft, fraud, forgery, embezzlement, etc.

Sex Crimes. Differences in the sex organs and sex functioning of males and females lead naturally to differences in the types of sex crimes each might commit (mainly, *rape* by males and *prostitution* by females). Otherwise, however, there is little relationship between heredity and sex offenses. Nor, as a rule, are sex offenses linked with other types of crime, except insofar as criminal conduct or a criminal environment may also lead to looseness or viciousness in sexual conduct. This is especially true of prostitution. In countries where prostitutes are not regarded as criminal (or in some places not even looked down on), there may be nothing in the way of abnormal tendencies to turn them toward this profession. But wherever prostitution is condemned by law and society, and where it is conducted in a criminal atmosphere, women who go into it, and stay in it, do tend to have abnormal or criminal tendencies. However, prostitution by itself, and other sex offenses (including *homosexuality*), might be more properly considered as types of sexual behavior. (See preceding chapter.)

WAR. Most of the facts with respect to crime in individuals can be applied to refuting the theory that in mankind as a whole there are "mass criminal" or "murder" instincts, which must burst out periodically into war, and that these "instincts" for war or aggression are very strong in some nations, whereas peoples of other nations are by nature peaceful. This theory finds no support either in scientific studies or in recent history. A first error is to assume that war is a "return to the animal state." Actually, while *individuals* among lower animals may fight—almost always males over the territory they have staked out, or over females— there is never any bloody mass conflict between two groups of the same species, as there is among human beings. Again, if in lower animals, those of different species or breeds are most antagonistic, so among humans one would expect any "war instinct" to show itself most between those of different races. Yet we know that many of the bloodiest wars in history have been between groups of the same race, and often also of the same stocks and nationalities (as in the civil wars in the United States and, most recently, in

Korea, Indo-China, and China.) Finally, the presumed "warlike" or "peaceful" nature of any people has often changed abruptly. Many primitive tribes (including American Indians) once considered "bloodthirsty savages" are now among the most peaceful of peoples. So, too, are the once-warlike Scandinavians. The Chinese, for centuries peaceful, are now highly war-minded. The Jews, warriors in Biblical times, were long thereafter thought of as "nonfighters," but back in Israel they have again become warriors. And so on. All of this has led the scientists who study human make-up to be among those most convinced that warfare lies not in our genes but in our thinking, and that if there is any "mass" instinct among human groups, it is for getting along with rather than killing one another. This might even be applied to crimes by individuals: the strongest desire in everyone is to get along with others—to be loved and respected, to be given a chance to be useful, to "belong," and to join both in producing and in receiving whatever the community can provide for happiness. It is only when individuals are in some way frustrated in achieving these ends that they turn to crime.

26

Human Evolution

EVOLUTION. To understand how human beings originated on this earth, one must have some idea of how life of any kind first began and how it led to the development of all the countless types and forms of other living things. The process by which scientists believe this was achieved is called "evolution." When people use this term they are apt to think of Charles Darwin, for it was his theories of evolution, published in 1859, that revised all previous concepts. What caused the most controversy and opposition was Darwin's contention that the different creatures were not created suddenly, at the same time and in their existing forms, but developed step by step, over very long periods, from other and simpler types, and, specifically, that *human beings* had also developed from lower forms of animals.

The Bible and Darwin. To many persons, the Darwinian theories may have seemed a direct contradiction of the Biblical account of Creation as having taken place in six "days," and of man in one "day." But others have realized that there actually need be no real conflict on this point if one interprets the Biblical "days" of Creation as meaning *stages* of indefinite length. By this definition modern science holds very closely in most respects to the Biblical concept of the successive stages of Creation: (1) The earth being "without form, and void," then being shaped into a mass covered by water, with "light"—the heat and energy from the sun—a first essential in all that was to take place; (2) land rising from beneath the waters, forming continents and islands surrounded by oceans; (3) the growth of vegetation; (4) changes in climate, environments, and food conditions; (5) the creation and existence of the simplest creatures, gradually developing into fish, reptiles, fowl, and mammals; (6) finally the evolution (or creation) of man. If scientists think of this as happening not in a "week," but in vast stretches of time—three billion years or more— and in endlessly remarkable ways, it can only add to the wonder of Creation.

THE FIRST LIFE-SPARK. In explaining evolution, scientists begin with the assumption that the first living thing was a single cell consisting of a *single gene*—or a section of DNA—housed in a blob of the life stuff, protoplasm. (This cell may have come from a simpler, viruslike cell, in between living and nonliving.) Endowed with the property of life and reproduction, the first gene cell could multiply itself endlessly. Very soon, among the millions of separate offspring cells, *mutations*—changes in genes (as described in Chapter 3)—began to take place, making some different from the others. As mutations increased, different genes began hooking up into chains to form chromosomes. And with each change in the types, numbers, and varieties of genes and chromosomes, there also were changes in the types and complexities of the cell formations, and of the creatures they produced. Not least important was the creation of *two sexes*. At the beginning creatures reproduced by dividing themselves, so hereditary changes from one generation to another were limited. But when mutations produced sex genes, then sex chromosomes, and thus individuals of two sexes, this greatly extended the possibility of making new combinations of genes with each mating, and of speeding up evolutionary changes.

Inventive Mutations. Altogether, in a rough way the process of evolution in living things was not too unlike that which came later in the evolution of man-made machines. From the first crude tools fashioned by man—chipped rocks—there evolved hand axes, spears, arrows, knives, needles, and tools and devices of innumerable kinds. From the first simple wheel there evolved vehicles and machinery growing ever more complex, until, with the discovery of engines, there came automobiles and huge airplanes. Tree-trunk canoes to battleships, windmills to giant power plants, bullets to atomic bombs—all of these were the results of countless successive inventive mutations. So, too, all the varieties of living and growing things in our world today are the products of vastly more numerous and complex *genetic* mutations. Just to produce the human eye alone, for instance, must have required thousands of mutations over millions of years.

STEPS IN EVOLUTION. Aiding continuously in the process of evolution has been the fact that as different mutations popped up, if they served some useful purpose or offered an advantage to a creature at a given time, they survived. But where mutations produced a defect or disadvantage (true in the great majority of cases) the creatures died off. In this process of "selecting out" the good mutations and weeding out the bad ones, *environment* was always a factor. Each type or change of climate, food supply, natural hazard, enemy, disease, or other condition demanded something special in an animal for survival and development. Different mutations answered these needs, in the forms of particular kinds of bodies, feathers, furs, skins, claws, teeth, coloring, internal organs, breathing apparatus, sensory equipment (eyes, ears, sense of smell), and not least, *brains*, as well as many other details. But if the right mutations did not come along, species of creatures could often also survive and thrive by *moving* to some new environment, or being moved there by the winds, water, earth upheavals, or climatic changes. Either way, groups of creatures originally of similar types (but perhaps with some differences in their genes) spread out and became *segregated* from one another. And again, over new long periods of time, in each group new mutations kept appearing, which, in their different environments, were selected out and adapted differently, making the isolated groups increasingly different from one another. These, plus other factors (including crossbreeding and various chance elements), can account for the innumerable kinds of birds, fishes, mammals, and other animals, and the varieties of each species that are peculiar to given regions and localities the world over.

Acquired Characteristics. The erroneous old theory that evolution proceeded because traits *acquired* by animals, through experiences and habits, were or could be inherited by their offspring was briefly discussed in Chapter 2. Here are a few more points. The most questionable part of the theory is that what an animal needed or wanted—or no longer needed or wanted—could *cause* a particular mutation to take place. If giraffes had to keep stretching their necks to eat high up on trees, they would somehow cause their offspring to be born with longer and longer necks; or if animals stopped using some part of their body, their genes would stop providing it. But there is just no way of explaining *how* this could occur. If an animal kept stretching its neck, how could that shake up or change its "neck" genes so as to put more "stretch" in their workings? If a red bird was too easily spotted by enemies in green trees, how could that *make* its color genes begin to produce green feathers? Obviously this is impossible. The probable fact, as already indicated, is that in each species mutations of every conceivable kind kept coming along purely through chance (as they still do, which can be seen by observing flies, mice, and other creatures in laboratories). With the desirable mutations being retained, the bad ones eliminated, for generation after generation, as one useful mutation was added to another, this could conceivably have produced in sufficient time any type of creature, or the particular inherited traits in all the creatures existing today.

Chicken or Egg First? The facts as science now gives them clearly answer that the *egg* came first. By the old "acquired characteristic" theories it would have been the chicken: that is, one would start with a type of bird that, through gradual changes in habits and environments, presumably turned into a chicken, which *then* produced the characteristic chicken egg. But modern genetics holds that mutations kept producing different kinds of genes in eggs of a bird species, which in time caused these *eggs* to produce chickens. As applied to persons and eggs, for instance, a blue-eyed baby does not result because its parents were blue-eyed persons (often they are dark-eyed), but because the *egg* from which the baby came carried blue-eye genes. Originally it is possible that there were no human blue-eye genes and that one suddenly arose through mutation. Thus again it was not the blue-eyed person but the "blue-eyed" *egg* that came first.

The Lysenko Controversy. This involved the revival of the acquired characteristic theories in the Soviet Union by certain plant breeders, led by Trofim Lysenko, and their attack, starting in the 1930's, on the basic principles of modern genetics. When, subsequently, the Lysenko theories were officially proclaimed by the Soviet Central Committee as the only "correct and acceptable ones," many leading Soviet geneticists were exiled or forced to recant their scientific beliefs. But in time, under the growing weight of scientific evidence, the Lysenko theories were discredited, and today modern genetics is again becoming an actively pursued science in the Soviet Union.

EVOLUTION OF PRIMATES. The scientific story of human evolution begins perhaps 50,000,000 years ago. By that time the earth was teeming with creatures of every kind. Among them were some now called "primates," who were smarter and nimbler than other animals. In succeeding millions of years innumerable mutations produced different types and branches of the primate family. Some were the monkeys—lemurs, spider monkeys, macaques, baboons. From the more "intelligent" branches came the great apes—the gibbon, orangutan, chimpanzee, and gorilla. And finally, from another *separate* branch, and "twigs" of this branch, there began to develop species of the brainiest of all creatures—*man*. In other words, *human beings did not descend from apes*, but both apes and men came from the same "primate tree." So while we and the apes of today have common ancestors, our relationship is millions of years apart, and the best any ape can claim is that he and we are very, very distant "cousins."

Apes and Humans. With all the manifold differences, we nevertheless recognize that monkeys and apes are far more like us than are any other animals. That is why we are so fascinated watching them in zoos or on television. From the scientific standpoint, the fact that human beings belong to the same primate family as do monkeys and apes (but with the apes more closely related) is proved in a great many ways: by unique similarities in their skulls, bones, teeth, eyes, hands and feet, and internal organs; by menstruation in their females (the only lower animals among whom this occurs); by closely similar periods of gestation (eight months for apes); by late onset of puberty (age nine or ten for apes); and, most recently discovered and perhaps most important, by *blood types* (those in apes being almost exactly like the A, B, O, Rh and other blood groups in humans). The one tremendous difference, though, is in *brains*. Mainly it was the series of additional brain mutations on the human branch of the primate tree (plus improvements in the hands and skeletal framework) that carried men so far beyond all other creatures, and left the apes and monkeys almost back where they were millions of years ago.

Earliest Man-Types. Between the time that the man family began to evolve, far in the dimmest past, and the point where

The Evolution of Apes and Man

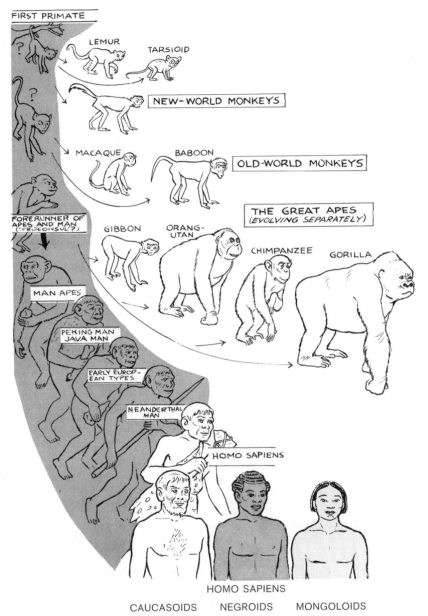

FIRST PRIMATE

LEMUR

TARSIOID

NEW-WORLD MONKEYS

MACAQUE

BABOON

OLD-WORLD MONKEYS

FORERUNNER OF APES AND MAN ("PROCONSUL"?)

THE GREAT APES (EVOLVING SEPARATELY)

GIBBON

ORANG-UTAN

CHIMPANZEE

GORILLA

MAN APES

PEKING MAN JAVA MAN

EARLY EUROPEAN TYPES

NEANDERTHAL MAN

HOMO SAPIENS

HOMO SAPIENS

CAUCASOIDS   NEGROIDS   MONGOLOIDS

(And Australoids, not shown here.) All existing human racial groups are of
the same species, descended from the same original ancestral group.

anything like true human beings appeared, there were a great many "experimental models" of ape men, part men, halfmen and near men, who died out or were killed off as improved types of man came along. We know of those man-types, fairly late in the procession (about two million years ago) only through a scant few of their skulls and bones which have been found. These earliest man-creatures have been named after the place where their relics were dug up: the East African ape man (or man-ape), the South African ape man, the Java man, the Peking man, the Heidelberg man, the Swanscombe man, etc. All of these were still heavy-browed, half-brained, stooped, and clumsy beings. But by 120,000 years ago a man almost like ourselves—the Neanderthal man—had appeared and was living in various parts of Africa, Europe, and Asia. He was about 5 feet 3 inches tall, had a big brow, a heavy jaw, and big teeth, but a good brain and capable hands, which enabled him to make wooden spears and flint tools, and to use fire. He also respectfully laid out his dead and must have shown other human traits.

Homo Sapiens. By about 100,000 B.C. a new man of our own present species, *Homo sapiens* ("wise man"), had evolved, possibly first in the region of Mesopotamia (which is where the Garden of Eden, Adam's birthplace, is supposed to have been). He was so superior to other types of men in brain power and skill that in time he alone survived. He may have killed off the cruder existing types of men (such as the Neanderthalers), or absorbed them by breeding; or they may have died off because of new diseases or conditions. About that we can only guess. But what we do know, from many scientific studies, tests, and observations is this: All the human beings in the world today, of all races and in all places, are biologically and genetically so much alike that they must be descendants of the same original stock of *Homo sapiens*. No matter how different they may seem to be (for example, tall blond Nordics and African pygmies), they all carry similar twenty-three pairs of human chromosomes with matching genes, and can mate and be fertile with one another (which would be impossible were they of different species). Thus, science now corroborates what most great religions have long been preaching: *Human beings of all races are equal "Children of God," descended from the same first man.*

27

The Human Races,
I: Physical Differences

THE ORIGIN OF RACES. Knowing that all human beings are of exactly the same species, descended from the same original man, how can the many differences among them in features, coloring, and other physical traits, as well as in behavior, culture, and achievement be explained? For the answer we return to the very beginnings of our species—*Homo sapiens,* about 100,000 years ago—and trace the story of racial differentiation as science now sees it. Starting with a single fruitful couple (Adam and Eve, if you wish), favorable conditions could have resulted in close to a million descendants in less than a thousand years. But in those early periods, with no fixed habitats, large groups would not have held together. So, moving wherever climate and the search for food led them, bands of people would have drifted apart, losing contact with one another, and spreading eventually to all habitable places of the earth. In time, then, these isolated human groups, multiplying and becoming fixed in different environments for thousands of years, would have developed various special hereditary characteristics through the continuing processes of evolution. We noted in the last chapter how *selection* and *adaptation* of gene changes as they came along in different environments, plus chance factors, could produce many varieties of birds or other animals of each species. The same factors could just as easily produce the many physical differences among human racial groups. (Their cultural and behavior differences, however, must be explained in other ways, to be dealt with later.)

THE MAIN RACES. The word "race" can be applied only loosely to human beings, because there are no large human groups all of whose members are completely different in any one trait from all those of other racial groups. We can make racial distinctions only with respect to *average* differences in a given number of inherited traits, to the extent that they occur in markedly different proportions in different groups. On this basis most scientists classify all human beings into four primary, or main, races (with the popular names given in parenthesis):

1. *Caucasoid* ("white") race, developing and concentrated largely in Europe, Asia Minor, India, and parts of North Africa. It is not known whether the white race was the first to develop; many authorities think the first members of *Homo sapiens* were dark, with Negroid features.

2. *Negroid* ("black") race, developing and concentrated largely in Africa, later spreading to some adjoining regions and then also being carried to the Americas and the West Indies.

3. *Mongoloid* ("yellow," or "yellow-brown") race, developing and concentrated mainly in Asia, and islands or regions adjoining it. Mongoloids are considered younger in evolutionary origin than either the whites or the Negroes.

4. *Australoid* race, comprising primitive peoples in and around Australia, with origins not too certain, but believed to stem from a very early mixture of Negroid and Mongoloid, and also some Caucasoid stocks.

The classifications by skin color, it should be kept in mind, are very questionable. As was pointed out in Chapter 8, people of all races have the same skin pigments, though in different proportions. Whites, for instance, are clearly not "white"-skinned. (They would look ghastly if they were.) What they themselves call their "flesh color" is actually pinkish-brown, as shown by the face powder or adhesive finger bandages they use. Further, many whites, such as swarthy Latins and Arabs, are very dark, and some in India have skins much blacker than many Negroes. Nor is "black" a correct term for many Negroid peoples who, without any mixture of white genes, have light-brown skins. So, too, the Mongoloids have a considerable range of skin colors, and while to some eyes their skins might seem to have a slight "yellowish" cast, this is only a variation of the basic human brown color.

Apelike Features. An old, false theory is that people of some races can be proved to be "less human" than others because their features are more "apelike." Although comparisons on this point have little meaning, it can easily be shown that persons of each race have some features which are farthest from the ape form, and some closest to it. For instance, the kinky hair of Negroes is less apelike than the straight or wavy hair of whites, and the sparse body hair of Negroes and Chinese is less apelike than the hairiness of whites. The full lips of Negroes put them farther away from the thin-lipped apes than are whites. This no more proves that whites are most apelike than broad noses of Negroes prove Negroes are, or Eskimos' thin noses prove they're least so.

SUBRACES. Each main race has (and had originally or developed in time) various subgroups, some being offshoots from the main race, and others blends with other races. Some examples:

American Indians and Eskimos. These are Mongoloid offshoots who, starting perhaps 30,000 years ago, began crossing over from Asia by way of a narrow strip of land then connecting Siberia with Alaska. The Mongols who formed or developed into the Eskimos and the various Indian tribes of North, Central, and South America (including the Incas and Aztecs), did not come all at once, but separately, at long intervals, and where they show marked differences they were probably already different Mongolian subgroups when they started out from Asia.

The Negroes. A common error is to think of Negroes in Africa (or in the United States) as all of one racial stock. Actually, they are of many racial subgroups, with differences going back thousands of years and greater than are found among whites. Some of the most striking differences are those between the tall, spindly, 7-foot Watusis of East Africa, and the stocky pygmies of the Congo, while the Bushmen-Hottentots of South Africa are so different in many respects from other Negroids that some anthropologists believe they constitute a separate race. Other African Negroes, the Zulus (Bantus), Sudanese, etc., also have distinctive physical traits. Thus, since American Negroes, whose ancestors were taken from many parts of Africa, are mixtures of many Negroid strains, plus some amounts of Indian and white genes, they might be considered in the mass as a new Negro subrace, genetically different from all other Negro subraces.*

The Japanese. Although a subgroup of the Mongoloids, as
are also the Chinese, the Japanese are distinct in various racial
respects from other Mongols. One fact is their part-white
ancestry through the Ainus, a short, hairy, Caucasoid people who
may once have been quite prevalent from Russia to northern
Asia, and primitive remnants of whom still live in northern
Japanese islands. Also mixed in with the Japanese strain are
genes from various Pacific islanders.

EUROPEAN ETHNIC GROUPS. When peoples are distinguished from one another less by inherited factors than by
differences in culture, history, and nationality, they are referred
to as "ethnic" groups. "Ethnic" is often confused with "racial"
(as are environmental traits with hereditary traits), especially
when applied to European peoples. Thus, mistaken references are
often made to the Nordic, Baltic, Alpine, and Mediterranean
"races," when they actually are ethnic groups with few clear-cut
genetic differences among them. This is seen when we look into
the origins of Europeans and find they are all highly mixed
peoples, not at all "pure" whites, but having both Mongoloid
genes, brought in through early Hun and African invasions, and
also some of the mixtures that went into the principal, European
nationalities.

English. Ancient Celts, Romans (and mixed Mediterraneans

---

* The arbitrary classification of individuals as "Negro" or "white"—varying
widely within the United States and in other countries—is scientifically un-
sound and determined more by social policies than by genetic facts. In view
of the high degree of white admixture among American Negroes (about 70
per cent having some white ancestry, and on the average, 20 to 30 per cent
"white" genes), skin color or surface features alone may be no clear guide
as to what relative proportion of the racial genes an individual carries. Through
the random process of parental transmission, in the very same putatively Negro
family—as of mulattos—one child may be much darker-skinned but have
less pronounced Negroid features than another, and in neither case can one
tell what proportion of the thousands of other genes involved in the body's
construction and functioning are derived from Negro or white ancestry. The
dubiousness of racial classification was exemplified by a Louisiana state law
introduced in 1970 (to replace an existing law that defined a Negro as anyone
with "any traceable amount of Negro blood"), whereby a person would be
declared "white" only if he had "no more than one-thirty-second of Negro
blood," and would not be designated by any public official as "colored,"
"mulatto," "black," "Afro-American," or a "quadroon."

including North Africans), Anglo-Saxons, Danish Vikings, Normans, Germans.

Irish. Ancient Picts, ancient peoples from France, Denmark, the Rhine (Celts) and Spain; Scandinavians, Normans, etc.

Germans. Unknown primitive tribes, ancient Celts, Romans, Huns, Slavs, Franks and Saxons, Vikings, Huguenots.

Norwegians and Swedes. Early Germanic tribes (through Denmark), Finns, Teutons, Lapps.

French. North Africans, North Italians, Celts (Gauls), Romans, Germanic tribes, Huns, Norsemen, English.

Italians. Ancient Sabines, Phoenicians, Etruscans, Greeks, Gauls, Goths, Lombards, Normans, German-Swabians, French.

Spanish. Iberians (from North Africa), Celts, Greeks, Carthaginians, Romans (Visigoths), Germanic peoples, Moors.

Russians. Finns, early Germanic tribes, Huns, Slavs, Turk-Tartaric peoples, Tartars, Vikings, Germans.

Hungarians. Celts, Romans, Vandals, Germanic Lombards and Goths, Huns and Avars, Slavs, Italians, French, Germans, Tartars, Turks.

KITHS. Some anthropologists believe this term may be applied to certain large groups of humans who are a sort of cross between "ethnic" and "racial"; that is, while originally of mixed stocks, they have held together for a long enough time, like large family groups, to develop various average hereditary similarities as well as common religious and cultural traits. Thus, the Jews, Irish, Scotch, and Rumanians are considered examples of kiths.

The Jews. That the Jews definitely do not constitute a racial group, but can be described more as a kith, is clearly shown by those collected in Israel today. The marked differences in physical appearance, features, and coloring among the various groups—Yemenite, Moroccan, Polish, Russian, Rumanian, German, Spanish, Italian, Syrian, English, and American Jews—not only reflect the different countries and environments from which they came, but also are proof that they are *genetically* different in various ways. Explaining this is the fact that continually through their wanderings they have absorbed genes of other peoples among whom they have lived (through converts to their religion, intermarriages, sometimes rape of their women, etc.). It is true that on the average some genetic characteristics are more common among Jews than non-Jews—including (as noted in Chapters 13, 15, and 17) Bloom's syndrome, dysautonomia, and Tay-Sachs disease. But in any Jewish population a very large proportion of the individuals can in no sense be identified as "Jewish" by any physical traits, and this proportion is growing, especially in new generations of Jews in the United States and other countries, as their training and living conditions become like those of other groups. (Supposed distinguishing features of Americans of Irish, Scotch, and other "kiths" are also becoming less and less marked in the newer generations.) Even in Israel visitors are struck by the fact that so many of the younger, native-born Jews ("Sabras"), reared and working in the Israeli farming communities, look so "non-Jewish" by former stereotyped ideas.

REASONS FOR RACE DIFFERENCES. As previously indicated, many of the main differences among races in coloring, features and even body types may well have evolved because they served some useful purpose in their original environments. As with lower animals, in early human history it may have been a matter of life and death whether individuals and groups had this or that type of physical equipment to cope with existing conditions. (Even in the United States today many people move from North to South, or vice versa, or from some other region to another, because they "can't stand the climate" where they are.) Thus, it is not mere coincidence that the darkest-skinned, blackest-eyed peoples arose and were long concentrated in the hottest climates (and for the most part still live there), while the lightest-skinned and lightest-eyed peoples developed and live in the more temperate regions. Although great improvements in housing, heating, refrigeration, clothing, and drugs, and in industrial devices have reduced the early importance of inherited race differences in various environments, they still have their usefulness, or may prove to be more useful than we have believed. Here are some recent scientific findings on these points:

Coloring. Negroes (and dark-skinned whites, such as those in India, the Arab countries, and North Africa) are best protected against the hot (ultraviolet) rays of the sun because of the heavier underlying deposit of melanin pigment particles in their skins. (Chapter 8.) Moreover, Negroes with the heaviest pigmentation have been found less likely than whites to develop skin cancer in the tropics; also, because Negro skin has an extra outer protecting layer, it is more resistant to germs and infections in hot, damp tropical climates, and to scratches in the jungles. Whites, on the other hand, have an advantage in cooler climates because their more lightly pigmented skins permit a maximum of the beneficial vitamin D irradiation from the sun. (The in-between, yellow-brown skin of the Mongolians or bronzed skin of American Indians may also offer some advantages in their native environments, but this has not been established.) Again, the heavily pigmented Negro eyes, with added pigment inside the retina and in the eyelids, are better adapted than white eyes to the glaring tropics.

Structural Details. The broader nostrils of the Negroes may permit better breathing in hot, moist climates, whereas in cool regions the smaller, narrower white nostrils are better adapted to warming up cold air before it enters the lungs. The Eskimos, it may be noted, have among the narrowest of noses. But also, some authorities believe, Eskimos have been aided in adapting to arctic cold by their fatty eyelids and underlayers of other facial as well as body fat, and by their stocky figures and stubby limbs and hands which do not permit as much heat evaporation as do long, thin parts. Contrariwise, the spindly legs, long, thin hands, and lanky figures of many Negroes are better adapted to heat evapo-ration in hot climates. In the matter of leg structure, some author-ities believe that the particular formation and musculature of the legs of some strains of Negroes may be assets in running ability, and may partly explain the upsurge of Negro champions in track and racing events, once they have had the chance to train and compete. It is also possible that the tightly curled or kinky Negroid hair may permit better scalp ventilation in the tropics.

Uncertain Factors. In addition to the race differences men-tioned there are others, some brought to light only recently (such as the blood types), whose usefulness or "adaptive" value remains uncertain or unknown. The Mongolian skin fold at the eye corner, some authorities believe, may help in protecting the eyes from the glare of the sun (or, with Eskimos, from ice and snow glare) by narrowing the slits through which the eyes are exposed. However, no good guesses have been made as to why Mongolians have such scant facial and body hair, or thick, black straight hair. Or why Negroes have thick lips. Or, among whites, what practical advantage or disadvantage there may be in straight hair, or wavy or curly, or brown, red, or blond hair. Or why women of some racial groups have much larger breasts, or different breast shapes, or more heavily padded buttocks, than others. Or why head shapes differ on the average among races. Many of these differences may be merely the results of nature's decorative whims, unrelated to usefulness; or they may prove to have once had practical value, in given environments, or to be related to some internal chemical or functional traits that still have meaning.

BLOOD-TYPE DIFFERENCES. Just as individuals and families differ in their blood types (*A*, *B*, *O*, or the Rh groups, or *M-N* types, discussed in Chapter 16), there are blood-type differences—though only in *average* incidences—among racial and ethnic groups. These differences have nothing to do with blood "quality" or "strength," but are of interest to anthropologists because of the clues they offer in tracing the origins and relationships of racial and ethnic groups, and may also be useful legally in disputed paternity cases. The layman, however, can be only mildly interested in such facts as that the blood type *O* occurs in about 35 to 45 per cent of European whites, 30 per cent among Asian Mongoloids, and 30 to 60 per cent among African Negroes (depending on regions), but is found in almost 100 per cent of most "pure" American Indian tribes; or that blood type *B* is most common in Asians (25 to 35 per cent), and ranges among Europeans from as low as 5 per cent in the Spaniards (but only 1 per cent in the Basques) and 7 per cent in the English to 23 per cent in the Russians; or that type *A* blood occurs in about 30 to 45 per cent of the Europeans, 25 to 30 per cent in Asian Mongoloids, and 20 to 25 per cent in African Negroes; or that the *M* and *N* types, or various subtypes of the main blood groups, have such and such incidences. More important to laymen are the *Rh* differences, where the 15 per cent incidence of Rh negative in whites, the 8 per cent in Negroes, and the almost total absence in Mongoloid peoples significantly affect the degrees of Rh disease threats to their offspring.

DISEASE DIFFERENCES IN RACES AND ETHNIC GROUPS. Because living conditions, diets, hygiene, and other factors may vary greatly among human groups, it is often hard to tell what part heredity may play in the different incidences of the major diseases (heart, cancer, diabetes, kidney ailments, etc.) among the world's peoples. We mentioned this with respect to Americans of different stocks (Chapter 19). However, in many less common inherited diseases the incidences are significantly different among racial and ethnic groups. Examples (cited in previous chapters) are sickle-cell disease, predominantly in Negroes, Cooley's anemia, predominantly in whites, and pernicious anemia, more common in whites than in other racial groups; primaquine sensitivity in Negroes and, favism in whites (Chapter 18); and color blindness, with an incidence of 8 per cent in whites, 3 per cent in Negroes. Other diseases and abnormalities with different racial distribution are Mongolian idiocy, harelip, and cleft spine, more frequent in whites than in Negroes; phenylketonuria (PKU), seldom found in Negroes; and extra fingers, occurring six times as often in Negro as in white babies. Within races, also, given ethnic groups or their subdivisions show differences in certain rare diseases and abnormalities which have probably arisen through unusual mutations in comparatively recent times. But on the whole, virtually all types of inherited diseases and defects are found among all racial and ethnic groups, and where conditions are approximately the same, most of their hereditary afflictions appear in much the same proportions.

Miscellaneous Race Differences. *Milk intolerance*—the inability to digest milk properly after early childhood, apparently because of an inherited lactase deficiency—occurs in a large proportion of Negroes and in many Mongoloid peoples, but much less frequently in whites. The *inability to taste* the PTC chemical (Chapter 15, p. 124) is rare among Negroes (2 to 4 per cent), less rare among Chinese (6 to 10 per cent), and common among whites (30 to 40 per cent). In *fingerprints,* racial differences have been reported in the relative proportions of whorls, loops, and arches. Reproductive differences exist too, Negro infants at birth weighing significantly less, on the average, than white infants, with those listed as premature (on the basis of weights under 5½ pounds) being 14 per cent among Negroes, about twice the white percentage. The lower *sex ratio at birth* of Negroes as compared with whites was discussed in Chapter 4, p. 31, and the racial differences in *twinning incidences* were discussed in Chapter 5.

Conclusions.   Looking at inherited physical traits as a whole, the racial or ethnic differences among human beings are extremely small, and what is most remarkable is that despite many centuries, or even thousands of years of living largely apart under disparate conditions in varied environments, human beings the world over are so much the same in all major physical respects.

28

The Human Races,
II: Qualities

RACIAL QUALITIES. Of all the facts dealt with in this book, what many persons may find hardest to accept is this: No race, ethnic group, or nationality (and specifically, their own) can be proved *better by heredity* in character or quality than any other. This statement strikes at deep-rooted conceits and prejudices which have caused countless bloody conflicts, which have brought death or suffering to untold millions of people, and which have been used to justify the enslavement or subjugation of some groups by other groups—not only in the past but in our own time, and at this moment. Fortunately, there is a growing realization that if mankind is to have a happier and more peaceful future, the peoples of the world must root out their old racial biases and adjust to the truths about themselves which science has been revealing. The most important of these truths we will try to present here.

Racial Stereotypes. The term "stereotype" is applied to particular traits of temperament popularly associated with specific racial or ethnic groups: English, "cool, reserved"; Germans, "militaristic," "systematic"; Latins, "excitable"; Irish, "pugnacious"; Swedes, "stolid"; Negroes, "childlike, uninhibited"; Chinese, "inscrutable"; Japanese, "sly"; etc. Whatever limited truth there may be in these stereotypes in any general sense, it is certain that they do not apply to a great many individuals of each racial group and in all probability have no hereditary basis. On the contrary, there is every likelihood that these group traits are purely the products of environment, habits, and training. This is clearly indicated in the United States by the fact that in a comparatively short time descendants of all races and nationalities have shed most of their supposed ancestral traits and taken on common characteristics of personality and temperament which peoples of other countries quickly identify as "American." (A significant story in reverse, of how an American reared from babyhood until age twenty among Chinese in China developed many characteristic "Chinese" traits, is told in the author's book *Your Heredity and Environment*, pp. 624 to 625.)

RACIAL CAPACITIES. The question of whether there are racial differences in thinking ability and in capacities for tasks of different kinds cannot be answered precisely, first, because environments are and have been so different among the world's peoples; and, second (as noted in Chapter 20), there are as yet no scientific tests by which any *inherited* racial differences in mental capacities could be accurately determined. Theoretically, certain types and degrees of "achievement" genes may have been and may even now be concentrated more heavily in one racial group than another. But the belief that any racial group is unique with respect to the genes making for talent, skill, or achievement in any particular field as a whole is refuted by history, past and present. As with other human behavioral traits we have dealt with, a basic fallacy has always been to confuse *performance*—what given peoples have or have not done, or are or are not doing—with *capacity*—what they are capable of doing.

Physical Achievements. One of the clearest examples of the distinction between racial *performance* and *capacity* has been provided by Negro records in American *sports*. Until a few decades ago, Negro athletes were almost completely absent from all professional sports except prizefighting (where it was thought that their more "animal" nature enabled them to excel), and only a relative handful were found on college varsity teams. In professional baseball, Negroes were relegated to the minor leagues of their own, and their total absence from the big leagues was taken as evidence that they somehow lacked the capacity for top professional competition. That notion was completely shattered once the barriers against Negro players were lowered in the big leagues (with the admission of Jackie Robinson in 1947), and in an amazingly short time Negro athletes began starring not only in baseball, but in professional football and basketball, far beyond their proportion in the population. Similarly, as opportunities increased for Negroes to enter colleges and be trained for varsity athletics, they swept to the top in almost every sport, particularly in track, in which they now dominate many of the events and have become mainstays of American Olympic teams. Although the theory has been offered that Negro body build, musculature, and special reactive capacities may have something to do with their athletic prowess, it is unquestionably the environmental change that has so suddenly moved them from the limbo of the sports world into brilliant eminence.

Cultural Achievements. As with sports, it may be hazardous to draw conclusions about the *inherent* abilities of different racial and ethnic groups on the basis of their accomplishments and state of advancement at any given time. During the thousands of years of man's cultural evolution, there has been virtually no racial group which at one time or another has not contributed greatly to progress in invention, industry, art, religion, science, social organization, and other fields. Changing places at the head of the historical procession of conquerors and cultural leaders have been Semites, Mongols, Egyptians, Greeks, Romans, Turks, and so on. And repeatedly, those out in front at one period fell behind later, and peoples who had long been backward or stagnant suddenly forged ahead of others. As recent examples, scarcely a century ago the Japanese, who had been living for many centuries in the most rudimentary technological stage, were considered to be technically incompetent; but once they set themselves to it, in a matter of decades they have become industrial and technological giants. The Russians as a people prior to World War II had a reputation of ineptness in the handling of sophisticated machinery—and then came their launching of the sputnik—the first space vehicle. The Jews, dispersed for almost two thousand years, were believed to be a non-fighting people—until they came together in their state of Israel. As for the black peoples of Africa, the fact is often overlooked that they had among them—and still have—highly organized political and social systems, had created intricate and beautiful works of art, and had devised various important technological processes, far back at a time when many European peoples were much less advanced. (Note also that much of the inspiration for modern art, dance, and music has been drawn from African peoples.)

The "Backwardness" of Black Africans. Whatever capacities they may once have manifested, a persistent question is why the African blacks stayed where they were and so far behind European and Oriental peoples in the march of progress. An answer could be that they were so distant and separated from the main path along which human cultural development had been proceeding—starting in Mesopotamia about eight thousand years ago, then spreading out slowly to contiguous areas, and not reaching the British and other peoples of northern Europe until the Romans came to them thousands of years later, in 55 B.C. (Cicero wrote to his friend Atticus shortly after that date, with the advice not to buy any Britons as slaves "because they are so utterly stupid and incapable of learning.") During all that long period the cultural advance was kept from penetrating to the African blacks by barriers of desert and jungles, and when the "enlightened" peoples finally did come a few hundred years ago, it was only to subjugate or enslave them and to stifle their opportunities for advancement. The equalization of environmental conditions, education, and opportunities for the black peoples is still far off, and only when it is achieved can any judgment be made as to their inherent capacities. What has been said of them can also apply to other present or recent primitive or backward peoples everywhere in the world—from the Eskimos to the South Sea islanders—many of whom have been proving that given the proper training they can brush aside supposed inborn shortcomings and quickly master complex technical know-how. (See also discussions of race differences in intelligence, Chapter 20; in musicality, Chapter 21; in crime, Chapter 25.)

RACIAL "SUPERIORITY" AND PREJUDICES. Not only the belief that one racial group is by *inheritance* "superior" in capacities and character to others, but race prejudice itself, dates back actually no more than a century or two. Among ancient peoples there was no such race consciousness or prejudice. Kings would marry princesses of any other races, and Caesar hardly felt superior to Cleopatra, nor Solomon to the dark Queen of Sheba. Divisions among ancient peoples were tribal or political rather than racial. For instance, the Biblical Hebrews thought of themselves as a "chosen people" mainly in the cultural and religious sense, and did not regard alien peoples as biologically inferior, nor ban intermarriage with those of other racial stocks who adopted their religion. Nor is there any evidence of any inborn or "instinctive" antagonism between racial groups. On the contrary, science has shown that people have to be *taught* to hate and look down on persons of other races, and that without this training white children, for instance, would no more shun black or yellow children than white birds, cats, or dogs shun those of other colors. As it happens, racial antagonism in recent times has stemmed mainly from whites. When African Negroes and American Indians first met whites they were very friendly; even today, "race prejudices" refer chiefly to the attitudes of whites toward those of other races. (See also "War" in Chapter 25.)

The Hitlerian Hysteria. An astounding and appalling fact is that at a time when myths about race had been exploded by modern science, racial fanaticism reached its most dreadful extreme in one of the presumably most advanced countries, Germany. Millions of people died, and millions more suffered horribly, before Hitler's reign of terror ended. That this was due purely to a "psychological sickness" in a warped environment is clear today, for there is no question that the German people are not *by heredity* any more cruel, militaristic, or intolerant than others. (Chapter 25.) But unfortunately it is not all past history, because the poisons of racial prejudice engendered by the Nazis have by no means been eradicated, and their false concepts continue to do harm.

Nazi Racial Theories. We have already shown that the basic Nazi ideas—that the Germans constituted a "race" of "superior blood"—were scientifically preposterous, since the Germans were (to cite three of their own top anthropologists, Baur, Fischer, and Lenz) no more than a "mishmash" or compound of many racial strains. (Chapter 27.) But also, the terms "Aryan," used by the Nazis to describe their "race," and "non-Aryan," to describe Jews and others, actually had no racial meaning, having been coined by scientists for the classification of large groups of *languages*. Thus, Aryan takes in not only many European languages, but also the Veddah tongue spoken by primitives in Ceylon. Likewise, non-Aryan refers to various other languages, including Arabic and Hebrew. But European Jews, who were the principal Nazi victims, were almost entirely Aryan in their language, since the overwhelming majority spoke not Hebrew but Yiddish—compounded of various European languages, mainly with an old German, and therefore Aryan, base—as well as the language of the country in which they lived. The Nazi racial doctrine reached its silliest stage when Nazi scientists obligingly proclaimed their allies, the Japanese, as also Aryans.

RACE MIXING. The strong feelings on this subject have been due to several beliefs. One, which we have just shown to be highly questionable, is that a given racial group is "superior" to another and will deteriorate if genes from an "inferior" racial group are mixed in with it. Second, if races are kept "pure," they will each be more outstanding in particular ways (presumably as pure breeds of cattle, horses, or dogs are each better for their particular purposes). But, again, we have seen that no human racial groups are pure, or ever have been or could be bred for purity the way domesticated animals have been. If at a given time any human group was or is superior in any respect, one could as easily ascribe this to their having been not pure but mixed, as in the case of Americans, one of the least racially pure and most genetically mixed nationalities the world has seen. The third is an old belief that crossbreeding between different human racial strains may result in misshapen offspring. But this also is contradicted by the many fine-looking mulattoes in the United States and South America (including some of the most beautiful actresses) and by handsome crossbreeds of many racial strains in Hawaii and elsewhere.

Hybrid Vigor. Opposite to the anticrossbreeding theories is the one that crossing different strains may produce hybrid offspring with greater vigor and other advantages. Livestock and plant breeders have long employed this principle to advantage in combining desirable genes from two different stocks. In early human evolution the same principle might have been effective, but with respect to the present situation we can only make these deductions as to when and how crossing between genetically different groups might be beneficial: (1) if a highly desirable trait (better physique, more efficient internal organs, a special talent, etc.) could be produced by a combination of genes only some of which were carried by one racial group and the rest by another, so that crossbreeding could bring the needed genes together; or (2) if one group had some hereditary weaknesses and the other group carried "gene antidotes" for it. However, in the matter of race-crossing (or intermarriage) we are confining ourselves here only to the genetic aspects. The question of whether these matings are socially desirable when they might lead to family and group conflicts, or personal maladjustment, is outside the field of this book.

Negro-White Mixing. Although many assume that Negro-white mixing has been highest in recent generations, the most race mixing actually took place in the Colonial days and up to the end of the Civil War. Moreover, where the earlier flow was of white genes into the Negro population, there has since been a considerable backflow of these white genes, plus some Negro genes, into the white population, by way of persons of mixed ancestry who could "pass." No accurate figures are available, but estimates (highly uncertain) are that perhaps two million persons of part-Negro descent are now in our white population, and that fifteen thousand or more go over to the white side each year. Since the genes for lighter skin and the less Negroid features are the ones being carried out of the Negro population, this should act to make American Negroes as a group darker and more Negroid, instead of less so, and to keep them racially distinct from the whites for a long time to come. At present it is estimated that the American Negro population has from 20 to 25 per cent white genes. In addition, it may carry a small percentage of American Indian genes—probably much less than 1 per cent. However, in the case of any *individual* classed as a Negro in the United States, by varying standards and where the degree of admixture is unknown, it would be impossible to say precisely what percentages of Negro and white genes he or she carries. Altogether, geneticists would strongly question both the social and legal definitions of Negro as currently applied to individuals in the United States and other countries. (See also "Racial Ancestry" in the next chapter.)

29

Ancestors
and Relatives

BLOOD KINSHIP. The term "blood" is merely a symbol with respect to the relationship of one person to another, since blood itself carries no hereditary factors. No one inherits anyone else's blood. As noted in Chapter 2, not even the mother's blood passes on directly to the child she carries, her blood being broken down into its elements before reaching the fetus. From the beginning the developing baby manufactures his own blood, and often his blood may differ even in hereditary type (A, B, O, Rh, etc.) from that of the mother. (Chapter 16.) Thus, sayings such as "The child carries my blood," or "Noble blood flows in his veins," or "He has common blood," are without meaning so far as heredity goes. Equally wrong is the assumption that a person's blood carries any traits of character, as when one speaks of "impetuous blood," "tainted blood," "honest blood," etc. The process of heredity, it must always be kept in mind, is solely and entirely one of passing on and receiving chromosomes and their genes.

Ancestral Relationships. Everything any person can inherit from an ancestor must be in the chromosomes received from each parent. No trait of itself can "skip over" from an ancestor to a descendant. Only chromosomes can be passed along, and these may or may not be the ones carrying the genes which can reproduce the trait of some ancestor. How much of a person's heredity stems from any given ancestor depends entirely on how many of the genes of that ancestor he received at conception. The further back the ancestor, the fewer of his or her genes a person is likely to have received, to the point where one may have virtually no hereditary link with a remote ancestor, regardless of what the "family tree" might show.

Estimating Hereditary Relationships. The only thing about

Ancestry Theories: Old and New

"BLOOD" THEORY
(wrong)

"JIGSAW" THEORY
(wrong)

**"CHROMOSOME"
THEORY**
(right)

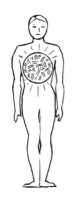

"A person is a mixture of the blood of all of his ancestors. No matter how far back an ancestor, some of his blood flows in one's veins."

"A person's ancestry consists of so many parts of this or that: For example, one-eighth Irish, one-eighth Scotch, one-sixteenth Italian."

"A person's ancestry consists solely of how many chromosomes of different ancestors he carries. If no chromosome came from an ancestor, there is no hereditary link with him."

one's heredity of which one can be certain is that exactly half of one's chromosomes came from each parent—twenty-three from the father and twenty-three from the mother. Tracing farther back, the number of chromosomes from any given ancestor can only be guessed. For, as explained in Chapter 3, each set of twenty-three chromosomes contributed to a child by a parent may be any one of millions of different combinations of the chromosomes from that parent's parents. Theoretically the twenty-three chromosomes received from one's father should include eleven or twelve from his father (one's paternal grandfather) and eleven or twelve from his mother (one's paternal grandmother). But actually, any number over half or less than half might have come from either grandparent. For example, among the twenty-three chromosomes received from one's father there might be, not eleven or twelve, but fifteen or sixteen of his father's, and only eight or nine of his mother's. Similarly, one might receive proportionately more chromosomes of one's maternal grandfather than of one's maternal grandmother, or vice versa. In extreme cases a person could conceivably have received not more than two or three of a given grandparent's chromosomes, which means that actual hereditary linkage with earlier ancestors on that side of the family might almost be broken off at that point. All we can go by, therefore, are these *average* possibilities of the number of chromosomes of each ancestor one may be carrying:

Grandparents: Avg. of ¼, or 11 to 12 chromosomes from each

Great-grandparents: Avg. of ⅛, or 5 to 6 chromosomes from each

Grt.grt.   "   : Avg. of 1/16, or 2 to 3 chromosomes from each

Grt.grt.grt.   "   : Avg. of 1/32—either 1 or 2 chromosomes from each

REMOTE ANCESTORS. Once one goes more than five generations back—beyond a great-great-great-grandparent—the chances become less and less of having a *full* chromosome of a given ancestor. Thus, in the case of a claimed ancestor six or seven generations back (such as, for Americans today, a Revolutionary War hero) the odds could be five to one against having received a full one of his chromosomes. For an ancestor of the early seventeenth century, such as a Pilgrim, the odds might be about forty to one against carrying a full one of his or her chromosomes. We speak of a "full" chromosome because *parts* of chromosomes might also be passed along. This involves a complex genetic process called "chromosome crossover," whereby every so often when sperms or eggs are formed in parents, and two chromosomes of a pair twist around one another, matching sections may be exchanged, or "cross over," when the chromosomes break apart. Such exchanges of parts of chromosomes over generations increase the chance that a person will have received at least a few of the genes of a distant ancestor. (See also the section following.)

The Crossover Process

How one can inherit part of a chromosome

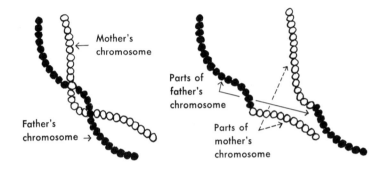

During the egg-forming or sperm-forming process, the paired chromosomes from the two parents may twist around one another.

In breaking loose, matching sections of the two chromosomes may be exchanged, so the new chromosomes formed thereafter have parts from different ancestors.

Increased Chances of Descent. When in any lineage there have been marriages between persons with the same ancestor, the chances of a descendant having received chromosomes of that ancestor are increased. For instance, if one's parents had an ancestor in common, this would double the chance of one's having received some of that ancestor's chromosomes. The more marriages between relatives there were along the lines of descent in a family, the more closely those coming later in the lineage would be linked to earlier ancestors. Thus, present-day members of the much-intermarried European royal families (such as children of Britain's Queen Elizabeth and her husband, Prince Philip, both descendants of Queen Victoria), have much closer ties to remote ancestors than have persons in general. This also applies, in a more limited degree, to descendants of any nonroyal close-knit groups among which marriages between near relatives were formerly common. (Colonial Americans, and members of many small communities in Europe, were among these.) Going back far enough into any lineage, of course, there must have been many marriages between relatives, for otherwise the number of anyone's potential ancestors—doubling with each generation back—would eventually reach astronomical and impossible proportions. Thus, it is estimated that all persons of English descent are at least thirtieth cousins, that there is fully as close a relationship within most other European stocks, and that with some smaller groups, such as the Swiss, Swedes, Danes, Dutch, Scotch, Irish, German Jews, etc., the cousin relationship for almost all may be no less than the twentieth degree.

Distinguished Ancestry. People who boast of descent from some famous remote ancestor usually overlook a number of the points we have stressed: (1) They ignore almost all the many other unknown ancestors who lived at the same time as the famous one and who contributed equally to their heritage; (2) they may have received not a single one of the noted ancestor's chromosomes (or only a small part of one), and thus have virtually no hereditary link with him; (3) if they did get some of the ancestor's genes, these may not at all have been those which helped produce his admirable qualities, but may as easily have been his worst ones; (4) traits such as high intelligence, courage, or unusual talent of any kind are so complex that it would be impossible for any combination of genes producing them to be passed along intact from a given ancestor—perhaps not even from a grandparent. The situation might be different for persons who have not one or two but many distinguished and worthy ancestors, and in whose family line for successive generations up to the present there were marriages between persons of unusual character and ability. In such cases the descendants might have well above average chances of carrying superior genes. (See Chapter 21.) But rarely do superior marriages or superior offspring continue for too long in any one family line. No human families ever have been or could be bred as were domestic animals—horses, dogs, cattle, poultry—with thoroughbred strains being produced by mating mothers to sons, fathers to daughters, or brothers to sisters, and selecting only those with the particular traits desired and discarding the rest. Because human beings have always mated any which way, there is no family that can consider itself as genetically anything but a "mongrel" mixture, with most of its genes unknown. In any individual case, human superiority or uniqueness rests not in one's claim to distinguished ancestry but only in what one can prove himself to be in character and achievement.

Inferior Ancestry: Jukes and Kallikaks. The many past misconceptions about superior ancestry were accompanied by equal misconceptions about inferior ancestry. In most countries certain family groups were held up (or still are) as horrible examples of inferior heredity. Most often cited in the United States were the Jukes, first brought to public attention in 1874, and the Kallikaks, publicized in 1912. Both families were reported as abounding in mentally defective, insane, alcoholic, degenerate, criminal, immoral, shiftless, and undesirable individuals of every kind—which was blamed almost entirely on their presumed "inferior" and "tainted" heredity, in turn attributed mainly to a few degenerate ancestors four or five generations back. Modern science sees the facts in a different light. What appears probable is that (1) the case histories of these families were considerably exaggerated and misinterpreted, since present-day techniques of making such studies were not then available, and (2) many of the traits blamed on inferior heredity were actually the result of *inferior environment.* This is not to say that the Jukes and Kallikaks may not have been more than ordinarily defective, or to deny that in some family groups genes for certain types of defects and abnormalities may collect and be passed on in above-average proportions, just as in other family groups superior genes may be more prevalent. But as noted in previous chapters, we are still far from knowing what part, if any, heredity plays in such traits as alcoholism, criminality, immorality, or degeneracy, and if these traits are concentrated in certain families, we may have to assume —unless proved otherwise—that this is mostly because of the bad environment running in these families. (For a detailed discussion of the Kallikak study see the author's article, "The Kallikaks After Thirty Years," *Journal of Heredity,* September, 1944.)

Racial Ancestry. One frequently hears a person say, "I'm one-fourth Irish," or "I'm one-thirty-second American Indian." In Nazi Germany many people were persecuted or exterminated because they were "one-eighth" Jewish. And in some parts of the United States the fact that a person is labeled "one-sixteenth" Negro, or less, is sufficient to bar him from white society and privileges. All such references to a person being precisely this or that fraction of a given ethnic group or race have little meaning genetically. The actual hereditary relationship of a person of mixed racial or ethnic descent to any of his ancestral groups depends entirely on the number of chromosomes of that group he carries, and it is impossible to do more than guess about this. For example, if a mulatto (half Negro), married a pure white person, all their children would be considered, technically, "one-fourth" Negro. Each child having one and the same Negro grandparent would, on the average, be assumed to carry eleven or twelve Negro chromosomes. But actually (as explained in a previous section) any given one-fourth Negro child could be carrying any proportion of the Negro grandparent's chromosomes. One child might be carrying many more than twelve, a brother or sister far fewer—to the point of having only one or two Negro chromosomes. Again it would be possible for a person who is technically one-sixteenth Negro to be carrying more Negro chromosomes than one who is technically one-eighth or even one-fourth Negro. Nor can anyone tell from a person's features, or from any known test, how many or how few Negro genes he is carrying. The genes that determine surface appearance are only a very small part of the total genes in a person, and these feature genes may work independently of most other genes. Thus, among offspring of mulattoes, a child who looks most Negroid might actually be carrying fewer Negro genes than a child who looks most white. All these facts apply equally to a person who had a grandparent, or other ancestor of any given racial or ethnic group—Chinese, Japanese, Indian or French, Irish, Jewish, etc.

RELATIVES: LEGAL AND HEREDITARY. Many of the facts about genetic relationships to ancestors apply to other kin— brothers and sisters, aunts and uncles, cousins, etc. The hereditary relationship between any relatives, as with ancestors, depends entirely on how many of their chromosomes are the same, which can only be guessed at in terms of averages. The exceptions, other than parents (with each of whom one has twenty-three chromosomes in common), are identical twins, who provide our first example of legal and genetic differences with respect to relatives.

Identical Twins and Other Siblings. The law makes no

distinction between (1) identical twins or (2) fraternal twins or (3) ordinary brothers or sisters. Yet in the first case there is a definite 100 per cent hereditary relationship—all the forty-six chromosomes in identical twins being the same—whereas in the other cases there is only an uncertain 50 per cent relationship. That is to say, nonidentical children in a family may be carrying any combination of twenty-three chromosomes from each parent; and although on the average half of these may be the same in any two of these children, it is possible that the proportion may be more or less than half. Thus, of several children in a family, two might have, not twenty-three, but thirty, thirty-two, or more chromosomes in common, and be genetically much closer than either of them is to another child, who might have only eighteen, sixteen, or fewer of the same chromosomes. Moreover, the degree of genetic relationship between any two children of the same parents cannot be proved merely by their similarity in surface traits, because genes in only a few of the chromosomes may be involved in producing these, and it is possible that two children who look less alike may be sharing more of the other chromosomes. In time geneticists believe, or hope, that there will be ways of knowing how many and which chromosomes of given parents the children are carrying.

The Sex-Chromosome Relationship Factor. Certain slight (but sometimes important) differences in the genetic relationships of parents and children, brothers and sisters, result from the way the X and Y sex chromosomes are passed along. For instance, in quantity of genes, a son is at least 5 per cent more related to his mother than to his father. Reason: Even though of the twenty-three chromosomes a son receives from each parent, twenty-two are the same in the number of genes they carry, the additional X chromosome from his mother has many more genes than the small Y from his father—enough to bring the total genes from the mother to at least 5 per cent over those from the father. (This accounts for the many sex-linked diseases and defects which sons inherit solely through their mothers. (See Chapter 11.) Daughters, since they receive an X chromosome from each parent, have genetically an exactly equal relationship to each.

Uncles, Aunts, Cousins, Nephews, Nieces, Grandchildren.

The general facts about chromosome relationships given for grand-parents and ancestors apply to all other relatives. One can make only an estimate in terms of *averages*, as follows:

UNCLE
AUNT
NEPHEW
NIECE
GRANDCHILD
} Each is a one-fourth relative, with the average possibility of carrying replicas of eleven or twelve of your chromosomes. Your uncle, for instance, if he is your father's brother, has an average of half of his chromosomes in common with your father, and since you have half your father's chromosomes, one half by one half = one fourth. The genetic relationship is the same to a grandparent (discussed on p. 258), to any blood-related aunt, and to a nephew, niece, or grandchild of yours.

FIRST COUSIN
GREAT-UNCLE
GREAT-AUNT
GREAT-NEPHEW
GREAT-NIECE
GREAT-GRANDCHILD
} Each is a one-eighth relative, with the average possibility of carrying replicas of six of one's forty-six chromosomes. (Further discussions about cousins in the next chapter.)

SECOND COUSINS
GREAT-GREAT:
UNCLE, AUNT,
NEPHEW, NIECE
} Each is a one-sixteenth relative with the average possibility of carrying replicas of three of one's forty-six chromosomes.

DISPUTED PARENTAGE CASES. The use of blood tests in many courts in the United States and Europe has already made it possible to clear more than half the men wrongly accused of fathering a child. The tests are even more effective in "inter-changed baby" cases, actual or alleged, when two sets of parents claim the same baby as their own. All these parentage tests follow the same principle: establishing the baby's inherited blood types in the different systems—A, B, O, Rh, M-N-S, etc.—and then find-ing out whether the man accused of being the father, or the couple claiming parentage, could have contributed these inherited factors. (See Chapter 18, Blood Types and Conditions.) The tests *cannot prove* that a given man is the father of a given child, or that a particular couple are its parents, because there may be many other persons in the population with the required blood types. But the tests can rule out a man as the possible father, or a couple as the possible parents, if they show that he or they do not have one or another of the blood types needed for the child to be his or theirs.

Exclusion Examples. (1) A child's blood is O and a man's blood is AB. The man *cannot* be the child's father. (2) If the man does have O blood, a second test might follow, with the MN types: should the baby have the M type, and the man the N type, this would exclude him. (3) If the man does have blood-type M, the tests would go on to the Rh series, and again there might be a chance that the man did not carry the particular Rh gene that would have had to be transmitted by the child's father. Tests of the mother's blood are necessary to give the most complete results. For instance, if a baby's blood is AB, a man with A blood could have been the father. But if the mother's blood is also A, then the father must have been the one who gave the child the B gene, so the A man would be ruled out. Altogether, with the principal blood tests employed today (A, B, O, Rh, and the M-N series), a man wrongly accused of parentage has about a 55 per cent chance of being cleared. This, however, is the average chance for a mixed American population, in which divergent proportions of the blood groups and blood types are represented. In a community or group here or abroad where most persons are of closely similar stock, and with small differences in blood types, the chance of parentage exclusion of any man would be greatly reduced. On the other hand, if a man has blood types that are infrequent in a given community or group, his chance of exclusion if wrongly accused of paternity might be very high. (See also Chapter 27, under "Blood-Type Differences.")

Changelings. Despite the many precautions taken by hospitals today, there are some rare instances of babies being given to the wrong parents. Since two babies and two sets of parents are involved, blood tests usually can establish whether there has been any interchange. In addition, footprints, handprints, and other traits of parents and children in which heredity plays a part can help to make the proof conclusive. (See also next section.)

Feature Clues in Parentage Cases. Occasionally rare inherited physical traits in a child may provide a means of proving or disproving someone's parentage. If a child has any unusual *dominant* surface trait listed in previous chapters (Hapsburg jaw, drooping eyelids, any of various hand abnormalities, etc.) and the mother does not have this trait, its presence or absence in a man accused of paternity might be significant. In some cases, also, certain features or coloring, if their inheritance is clear-cut, might carry weight with respect to parentage. Obviously, if a baby has black hair, dusky skin, and jet-black eyes, and the mother is a fair-skinned blue-eyed blond, a man who is also fair, light-haired, and blue-eyed is hardly likely to be the child's father. However, one must be extremely cautious about forming judgments or suspicions regarding parentage on the basis of a few surface traits. Many hereditary traits do not show themselves or become set until late in childhood, or in the mature years, and thus have no value if decisions must be made regarding an infant's parentage. Further, the mere resemblance or lack of resemblance between a person and a given infant need not offer proof or disproof of parentage, since a child may sometimes be quite unlike either of its true parents in coloring and other feature details. (Chapter 6.) But taken altogether, a number of inherited feature traits could have a bearing on parentage cases where the blood tests are inconclusive.

30

Parenthood
Problems

APPLIED GENETICS. Interesting as the subject of human genetics may be, its main importance lies in the practical contributions it can make to human welfare and happiness. True, the application of genetic principles has led to vast improvements in plant and animal breeding, with better quality and increased production of grains, fruits, vegetables, beef, poultry, milk, and virtually every other major cultivated food product on today's tables. Further, applied genetics has greatly increased the production of penicillin, streptomycin, and other disease-fighting antibiotics. But in these and many other ways, the achievements of genetics have come through working with *nonhuman* genes. What has been, or can be, accomplished by applying the principles of genetics directly to the improvement of human genes and human breeding? In this and the next chapter we will present some of the answers.

Uses of Human Genetics. At various points in this book it has been shown how the knowledge of human genetics has swept away many superstitions, false beliefs, fears, and harmful theories about heredity that have plagued people for ages; how it has helped to give parents and children a better insight into their biological relationships; how it has clarified the nature and causes of many diseases and defects and made possible better medical diagnoses and treatments; how such specific findings as those relating to the Rh factor have aided in saving the lives of thousands of babies; how with respect to traits of intelligence, achievement, talent, and behavior, we are now better able to identify the relative roles of heredity and environment, and deal more fairly and sensibly with individuals; and how the facts regarding race and ancestry are all working to promote better understanding among human beings in general. Now we will take up some of the ways in which human genetic findings can guide persons in important individual situations.

PERSONAL HEREDITY PROBLEMS. The most common of these involve fear of inheritance or transmission of defects, diseases, or other undesirable traits. In each case, once it is clear that a given condition is hereditary, decisions must be governed by its severity; the nature of its inheritance and the risk of transmission; the stage of life at which it appears; the degree of its interference with happiness, work, or adjustment; and the degree of the parents' preparedness to have and rear a child so afflicted. Further, whether or not there is immediate danger of a defective child, socially minded persons might be concerned about passing on the defective gene to future generations. (See next chapter.) With respect to many of these points, the general answers can be found in preceding parts of this book. Where more specific guidance is needed, it may be obtained from various qualified persons, depending on the nature of the problem: if chiefly medical, from physicians specializing in the disease or defect; if chiefly genetic, from medical geneticists; if chiefly ethical, moral, or social, from one's spiritual adviser or a qualified marriage counselor. Here are some of the situations for which advice is often sought:

1. *A couple has had one seriously defective child.* Should they risk having another? One must first be sure about the nature of the condition. Many congenital abnormalities are purely environmental, due to prenatal accidents or the mother's temporary state, and some to chromosomal aberrations in sperms or egg which seldom occur again in a family. If the condition is clearly hereditary, the chance of a repeat with another child will depend on the method of inheritance, as shown in the accompanying table of "repeat threats." In any case, one should not make the common error of thinking that "lightning doesn't strike twice," or that if the risk of having a defective child is one in four, for example, once one has appeared the next three will be normal. As with a dice number turning up, two or three genetically defective children may appear in succession, for the result of one toss of the dice

CHANCES OF A "REPEAT" DEFECTIVE CHILD
(Whether hereditary or not: selected examples)

If a couple has had one child with this defect:	*The chances of having another child with the same defect are:*
Idiocy	
Mongolism (Down's syndrome)	
(1) Average risk, rising with mother's age	1 in 200 to 1 in 35
(2) If mother has abnormal chromosome (rare)	Up to 1 in 3
Phenylketonuria (PKU) ⎫	1 in 4
Tay-Sachs disease (amaurotic idiocy) ⎬	
Cretinism	Up to 1 in 4
Schizophrenia	Up to 1 in 12
Harelip (with or without cleft palate, or cleft palate alone)	
(1) If neither parent affected	1 in 28
(2) If one parent affected and an affected child appears	1 in 7
Spina bifida	1 in 20
Cystic fibrosis ⎫	1 in 4
Kidney, polycystic congenital ⎬	
Dwarfism (achondroplastic)	
(1) If one parent affected	1 in 2
(2) If neither parent affected (but probably a mutation in one child)	Very small chance of a repeat
Extra fingers and toes	1 in 2
Malformed hands or feet (hereditary type)	Up to 1 in 2
Clubfoot	1 in 30
Any other hereditary defect or abnormality	
If simple recessive	1 in 4
If simple dominant	1 in 2
(But if neither parent affected, probably mutation, with little repeat risk)	

Note: Risks for any recessive or dominant condition are much reduced where listed as "qualified," "irregular," or "multiple." For chromosome abnormalities, see text.

does not affect the next throw. On the other hand, the risk of a repeat is often so small that parents need not be concerned too much about future affected children.

2. *A couple who have not yet had children are hesitating about having any*, because one mate is afflicted with an extremely serious hereditary condition.

a. If the condition is a clear *dominant*, it will probably be transmitted to *one in two* children. With the risk so great a couple must consider the possibility of not having children. For *dominant-qualified* conditions the risks are smaller, but still ominous.

b. If the condition is *recessive*, there will be no defective child unless the other mate is carrying a gene for exactly the same defect. Clues as to whether this is so may come from that mate's family history and, in the case of some diseases, from tests. (See under item 4 below.)

c. If the condition is *sex-linked* (with the gene on the X chromosome), and if the husband is afflicted, there will be no children with the defect, but there is a fifty-fifty threat for each of his daughter's sons. In some of the very serious sex-linked conditions (hemophilia, certain muscular atrophies, certain blindness conditions, etc.) there would be every reason for afflicted men not to have children.

3. *Both members of a couple have serious hereditary defects.* If these are *dominant*, the facts in item 2a apply even more strongly. If the defects are *recessive*, the important point is whether they are exactly the same ones in both mates. If they are, *all* the children might be affected. But if the husband's and wife's hereditary afflictions are entirely different, *none* of the children are likely to have either defect. However, every child would become a carrier of two different harmful genes.

4. *Neither member of a couple (married or contemplating marriage) is defective*, but serious hereditary defects have appeared in close relatives of each. Here again, the question is whether the defects on both sides are the same or not, and how they are inherited. If the defects are the same, and *recessive*, there is a chance both mates are carrying genes for it and might produce a defective child (but with the risk no more than one in four). In many conditions (as noted in Chapter 11) screening tests can now reveal carriers of the single genes. If the mates differ in the condi-

tions for which they carry genes (for instance, some forms of recessive blindness on one side, and recessive deafness on the other), no child would be likely to have *either* defect, since matching genes would be required from both parents. If the conditions running in both families are clearly *dominant*, the fact that both mates are free of the conditions would strongly suggest they are not carrying the genes involved, so there would be almost no threat to their children. However, in *dominant-qualified* conditions, or those with late onset, there cannot be equal assurance. (See "Guide to Gene Types," Chapter 11.)

5. *A couple with all the children they expect, and none yet defective, are nevertheless concerned for the future because of hereditary defects in close relatives.* Is there reason for such concern, and does it help any to worry? Sometimes, yes, if the hereditary defects or diseases are among those whose appearance depends on environmental factors, or on age, or both. For instance, if diabetes, or certain forms of heart disease, biochemical disorders, cancer, mental diseases, etc., have appeared in families, there should be alertness to possible symptoms in the children, and special precautions should be taken if needed. Particularly hopeful is the fact that as medical science has been tracking down the causes of various hereditary defects and diseases, and linking some of them with abnormalities or upsets in the body chemistry, the chances of reducing their seriousness through early detection and treatment is increasing.

6. *A young man and woman, much in love, are hesitating about marriage because of certain bad social traits in relatives of one or the other*—criminality, drunkenness, sexual deviation, etc.—which they fear might crop up in their children. As we saw in previous chapters, there is little evidence that such behavior traits are hereditary, and even if they were, their transmission would be so complex that a child would run virtually no chance of "inheriting" these tendencies of a grandfather, uncle, or aunt. Nothing in the situation as stated would prevent a marriage; in fact, if the man and woman are themselves normal, of good character, and well adjusted, any genetic risks would be outweighed by the advantages they bring to a marriage.

7. *The man and woman are cousins.* Popular fears that cousin marriages run a high risk of producing defective offspring have

Cousin-Marriage Risks

FIRST-COUSIN MATES

OFFSPRING

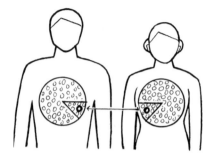

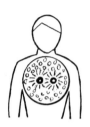

One eighth of the genes of first cousins are the same. If one cousin carries a hidden (recessive) bad gene, the chance is one in eight the other has the same gene.

If first cousins marry, the risk is thus much above average that a child will receive two of the same bad genes, and will develop the recessive defect.

some basis, though not nearly so great as supposed. In the case of first cousins, *one in eight of their genes is the same* (as told in the preceding chapter). Thus, if some recessive genes in their families, hidden or revealed, are defective (as for hereditary blindness, deafness, feeble-mindedness, albinism, biochemical deficiencies, or other abnormalities), the odds are far greater than average that the cousins will carry matching genes for the given defect, and that it will afflict a child of theirs. In marriages between second cousins, with only one in sixteen of their genes in common, the risks to offspring are much less, but still considerably greater than for two unrelated individuals. But this is speaking in general terms. In individual cases—unless family histories give special cause for worry—most cousin marriages do not present too great genetic risks.

Evidence for Inbreeding Effects. In groups where there has been much inbreeding, the incidence of hereditary defects is usually much above average, particularly in the case of the rarer conditions. This has been found true in certain isolated American rural communities, such as those on Martha's Vineyard (lying off

Massachusetts), the Chesapeake Bay peninsula, and the Kentucky mountains; in closely knit religious groups, such as the Amish and Hutterites; and in some sections of Switzerland, Sweden, Japan, and other countries with high cousin-marriage rates. However, in most groups and parts of the world there has been a steady decline in the incidence of cousin marriages, resulting from the increased opportunity for people to move about and to go afield for their mates.

Good Cousin Marriages. Where related individuals are unusually healthy in body and mind, and there is reasonable assurance that no serious hereditary defects have been running in their mutual family line, the genetic risks to their offspring may be relatively small, and in some cases their marriage may even produce superior children. That is to say, where there are concentrations of genes making for high intelligence, musical talent, artistry, or other good qualities, marriages between cousins can increase the chances that desired gene combinations will be passed on to offspring. In some families, therefore, the possible good results might offset the risks. One might note that Charles Darwin was married to his first cousin, Emma Wedgwood (of the famed china makers), and had many distinguished descendants. Abraham Lincoln was also the product of a cousin marriage. In the Bible there are many examples of close-relative marriages with notable descendants: Jacob, married to his first cousins, Rachel and Leah; Abraham married to his half sister; and Amram married to his aunt, Jochebed, and siring Moses, Aaron, and Miriam. In the Rothschild family for generations a large proportion of the marriages have been between first cousins. And in the royal families of ancient Egypt, marriages between brothers and sisters were the rule (Cleopatra having descended from six generations of such marriages), with apparently no undue serious consequences to offspring. The foregoing, incidentally, would suggest that there is no natural instinct against incest among human beings (any more than in lower animals) but that prohibitions against near-relative matings may have been largely social and psychological in origin, although not entirely excluding the possibility that people may have become aware of a higher than average incidence of defective offspring in incestuous marriages.

8. *A couple have decided for one reason or another not to have a*

child, or any more children. Of various contraceptive methods available there are personal or medical objections to some, and others are not considered reliable—the "rhythm" method especially so, since it is based on the timing of the menstrual cycle which is very often irregular and makes the so-called "safe period" undependable for about two out of three women. A general discussion of birth control methods is not within the scope of this book, but it may be said that one completely certain method at present is *sterilization* of either of the mates, which involves cutting and blocking of the ducts in a man through which the sperms are emitted, or the fallopian tubes in a woman through which eggs descend from the ovaries. (Sexual feelings or performance are in no wise affected.) The operation is quite simple (most so for the man). The effects are usually permanent, but if desired, another operation can restore fertility in about 20 to 30 per cent of the cases for women, and about 10 per cent of the cases for men.

9. *A pregnancy is already under way when fears arise that the fetus may be genetically defective or abnormal.* Certain facts can now be ascertained after the first few months by *amniocentesis*—inserting a needle into the woman's abdomen and withdrawing some of the amniotic fluid containing cells shed by the fetus. Tests may then show (*a*) if there is a chromosome abnormality, (*b*) *possibly* if there is some biochemical abnormality, or (*c*), if the fetus is male, which is very important when the mother is known to carry a gene for some serious sex-linked condition (hemophilia, the Lesch-Nyhan syndrome, or one of many others) which poses a fifty-fifty chance that a male child would be afflicted. (A girl would be normal, but with an even chance of being a carrier of the gene.) In any of the foregoing situations, an *abortion* could be considered, depending on the parents' attitude.

10. *A couple who very much desire children are apparently unable to produce them.* In about one third of the cases the problem lies with the husband's sperms (inadequate or abnormal) or difficulties in inseminating his wife. If the problem relates to the wife's condition, it may involve failure to ovulate, hormonal insufficiency, blockage of the fallopian tubes, chemical conflict with the husband's sperms, unreceptiveness in the womb to egg implantation, or inability to carry through a pregnancy properly. In many of the

foregoing situations the obstacles may be overcome by medical treatment. (If one's own doctor cannot advise, see item 13 at the end of this chapter.) Where ordinary procedures are ineffective, there are these possibilities:

Artificial Insemination. (*a*) When the husband is fertile but the wife cannot be successfully impregnated or cannot conceive through the usual means, the husband's sperms may be withdrawn by the physician and introduced in her at the time of the month and under conditions that are most propitious. The use of the *husband's* sperms is the most frequently employed form of artificial insemination and encounters no religious or personal opposition.

(*b*) The second method, *where the husband is sterile or unremediably impotent*, or there are fears of his transmitting some serious hereditary defect, is to use the sperms of another man—an anonymous donor carefully selected by the doctor and with no sexual contact.* This donor method—ensuring for a couple a baby who is genetically "half theirs"—has been successfully employed in the conception of vast numbers of babies (estimated to be over 100,000 in the United States to date), and would be much more widely used were it not for personal objections (mainly of husbands) or religious opposition (chiefly Catholic and Anglican). Of less concern have been unresolved legal problems: Is an artificial-insemination baby born through the donor method *illegitimate?* † Is the wife technically guilty of adultery? Is the child a legal heir of the husband's? Is a crime committed when the birth certificate names the husband as the father? In the scattered few court tests of these and related questions, conflicting judgments have been rendered, so the issues remain legally unresolved. However, various means have been resorted to by participating parents and doctors to overcome the possible legal difficulties. Moreover, studies have indicated that in the over-

---

* If the husband's sperms are not genetically undesirable, though inadequate, some of his seminal fluid is usually mixed in with that of the donor, so the possibility of his paternity of the child conceived still exists.

† In one of the first state actions, Oklahoma in 1967 ratified the legality of children born through artificial insemination, but with the provision that husband and wife obtain prior certification of their agreement to the procedure.

whelming proportion of cases, babies born through the donor-insemination method have brought happiness and greater solidarity to couples, without any subsequent complicating problems.

(c) *The husband is fertile, but the wife cannot conceive or carry through a pregnancy and safe delivery.* The possible procedures in these cases are still in the future for human beings, although they have been successfully employed with cattle and experimental animals. They would include: (1) If the wife can produce a fertile egg, having it withdrawn from her, fertilized by the husband's sperm in a test tube, and then implanted in the receptive womb of another woman—known only to the doctor—who will serve as a "proxy" mother, and when the child is born, will turn it over to the couple. The child would be *genetically* as much the couple's own (with no genetic traits acquired from the proxy mother) as one borne by the wife herself. (2) If the wife cannot produce fertile eggs, the husband's sperms could be artificially inseminated (with no sexual contact) into an anonymous woman selected by the doctor, who had agreed, with payment, to carry through a proxy pregnancy as in the preceding situation. In this case—the reverse of the results in artificial insemination—the child would be genetically the father's, but not the mother's. However, for the immediate present, no proxy-mother procedures are available, and the only alternative when the wife is wholly infertile is to adopt a baby.

11. *Adoption: A couple would like to adopt a child but have fears as to what it may turn out to be.* The major concern regarding babies of unknown or uncertain parentage offered for adoption is that they may have undesirable hereditary traits. The fears tend to be exaggerated. If there is a genetic risk in an adopted baby, it must be recognized that even a child of one's own may also be a genetic gamble to a considerable extent. (Nor is any child ever a true "chip off the old block," for the random combination of half of one parent's chromosomes and half of the other parent's chromosomes can never reproduce the composite genetic characteristics of either.) An offsetting advantage in the baby offered for adoption is that the prospective foster parents can at least see that there are no obvious defects to begin with. Assurance to this effect has become increasingly greater as the result of

new techniques to identify genetic and other abnormalities. In any case, reputable adoption agencies will report any risks that the baby may present, and permit its return if some serious inborn defect shows itself within a given period. With respect to the ultimate character and behavior of an adopted child—granted that it is mentally and physically healthy—the prevailing belief is that it will generally be determined much less by the traits of the true parents than by those of the foster parents, and by the environment and training they provide. However, the major problem now is getting babies to adopt, as the available supply is being steadily diminished by increasing contraception and abortions, fewer children orphaned, welfare aid enabling mothers to keep their children and less stigma attached to unmarried mothers who wish to do so.

12. *What is "genetic counseling," and how can it be of service?* With problems of the inheritance of diseases, defects, and abnormalities becoming more technically detailed, complex, and important—and bringing up psychological and social problems as well —specialists are needed to clarify relevant situations confronting many parents, prospective parents, and concerned individuals. Those engaged in genetic counseling are specially trained medical men and geneticists who are qualified to deal with these problems. Such specialists are usually affiliated with medical or other colleges, hospitals, and clinics. As a rule, they do not directly advise or *tell* people what to do. Rather, they explain the facts—such as the risks or chances of developing or transmitting a given disease or defect, or answer questions relating to cousin marriages, adoptions, or other situations we have discussed—and then leave it to the parents or individuals to make their own decisions. (More on this subject in the chapter following.)

13. *Where can one obtain specific information with regard to the parenthood problems discussed?* These important national agencies can direct one to this service:

Genetic Counseling. For information regarding the human genetics clinic and/or genetics counselors nearest to you, write to The National Foundation–March of Dimes, 1275 Mamaroneck Road, White Plains, New York 10605. (The Foundation publishes a Directory of Genetic Services as well as many valuable monographs and books on congenital malformations and inherited diseases and defects.)

Birth Control and Other Parenthood Problems. Planned Parenthood clinics or bureaus now exist in a great many cities and are listed in telephone directories. If there is none in your community, write for the address of the one nearest you to Planned Parenthood, Inc., 810 Seventh Avenue, New York, New York 10019.

Infertility Problems. For the name and address of a specialist nearest you, write to Secretary, American Fertility Society, 944 18th Street, Birmingham, Alabama 38205. If you are in the New York City Metropolitan area, contact Margaret Sanger Bureau, 17 W. 16th Street, New York, New York 10011.

31

The Changing
Human Species

HUMAN EVOLUTION, PAST AND PRESENT. Contrary to what many believe, the biological evolution of human beings did not all occur in the dim past, with mankind remaining genetically the same since its recorded history began. However, the more recent evolutionary changes may not have proceeded at the same rate or in the same way as they once did, for several reasons: (1) In the earlier stages of man's evolution, more unsettled climatic conditions, higher temperatures, and more intense radiation may have induced more frequent changes; (2) human groups have ceased being isolated as they once were for very long periods, which gave greater chance for new hereditary traits to become adapted and fixed in given environments; (3) the process of selecting out for survival the "fittest" persons reproductively, or those with special hereditary traits, has been greatly held down by social changes which permit individuals of all types and kinds (including *genetic defectives*) to survive and reproduce themselves.

The New Mutations. These have been constantly occurring in human beings, perhaps at the rate of one changed gene in at least every tenth egg or sperm; or, taking sperms and eggs together, at least one in every five fertilized eggs (or children) would be carrying some newly mutated gene. The great majority of these changes are very slight, but often are harmful—some extremely so, being newly produced genes for many of the serious hereditary diseases and defects we discussed in earlier chapters. Only here and there do *desirable* mutations occur, which, if the changed genes are passed on and multiply, might lead to hereditary improvements. But whatever new human evolutionary changes may have taken place in recent generations, they could hardly have been very great or easy to detect, considering that a century is the merest tick of time in the vast stretches of man's evolutionary history.

Continuing Animal Evolution. In lower animals it has been much easier than in humans to see continuing evolution at work, because they have many more generations in a given period (weeks, months, or a few years) and are less flexible in their capacities to adjust to changed conditions—especially those which are man-made. Thus, within our own time, scores of bird and animal species have become extinct or are on the verge of becoming so. On the other hand, many *useful* new mutations in various animal species have been taken advantage of by breeders, resulting in new types of fox and mink furs, improved types of cattle and fowl, and many new strains of laboratory animals (mice, guinea pigs, fruit flies, etc.). In plants, fruits, flowers, and vegetables, innumerable new mutations have also led to the evolution of many important new varieties. Such man-induced or man-propagated changes in lower animals have brought up the question we will now discuss, *Why can't human beings also be improved genetically?*

HUMAN INEQUALITY. When governments and religions avow that "all men are created equal," it is recognized that this refers to the rights of all human beings under the laws of God and man to be given fair and equal treatment. No one can be unaware that nature does not follow this principle in fashioning people's minds and bodies, but brings individuals into the world with many inequalities in their inherent make-up and chances for survival, achievement, and happiness. This fact has been a troubling one throughout history, and has given rise to various notions, practices, and plans. In some groups, such as the Spartans, defective offspring were killed (as they still are among various primitive peoples). Other groups have assumed that they could grade themselves into "superior" and "inferior" hereditary classes, born and bred for different roles and stations in life. Still others have felt that their own racial or ethnic group was inherently destined to dominate—and if they wished, to exterminate—"inferior" peoples (as did the Nazis). Beyond this the thought has always persisted that, inasmuch as human beings could successfully breed lower animals for improved and special qualities, why could they not control their own breeding toward more desirable goals? Some of the many problems raised by this question will be dealt with now.

EUGENICS. The term "eugenics," derived from the Greek *eugenes* ("wellborn"), refers to measures for improving the hereditary make-up of the human species. Eugenics is not a science, and should not be confused with "genetics" (as it often is), although it has drawn on genetic principles. However, when the eugenics movement was launched and named by Sir Francis Galton, in England in 1883, the science of genetics had not yet come into being. Thus, at the beginning, the eugenics program was based on many wrong beliefs regarding the inheritance of human traits; the division of people by birth into "superior" and "inferior" groups, classes, and stocks; and the manner in which mankind could be rapidly improved by extirpating the undesirable genes and propagating the desirable ones. Because of the extreme attitudes and proposals of many early eugenicists and their failure to distinguish between the effects of bad environment and bad heredity, the original movement met with much opposition. But as the science of human genetics developed, the eugenics proposals became sounder, more moderate in their approach, and better adapted to the social realities. Thus, modern eugenics—which aims for the betterment of human beings by improving their genes so far as possible, but perhaps more by improving their environments so that the greatest potentialities of the existing genes can assert themselves—has enlisted the support of many respected geneticists, social scientists, and laymen.

Population Quality. Previous concerns that human populations were deteriorating genetically because the "unfit" groups were outbreeding the "fitter" ones have given way to the realization that the most imminent danger facing mankind is the continuing "population explosion." For regardless of the genetic make-up of human beings anywhere, their quality and welfare with respect to health, nutrition, living standards, education, and achievement potentialities would be steadily worsened if the earth became glutted with more people than it could properly sustain. That this was threatening was obvious in the huge universal population growth which had come as environments and medical improvements had sharply reduced death rates while correspondingly increasing life expectancies. Where the world's population had been only about three quarters of a billion in 1800—grown slowly from an estimated 250 million at the time of Christ—it had swelled to two billion in 1940, and to over three and a half billion at this writing. In many countries of Central and South America, Africa, and Asia, with birth rates of 40 to 50 or more per 1,000 annually (and death rates half that), the populations are doubling every twenty or twenty-five years. Even in the United States, with a birth rate now down to about 18 per 1,000 (and a death rate of about 9.5), the population could double in forty years or so. In general, at the present rate of increase the world could have seven billion people by the end of the century, fourteen billion a generation later, and so on—into completely unsupportable numbers no matter how great the technological advances or the means employed to increase food supplies. Thus, there is an imperative, imminent need for controlling population growth, and as opposition on religious or other grounds has dwindled, the only question is what means should be employed.

Genetic Improvements. Although the major concern is with population quantity, there still is a need to do everything possible to improve the *quality* of mankind's genetic heritage. The measures proposed are of two kinds: *negative* eugenics, involving all steps that could prevent or reduce the births of seriously defective individuals (those who would be a burden to their families and society and find no happiness in being born); and *positive* eugenics, comprising both genetic and environmental measures that could improve the human stock by increasing the proportion of healthy, intelligent, capable, and useful persons. Taking up negative eugenics first, the specific steps would include those discussed in the preceding chapter with respect to (1) curbing the reproduction of individuals with high risks of transmitting serious hereditary defects; (2) identifying through prenatal tests fetuses likely to be seriously abnormal and aborting them at an early stage; and (3) limiting excessive childbearing. Also discussed was *sterilization* of individuals who were genetically defective (or preferred not to reproduce at all or further). Here we will deal in more detail with the latter question.

STERILIZATION: EUGENIC RESULTS. Any hopes that the worst human hereditary diseases and defects could be largely wiped out—and in a short time—by sterilizing the afflicted persons have been much deflated by these findings:

Recessive Conditions. In these—the most common serious ones (with two matching genes required)—the afflicted persons are only a small percentage of those carrying the genes. For example, it is estimated that if a recessive condition afflicts 1 in 10,000 persons, about 1 in every 50 persons is carrying a single gene for it; and if it afflicts 1 in 1,000 persons, then about 1 in 16 persons is a carrier of the single gene. In short, with many hundreds of serious recessive defects afflicting human beings, the probability is that every normal individual is carrying, on the average, several hidden recessive genes for one condition or another. Thus, even wholesale sterilization of all persons who actually have a recessive hereditary disease or defect would not prevent the vast majority of the genes involved from continuing to be passed on.

Sex-Linked Defects. In these, which afflict chiefly or only males, sterilization of all defective males would still leave the largest proportion of the genes to be transmitted by the female carriers. While the latter could often be identified if a woman's father or grandfather had the condition, or if she had already borne an afflicted son, sterilization might be justified only in extreme cases.

Dominant Defects. These could unquestionably be greatly reduced in incidence by sterilizing the afflicted individuals. But the serious simple dominant conditions are rare, and the irregular or qualified dominants, which often do not reveal themselves in carriers of the genes, would present problems similar to those of the recessive defects. A special difficulty would arise with conditions having late onset, which may not appear until after the person's children have been born.

Chromosome Abnormalities. Almost all of these—except perhaps 2 or 3 per cent—are due to accidents, of egg or sperm formation or during conception, and are not transmissible by the afflicted persons. However, inasmuch as the threat of producing chromosomally abnormal offspring—especially mongoloid idiots, and those with the Klinefelter or Turner syndromes—increases sharply as mothers reach or pass their late thirties, sterilization of women in those ages who have already produced an adequate number of children could considerably reduce the numbers of individuals with these defects.

Compulsory Sterilization? Granted that sterilization on a large scale would bring a significant decrease in the proportion of defective individuals—with a saving of much heartache and vast public expense—there is the question of how far society and the state could or should go in this regard. The question was first raised in the early part of the century when sterilization laws in many states (beginning with California and Indiana in 1907) authorized the sterilization for eugenic reasons—real or assumed— of mentally defective and diseased individuals (the majority of these females) and, to a limited extent, of epileptics and criminals. (Even sex offenses or misbehavior were grounds for sterilizing girls in a Kansas reformatory for a short period.) The legality of state sterilization laws was upheld by the Supreme Court in 1927, although more restraint began to be exercised in enforcing the laws (some states suspending them) as doubts increased about their genetic validity and social desirability. The extreme dangers of compulsory, state-enforced sterilization were shockingly revealed during the Nazi terror reign when hundreds of thousands of persons were sterilized on the flimsiest eugenic grounds, or purely out of malice or racial hatred. Since then emphasis on sterilization for eugenic reasons or birth control has shifted from the compulsory to the voluntary, with the hope that increasing education and feelings of social and personal responsibility will induce individuals with high risks of transmitting genetic defects to take the initiative in having themselves sterilized or, in the case of serious defectives who are incompetent to act for themselves, having parents authorize their sterilization. In any event, and for one reason or another, it is estimated that up to 200,000 sterilizations are being performed in the United States annually. (In India, hundreds of thousands of men, spurred by a small monetary inducement, have had themselves sterilized.)

POSITIVE EUGENICS. Many of the most feasible measures to improve human quality are already being carried out in advanced countries. Earlier childbearing, the limitation of family sizes, and better prenatal and child care are resulting in healthier, abler children in all groups. Further, economic, social, and educational advantages, spread more evenly over populations, have decreased the reproductive differences between the previously labeled "fit" and "unfit" groups, particularly as many college-educated parents are now having more children than their counter-parts in preceding generations, and parents in the less-advantaged groups are taking advantage of contraceptive methods to have relatively fewer children.

Breeding Superior Humans. Suggested by the remarkable breeding techniques now widely used to improve the quality of livestock and poultry is the thought that they could also be applied to produce superior human beings in increasing numbers. For instance, sperms of prize bulls and champion race horses are being preserved by quick-freezing processes, stored for long periods in "sperm banks," and often transported great distances to insemi-nate females as desired (one prize animal's sperms being capable by this means of siring vast numbers of progeny). Could not the same procedure be used for the siring of innumerable children by a genius or other outstanding man, even long after his death? In the case of a woman with demonstrated exceptional qualities, we told in the preceding chapter of the proxy-mother techniques by which her eggs could be withdrawn, preserved, and implanted in many other women to produce a great many children with her genetic qualities—the same as if she had conceived and borne them herself. (This proxy-mother technique has already been suc-cessfully used in livestock and other animals, but so far only to a very limited extent, because the process is much more involved than is that of artificial insemination of a selected male's sperms.)

What Is Meant by Superior Humans? The big deterrent to any program for breeding superior human beings by the methods suggested is the question of deciding *what types* of human beings to breed for? Lower animals are bred for only a few specific traits; one is not concerned with other traits. A horse may be a speedy racer, but no good for heavy work. Or a dog may have a fine-shaped head and body, but be unfitted for hunting or for protection. A desirable and successful human being, however, must have a great many unique qualities, adapted to special requirements, each of them highly complex and dependent on a great many genes. We have seen how difficult it would be merely to breed out serious defects—even those produced by a few simple genes. There would be far more difficulty in trying to *breed in* almost any of the human "desirable" traits—superior minds, great talents, fine char-acter, bravery and enterprise—the complex genes for which have not even been discovered. Most difficult of all would be trying to combine in one stock of humans not merely these traits but also beauty, strong physique, and superb health. Finally, when we consider that thoroughbred cattle, horses, and dogs are the products of hundreds of generations of selective breeding—and that a generation for these lower animals is a fraction of a human generation—any extensive plan to breed superior human beings must seem remote if not also dangerous.

ATOMIC MUTATION THREATS. Overshadowing the thoughts of greatly improving human genetic make-up have been the fears of man-induced genetic *deterioration*. Such fears became formidable with the dropping of the first atomic bombs. As far back as 1927, before these bombs were ever dreamed of, the late Prof. Hermann J. Muller proved that the natural radiation rate—always going on through cosmic rays, rock and earth chemicals, and spontaneous changes—could be increased 150 *times* by ordinary X rays. This discovery (which brought Muller a Nobel prize) assumed awesome significance with the development of the atomic bomb and the finding that the radiation it set loose could produce infinitely more mutations than could X rays, as well as bringing death or serious injury to those within range of an explosion. The first actual evidence on these points came with the dropping of the bombs on Nagasaki and Hiroshima, Japan, in 1945. The immediate effects, in addition to the vast death toll, included a greatly increased incidence of congenital abnormalities (microcephaly for one) among babies who had been carried by pregnant mothers in the blast areas, as well as numerous cases of skin cancer, cataracts, and blindness among other survivors. (A high proportion of the survivors were also found later to have chromosome abnormalities in their cells, which offered potential threats of malignancies.) However, the extent of the genetic mutations which may have occurred cannot be known for a long time, inasmuch as the great proportion of these would have been in genes for recessive or other multiple-gene conditions requiring several generations to manifest themselves. But geneticists are quite sure that eventually many mutations which resulted from the first atomic bombings will show up in later offspring and descendants of exposed individuals.

Fallout Effects. Added to the immediate results of direct exposure to atomic bomb blast, there have been the wider and more continuous threats of *fallout*—the rain of radiated particles set loose and spread afar through winds and waters, contaminating plants, fish, and food animals, and capable of causing mutations among people over vast areas. Similar effects, but in a reduced degree, could come from the unguarded release of radiated waste substances of atomic-energy plants. In any case, the enormous threats presented by atomic radiation have been a potent restraining influence on great-power conflicts and are causing—or should cause—every precaution to be taken in the development of atomic energy for peacetime uses.

Other Genetic Pollutants. Atomic or X ray radiation are not the only new causes of human gene mutations. Mutations can also be induced by a wide variety of present-day chemical substances, including some of the industrial waste products and gases spewed into the air or poured into streams, rivers, lakes, and oceans, as well as insecticides and pesticides, which all can be absorbed by edible plants, fish, and food animals, or which may reach human beings directly. Further, many drugs (some previously described), and some of the chemical food additives used to preserve or flavor foods, can be or are suspected of being mutagenic in some degree. The full facts about the effects on human genes of various environmental pollutants are still to be established.

32

Mankind's Genetic Future

Assuming that mankind will not destroy itself or damage its genes irremediably, scientists are looking ahead to the possibilities of eliminating or reducing in severity many of the present human genetic defects and, at the same time, greatly improving the functioning of existing normal genes. We already have discussed various negative eugenics and positive eugenics suggestions. Here are some other proposed measures—all still far short of realization:

GENETIC ENGINEERING. On the basis of successes to date in synthetically fashioning elementary genes (or sections of DNA) and altering or replacing genes of simple one-celled creatures, the hope is held out of eventually applying the same techniques to human beings. For example, where there is a defect in the DNA coding of a gene, correcting the error by reinforcement with or substitution of a properly coded gene, or supplying the individual with a corrective chemical, may be possible in the future. Actual gene substitution, while experimentally possible with simple creatures, might prove much too involved and costly for any wide use in human beings. Much more feasible may be the chemical alteration or reinforcement of defective genes by addition of new genetic material. This technique could be applied most importantly to the mental deficiencies that are directly due to inherited biochemical abnormalities. It might also be used, theoretically, in speeding up the workings of normal brain genes, or memory genes, so that ordinary individuals could reach higher levels of mental achievement. Further, in regard to special talents, such as for music, art, mathematics, and science, when and *if* the chemical bases for these capacities are identified, prescribed treatments might produce bumper crops of geniuses in these areas.

(All of which, geneticists warn, is still highly speculative and if not, may be a long way off.)

ORGAN TRANSPLANTS. More imminent is likely to be the widespread transplanting of vital organs and parts of the body, stored in "banks" for use as needed. The major present obstacle —that of rejection by transplant recipients because of genetic tissue incompatibility—is expected to be overcome to a great extent. The new techniques could be especially well applied at early ages in cases where inherited defects in the functioning of the kidneys, liver, pancreas, or endocrine glands now bring serious impediments or premature death.

SEX-DETERMINATION CONTROL. An especially definite possibility in the not too distant future may be the means that will enable prospective parents to have a child of the sex they desire. The simplest method would be that of separating out the husband's X-bearing (girl-producing) sperms from the Y-bearing (boy-producing) sperms, and then inseminating the wife with the one or the other kind. Less certain would be treating the uterus chemically in some way so that either the X-bearing sperms or the Y-bearers would have a clear-cut advantage. More difficult and complex would be fertilizing a number of eggs in a test tube, culturing them to the point where one could distinguish the male from the female, and then implanting the desired embryo in the womb. If any of these methods prove effective and generally available, it is estimated that perhaps 10 per cent more boys than girls would be brought into the world, which could help to make up for the heavier toll of males in later years and come closer to equalizing the numbers of adult men and women.

"VIRGIN" BIRTHS. Another possibility held out is that a woman who so desires may be enabled to conceive and bear a child genetically all her own—*with no contact whatsoever with any man or with his sperms.* The process, called *parthenogenesis* —which sometimes occurs spontaneously in poultry, and has been induced experimentally in rabbits—involves activation of a female's egg so that its one set of chromosomes becomes double, and then proceeds as if a second set had been brought in by a sperm and had initiated conception. Inasmuch as the mother carries only X chromosomes, her self-fertilized egg could produce only an XX baby, a girl. Further, women who see in the process a means of liberating themselves from reproductive dependence on men may be unaware of the grave genetic dangers. For doubling of the same chromosomes of a woman to produce a child would also mean doubling any defective recessive genes she may carry—especially genes on the X chromosome for sex-linked diseases and defects—thus greatly increasing the risk that a "virgin-born" child would not be normal.

FATHERS WITHOUT GENETIC MOTHERS. Also theoretically possible would be the production by a man of a child genetically all his own. This process would involve taking an egg from a woman, withdrawing her chromosomes from its nucleus and substituting the man's chromosomes from one of his X sperms, then inducing conception by another of his sperms either before or after implantation in a host woman who would bear the child. While a man by this process could produce either a boy or a girl, depending on the fertilizing sperm selected, the great added risk of the child's being defective because of getting a double dose of any bad genes carried by the father would be similar to that referred to in the case of virgin births.

TWINS AND SUPERTWINS. Future parents should be enabled to have twins or higher multiples if they desire should the procedures mentioned in Chapter 5 be developed with more certainty. Producing fraternal multiples to order would require accurate control of the hormonal dosages given prospective mothers. For identicals a much more difficult process would involve induced splitting of a fertilized egg and separating the halves (or further subdivisions for higher multiples)—all probably to be done in a test tube—with subsequent implantation in the woman. The test-tube conceptions would further make possible selection of the sex of the twins or supertwins.

MEN BEYOND THE EARTH. Is there a possibility that men—or some superior type of humans or humanlike beings—exist on other planets? That they could communicate with us and enable us to vastly improve ourselves? Or that if earth men become extinct, these other beings may some day replace our species? Speculating on these points, authorities seem to agree on the fact that no manlike creatures, or other higher animal forms, exist or could exist on any planet now even remotely accessible to our earth. Old beliefs that there might be men on Mars, Venus, Mercury, or some other planet in our solar system, have already been dashed by space explorations which have shown that none of these planets has an environment that could sustain higher animal life. Quite probably, among the billions of other planets farther off in outer space—so far away it could take a thousand or thousands of our lifetimes to reach them—there might very well be high forms of life, although it would seem almost impossible that the same environmental conditions and the myriads of evolutionary steps which on this earth produced our human species could have been precisely duplicated elsewhere. Even on this earth, should a radical change in natural conditions completely wipe out human life (as happened with the dinosaurs and innumerable other now extinct species), or should atomic warfare achieve much the same ends, scientists doubt greatly whether a species exactly like our *Homo sapiens* could again evolve through the chance processes of evolution. If one believes in Divine Creation, of course, it could be assumed that the creation of man— possibly an improved, superior man—could again be achieved, or could just as easily have already been achieved on some other planet. All that now seems certain is that whatever may be Earth Man's future destiny, it will be governed by how intelligently he himself can utilize the genetic and environmental resources within his range and command.

CONCLUSION. We have sought to bring out in this book how all human traits and all human beings, individually and collectively, are the end results of a constant interaction between the effects of heredity and environment. The unique hereditary endowments of human beings have enabled them—alone among all other animals—to consciously shape their environments and control their lives, carrying them an enormous distance from their original state. But this same advancement—technological and cultural—has brought with it, increasingly, both environmental and genetic pollution. What will matter most from here on is not—or not merely—how much more technological or scientific progress is made, but how far it will go toward providing saner, healthier, more enlightened, fuller living and peaceful coexistence for the world's peoples. To achieve this will require no great improvement in human genes—although there will be the utmost need to ensure against deterioration of the existing genes—but only the release of the tremendous potentialities that have yet to be utilized in man's genetic heritage.

Index